Inside
Shelby
American

Inside Shelby American

Wrenching and Racing with
Carroll Shelby in the 1960s

John Morton

motorbooks

Dedication

To Sylvia Wilkinson,
whose invaluable help and experience made it possible for me
to write this book. I hope this is my last one and so does she.

To my brother Lyman,
who drove as well as I did and writes much better.

To Peter Brock and George Boskoff,
both of whom had more faith in me than I had in myself.

To the memories of my best friends:
Dan Baker, Johnny Opitz, and Earl Jones.

Acknowledgments

*Thanks to all of the photographers and friends
who helped bring this story to life. Thanks also to Steve
Johnson for bringing old photos back to life.*

*A special thanks to Louis D. Rubin Jr.
for his insight, to Ted Sutton for his recollections, and to
Buck Trippel for his research.*

First published in 2013 by Motorbooks, an imprint of Quarto Publishing Group USA Inc., 400 First Avenue North, Suite 400, Minneapolis, MN 55401 USA

Motorbooks titles are also available at discounts in bulk quantity for industrial or sales-promotional use. For details, write to Special Sales Manager at Quarto Publishing Group USA Inc., 400 First Avenue North, Suite 400, Minneapolis, MN 55401 USA.

To find out more about our books, visit us online at www.motorbooks.com.

Library of Congress Cataloging-in-Publication Data

Morton, John, 1942- author.
    Inside Shelby American : wrenching and racing with Carroll Shelby in the 1960s / John Morton.
        pages cm
    Includes index.
        Summary: "An account of sports-car builder and racing team Shelby-American through the eyes of John Morton, who worked his way up from shop janitor to team driver to launch a racing career spanning forty years"-Provided by publisher.
    ISBN 978-0-7603-4394-4 (hardcover with jacket)
    1. Morton, John, 1942- 2. Shelby, Carroll, 1923-2012. 3. Shelby American, Inc.--History. 4. Automobile racing drivers--United States--Biography. 5. Automobiles, Racing--United States--History. I. Title.
    GV1032.M57A3 2013
    796.720922--dc23
    [B]
                            2013021590

Editors: Zack Miller and Kris Palmer
Art Director: Rebecca Pagel
Cover design: Faceout Studio
Layout: Helena Shimizu
Front cover image: Ron Kimball/KimballStock

Printed in China

Contents

Chapter One
Learning to Drive the Shelby Way 1

Chapter Two
Racing from the Wrong End of a Broom 37

Chapter Three
Midwest Racer 81

Chapter Four
Cobra Pilot 105

Chapter Five
Shelby Expands 171

Chapter Six
The Shelby Shadow 203

Epilogue 241
Index 246

Learning to Drive
the Shelby Way

It's a stretch, I suppose, to claim that my racing DNA goes back more than a century, but it appears that my father's strange attraction to auto racing began in Savannah, Georgia, more than a hundred years ago. He was not a race fan, didn't follow the sport, and knew very little about it. But as a boy, he attended the American Grand Prize race in 1910 and the Vanderbilt Cup race in 1911. Perhaps this explains

My brother Lyman (driving) and I sharing our first four-wheeled vehicle in 1945, a Graham-Bradley pedal tractor. *John Morton Collection*

We were rewarded with two three-wheelers on Christmas morning 1946 but still couldn't reach the pedals. I routinely claimed that my tricycle could go 100 miles per hour. The racing exaggerations began young. *John Morton Collection*

why my father took my brother and me to auto races when we were little kids.

I grew up in Waukegan, Illinois, about half-way between Milwaukee and Chicago. In the late 1940s there were a number of racetracks within easy driving distance of our home. The first race I ever saw was a dirt, short-track modi-fied race, probably in 1948. I remember asking my dad how the drivers knew how many laps they had to go until the end of the race. He hypothesized that "they must mark the laps off on a piece of paper they carry with them in the car." As I mentioned, my father knew very little about racing.

Dad also took us to a midget race. I still recall the wonderful smell of these pint-sized racers. My father explained the smell was the fuel they used. When the races were over, fans were allowed to cross the track and enter the pits. I had never been so close to a race car. A beautiful light-tan-colored car, No. 10, caught my eye. Its long, shiny exhaust pipe passed dangerously near the cockpit and seemed to beckon me. I put my hand around it. The car must have just finished the last race because it burned the hell out of my fingers. As I cried, someone poured motor oil over my burns in an attempt to relieve the pain. My first racing injury!

In the summer of 1949 my family drove to Milwaukee to see the Indy car race on the 1-mile oval. At that time Milwaukee was still a dirt track, as were all Indy car tracks of that era with the exception of Indianapolis. From the infield we watched the cars roar down the straights. Excitedly, I told my dad, "Tell me when they are going a hundred miles an hour!"

"I think they are going a hundred now," he replied.

I was disappointed because from our distant vantage point, they didn't look so fast. A hundred miles per hour was a magic speed in my seven-year-old mind.

Later in the race, we moved to a vantage point closer to the track where the cars entered the turn after the backstretch. One of the race cars stood out from the rest, making a lasting impression on me. It had six wheels. Many years later I tried to find out if this car had really existed or if it was a figment of my imagination. No one could give me a positive answer until 1974 when a man helping me with my own race car explained that the six-wheeler was the *Pat Clancy*

The very unique *Pat Clancy Special* Indy car left a lasting impression on me. It competed in July 1949 at the Milwaukee Fairgrounds in the first big race I ever witnessed. Here it is being readied for the race with driver Jackie Holmes in the cockpit. Holmes and the *Special* finished fourth, the best performance of the car's career. *Armin Krueger: photographer, Greenfield Gallery Collection*

Headed out on a boat camping trip in coastal South Carolina with my father and Lyman.
John Morton Collection

Special. I did some research and discovered that the car had been driven to fourth place that day by Jackie Holmes, the best finish it ever had.

My father was more jock than car nut. An all-around sports fan, he had been a long-distance swimmer and a handball champion. We attended Cubs, White Sox, and Milwaukee Braves baseball games as well as a Chicago Bears football game at Soldier Field. My most vivid memory relating to the baseball games was in 1955 on our way to watch the Cubs play on Memorial Day, listening to the Indy 500 on the radio as we drove. Bill Vukovich was again leading the race for the fourth year in a row. After a station break, the announcer gave the running order. Bob Sweikert was leading, but Vukovich wasn't even on the list. We wondered what happened, until it was announced that Vukovich had been killed. At 13 I learned that even the best can die.

Waukegan Speedway opened in the fall of 1949, bringing us both modified races and motorcycle races. Here we watched top local drivers like Eddie Stillman, Elmer Musgrave, and Miles "The Mouse" Melius. Though none of them made the step to big-time auto racing, all three were skilled drivers and, save for the elusive lucky break or perhaps the ambition to move beyond their local tracks, might have been stars on a grander scale. My guess is that it just didn't occur to them to try.

Savannah and Beyond

Almost every Christmas our family would drive a thousand miles to Savannah, Georgia, to spend the holidays with my grandparents and other relatives on my father's side. We also spent part of every summer down there. By the time I was 11 years old, my father had me helping with driving duties.

In the 1940s and 1950s, highways in America were still two lanes; the project that would produce the Interstate Highway System didn't even begin until the late 1950s. Highway driving was much more challenging then, particularly passing. My father had honed his passing to an art form, often to the horror of oncoming drivers, not to mention the occupants of his car. Close calls and hair-raising lane changes were part of every road trip. I actually learned quite a bit about driving on those trips.

I was behind the wheel on one trip to Savannah in 1954 when my father began complaining that I wasn't steady on the accelerator. "Let me have the gas. I'll show you what I mean," he said. My mother protested from the back seat that she thought it was awful for a 12-year-old to be driving 80 miles per hour. Dad paid no mind as he slid over to work the accelerator as I steered. Now we were at a steady speed—a steady 93 miles per hour! My father was always the boss, and he was working the gas.

My brother and I took turns spending our summer vacations in Savannah. In 1955 it was Lyman's turn, so I went with my mother to visit her sister and cousins in California. We stayed in Oxnard with my aunt and uncle. Oxnard had a distinct smell—a combination of hot asphalt and eucalyptus, with a hint of insecticide. I loved it. I hung out with some kids who were involved in flying model airplanes, which was right up my alley, as I loved airplanes nearly as much as cars.

One of the best days of my young life was the day my uncle took me to Ventura to watch my friend fly in a model airplane contest. As luck would have it, there was a motorcycle scrambles race happening just across the road. There were Triumphs, BSAs, and all sorts of fabulous bikes unknown in Waukegan, Illinois. I ran back and forth between the two events all day.

To the Cubmobile!

My first official race was in 1951. I was a Cub Scout, and there was an event called the Cubmobile Derby. The rules were similar to those

of the Soapbox Derby, with the cars supposedly built by adults working with kids. Each Cub den could enter a car in the race. Unlike the basic and relatively crude Cubmobiles of today, our cars were quite elaborate, and some of them were beautiful. My den had a car, but no scout I knew had a hand in it; it just seemed to appear.

In Waukegan the race was run down Johns Manville hill, a fairly steep grade a quarter mile long with a finish line near the infamous-to-be asbestos factory. I finished third in my race, and our car was taken home. Later we were told we had been fast enough to get another run. In a panic I borrowed a dime for the payphone at a nearby res-

My brother ready for the start of his heat in the 1952 Cubmobile Derby down Johns Manville hill in Waukegan, Illinois. *John Morton Collection*

taurant and through tears pleaded with someone's dad to bring the car back. The car got back in time only to be soundly beaten again. Maybe I should have gotten the message at that point that racing could be a cruel sport.

Under the Influence

I never knew who built the Cubmobile, but MG made the first real sports car to capture my attention. It was a 1954 TF owned by Ryser Ericson. His family lived across the street from our house in Waukegan. Ryser was about to graduate from college when I was in eighth grade. He loved sports cars, so his parents gave him a 1954 MG TF as a graduation present, a gift that would have a huge effect on my life. Sports cars were rare at that time, particularly in the Midwest, so I was thrilled to be living across the street from one. When it came to keeping his car clean, Ryser was something of a fanatic. At least twice a week he would be in his driveway meticulously washing and polishing his car. And each time I walked over and annoyed him with questions while he cleaned.

Ryser was active in a local sports car club, called FAST (Foreign Auto Sports Team), and he followed the local road racing circuit closely, as well as the international scene. Through our impromptu discussions during Ryser's car-cleaning sessions, I developed a real interest in sports car racing, attempting to follow the sport through magazines like *Road & Track* and *Sports Cars Illustrated*. It was difficult to follow racing in the 1950s because the magazine reporting lagged the actual events by a month or more and newspapers offered little if any motor racing coverage.

Occasionally Ryser would take me for a ride, which always ended far too soon for me. One brisk fall morning, several of Ryser's sports car friends met at his house to go, I assume, on a drive in the country. I wasn't old enough to drive yet, and I thought that those were the luckiest guys in the world.

Ryser sold the MG and bought a black 1955 Jaguar XK140. Sometime later, the Jaguar was replaced with a new Austin-Healey. The Healey was then displaced by a Porsche 356 coupe. It's amazing that a person can have such an impact on someone else's life and never even realize it. I've often thought that if I'd grown up on another block, my life would have followed a different path.

Neighbor Ryser Ericson was a huge influence on my interest in sports car racing. His 1954 MG TF was a college graduation gift. It was pure magic to me at 12. *Jill Ericson Collection*

Determined to Race

By 1957, when I was 15, I had acquired some knowledge of sports car racing through the magazines—reading about Juan Manuel Fangio and Stirling Moss and Americans Phil Hill and Carroll Shelby—and from my conversations with Ryser, but I had yet to see racing anywhere except on an oval track. As luck would have it, I talked my father into taking us to Elkhart Lake, Wisconsin, to see the 500-mile sports car race in September.

Reading magazines hadn't prepared me for what I experienced that day—sounds I never imagined and smells. How could cars smell so good? Phil Hill won the race in a Ferrari, with

Ericson practicing his Le Mans start technique. He and his friends would find a secluded spot for this activity so as not to make a spectacle of themselves. *Darrell May Collection*

Carroll Shelby second in a Maserati, and Eddie Crawford taking third in a Porsche Spyder. That day—at age 15—I decided I would become a race driver. On the way home, I worked out how many years it would take before I would be doing what I'd just watched.

Obviously, I would need a driver's license. Nearly every teenager about to turn 16 was excited about getting a driver's license, but that milestone was an even higher priority for me because I had picked driving as a career.

On my 16th birthday my father took me to the National Guard Amory, where the driver's license tests were administered. We had a 1955 Buick Super Riviera, which I could drive damn well thanks to five years of illegal behind-the-wheel experience. After passing the written test, Mr. Babcock, the examiner, directed me through the required driving tasks. As I drove, parallel parked, backed up, etc., Mr. Babcock wrote on his clipboard without giving a verbal critique. After arriving back at the armory, he explained what I had done wrong. I had been asked to turn into a driveway, back out into the street, and then continue in the opposite direction. He said I should have pulled far enough into the driveway to clear the sidewalk in case someone wanted to walk past. This seemed stupid because it increased the chance of backing over a pedestrian.

My dad, who had been listening, sensed I was about to be told that I'd failed.

"Mr. Babcock," he said, "is the Babcock I see on the billboards running for sheriff any relation to you?"

Babcock beamed. "Why yes. He's my son."

"Your son is quite a guy," Dad said. "He's going to go places in this world."

Mr. Babcock turned to me. "You know what your mistake was, don't you, son?"

"Yes, sir," I replied. He signed me off and handed me my temporary license. My father wasn't really a bullshitter, but this time he rose to the occasion.

Dad was also very reasonable about letting me use the family's only car, even after I destroyed low gear in the Dynaflow transmission. After I confessed and explained that I was, in fact, trying to burn rubber, my father said that what I did should not have caused the problem. I decided to drop the subject.

That old Buick afforded me my first opportunity to drive 100 miles per hour. The site of the feat was Western Avenue, which ran for about a mile between Greenwood and Glen Flora Avenue. I got the needle up to 1-0-0 and then hauled down to a stop. The latter was just as important as the speed mark because Western Avenue ended at Glen Flora.

No More "We'll See!"

Ever since one of our trips to Savannah in 1948, I had pestered my father to let me have a motor scooter. We had stopped at a repair shop during our trip because the horn on our car was stuck on. As we waited, I spotted a tiny motor scooter against a wall in the shop. Being tiny myself, it was the perfect size. The mechanic called it a Doodle Bug, and I told my dad I wanted one. "We'll see," he said. But seeing was all I got. He said, "We'll see" about the Doodle Bug and then the Cushman, the Whizzer, the Moto-Scoot, and the Vespa. "We'll see" came to mean no. Now that I was 16 with an automobile driver's license, I didn't want to hear "We'll see" anymore.

Dad seemed resigned to the idea that I would get a car, so haunting used car lots became my number-one pastime. A sports car was out of the question—or at least our price range. I pushed for a red Isetta 300, which Dad nixed as too dangerous. He also vetoed a Renault 4 CV, another smart decision on his part. When a very cool powder-blue '53 Mercury two-door stick shift appeared with 73,000 miles for $300, I thought the search was done. But I let the clutch out too fast and squealed the tires on the test drive. My mistake. Dad nixed the Mercury as too powerful. On another car lot he spotted the perfect car for me: a light gray '54 Dodge four-door sedan with a flathead six-cylinder engine that couldn't have spun its tires if its life depended on it. This was not the car of my dreams, but it was by the time I drove it home. I loved it.

The car cost $600, which was more than I'd expected. Dad said, "I'll pay for the car, but you have to buy the gas." He helped me earn the money, though. He was a realtor who developed a small rural subdivision on which he would occasionally have a spec house built in partnership with a carpenter. He got me a job as the carpenter's helper and asked him to pay me 75 cents an hour. The carpenter raised me to a $1.25 by lunch on the first day. He said, "I can't pay you seventy-five cents an hour. You work too damn hard."

It was well understood that if a guy had a car, he could attract girls, but my car seemed to attract only guys. Almost every summer evening, several male friends would show up at our house to go riding around in my car. They were not very forthcoming with gas money, so I seldom put more than $2.00 in the tank, more often 50 cents to a dollar. Running the tank dry became pretty commonplace. In fact, I once ran out three times in one week, and two of the times were consecutive tanks. I had a lot to learn about fuel management if I was going to be a successful race driver!

I drove the Dodge to the inaugural race at a new road course near Chicago called Meadowdale Raceway. The event was well promoted with ads in all the Chicago area papers. The 3.27-mile course had a unique turn called the Monza Wall: a very highly banked, large-radius 180-degree turn with a steel boilerplate guardrail to keep a car from going over the top if the driver lost control.

Two Scarabs dominated the main event. I had read about these amazing Chevrolet-powered specials built by a California team called Reventlow Automobiles Inc. Chuck Daigh finished first, with team owner Lance Reventlow second. Those Scarabs had an aura about them I would never forget. They beat Chuck Rickert, who finished third in a Porsche.

Off the Front

In grammar school my brother and I and our friends would ride our bicycles to Kenosha, Wisconsin, about 15 miles north of Waukegan. Our destination was the Washington Bowl bicycle track—a banked clay oval about one-fifth mile long, which held championship bicycle races every week in the summer.

Bike riding was passé after I got the Dodge—until I learned that the Washington Bowl had a bicycle race every Wednesday night that I could enter all summer long. It was the two-wheeled equivalent of the hobby stock or jalopy class, reserved for rank amateurs. I loaded my purple Schwinn Sport into the Dodge and drove to Kenosha.

Races were three laps, and on the last lap a bell rang, which I think meant, "Now's the time to go like hell!" There were lots of entrants in my class—maybe 20—mostly kids my age or older. When the race started, I took off as fast as I could go, which was not how bicycle races were supposed to be run. Normally they rode at a fairly fast pace until the bell lap, at which time they sprinted. By the bell lap I was so far ahead nobody could catch me. I won $3.00. If I was class champion for the season, I would receive a Schwinn Paramount track bike. Second place won some sort of watch.

The next week I pulled off the same stunt and won again, only this time, some of the riders were yelling at me to slow down. I was actually making money bicycle racing, but the third week, they had my number and took off fast with me, running me into the ground by the end. I finished about eighth, though still led the points. But our family's summer Savannah trip ended my quest. I was pretty sure my winning ways were over anyway.

Although my main interest was car racing, where a small frame is no disadvantage, I still wanted to do a sport in high school. Any ability I had at basketball or baseball was well hidden, and I was much too small for football. Swimming, however, was another story. I had been city diving champion in grammar school, so swim team it was. I also ran cross country, a painful, thankless running event that was so unimportant in our school that even parents didn't come to the meets. We almost never won, and my only achievements I could look back on after four years on the team were that I never walked and I never puked.

Basketball and football were the important sports at Waukegan High. Swimming was not, although a parent or girlfriend would occasionally show up at the meets. I dived and swam all four years of high school and as a senior was voted most valuable swimmer by my teammates—a big diver in a little pond. During the end-of-the-year assembly, all the sports teams' most valuable players were given their awards before the entire student body of about 2,500 people. As I stood on stage basking in my glory, a friend in one of the rows near the stage motioned something to me, but I couldn't understand the signal. As I took my seat, he informed me that my fly was down.

A Brotherly Scheme

Motorsports dominated my thoughts more than running through the woods or diving into a big pool of water. Lyman, who is a year younger than I am, got an Allstate moped in his early teens. We would often make up a course of some kind and have time trials. He beat me as often as I beat him, but when he turned 16, his attention shifted to cars. We found a nice 1952 MG TD on the used car lot at the foreign and sports car dealer in town for $795. I agreed to donate my Dodge as my half if Lyman could talk our father into paying the difference. We would then share the MG.

It was winter, and I remember that there was lots of snow on the ground. I had swimming in the afternoons, so I asked Lyman to drive the Dodge home from school that day to try to put our deal together with Dad and then pick me up after practice in the MG. It was a great plan, but I had little hope that Lyman would succeed. As I sat in the school hallway looking out at the street for my ride, I saw an unforgettable sight: Lyman pulling up in the MG.

Bashing with the VSCC

The Chicago paper had a section every Sunday listing all the sports car events in the greater Chicago area. The Village Sports Car Club often put on competitions. A few weeks after getting the MG, we read that the VSCC was having a bash. Lyman and I had no idea what a bash was, but we had directions from the paper and a plan to find out.

It was early spring, and spring in the Chicago area means wet and cold. Lyman and I arrived at the scene of the advertised bash to learn that it was a timed event through a wet, muddy, wooded area. The course covered about a mile of narrow, rutted dirt trails. A large variety of British sports cars were entered, plus some Corvettes. After registering, all entrants were given a practice lap or two before official times were taken. I was to drive the first practice lap, with Lyman in the passenger seat. After only a very short time at the wheel, I told my teammate, "We're catching that Corvette!" In my excitement I braked too late for a tight left-hander and hit a tree. Lyman, who hadn't fastened his safety belt (remember, this was 1960), smacked his head on the windshield wiper motor, which on an MG TD was just above the windshield on the passenger side. His head was bleeding and the bumper was rubbing the tire, so we limped back to the parking area and removed the bumper. Fortunately, Lyman's bleeding stopped as well.

We both made official laps with mediocre results and headed home to try to explain our day to our parents. We couldn't agree on a convincing lie, so we decided to tell the truth. Our father didn't even get mad.

After the damage was repaired at a local body shop, we were eager for another event. The paper's sports-car section announced another VSCC at Meadowdale Raceway. For three bucks, a person could enter a sports car and run it on the racetrack.

This was serious business. A year earlier on this same track I had been a spectator watching Ricardo Rodriguez, a boy of my exact age, race his new Porsche RSK. Jim Jeffords won the race in the same Scarab that Chuck Daigh had driven to win the inaugural race in 1958. Rodriguez ran second in his underpowered car until, trying a little too hard, he left the road and turned over but was not seriously hurt. It was hard to accept that a fellow 17-year-old was competing in a professional race in America when I would have to wait four more years even to get a racing license. Regardless, Lyman and I were excited for the opportunity to drive on a real racetrack.

Club officials inspected our car and concluded that our tires were too worn for high-speed driving—but somehow they let us run anyway. Some serious cars and drivers showed up for the event. Harry Heuer, who had recently purchased a Scarab for his Meister Brau Racing Team, used the day as a test session. Another prominent local driver named Tossie Alex was running his Jaguar XKSS. All of the participants were allowed to run on the track anytime they wanted. It was quite a feeling, and very eye opening, to be blasting down the nearly mile-long Meadowdale straight, faster than the MG had ever moved—80 miles per hour—and have the Scarab rocket by at 165 as if we were parked.

At the end of the long main straight was a fast right-hand turn called Greg's Corkscrew, with a very unforgiving guardrail around the outside and no escape road. Lyman spun the MG there, but it was a harmless spin to the inside. When Heuer passed in the Scarab, he wagged his finger at us, not so much in anger but to say, "You boys better be careful."

We finished our exciting day unscathed.

Fast Girls

I never had a girlfriend in high school and managed only four dates—three of them for the big school dances: homecoming, military ball,

My pride and joy in high school was this MG TD I co-owned with my brother. It cost $795, but no street car since has been as much fun. That's Ryser Ericson's house directly behind me. *John Morton Collection*

and the junior prom. Each date was a different girl; number four was a girl I took to Meadowdale.

My first high school date was with a girl named Virginia. Probably my most difficult moment in the four years at Waukegan High was dancing at homecoming in the dimly lit gymnasium with Virginia, whom I barely knew, while trying to keep her from knowing that I had an erection and that her hairspray was making my eyes water so badly I could hardly see.

At one of the high school graduation events a girl named Carol and I got to know each other better and started going out. She was a tomboy who liked cars and wasn't afraid to see what they could do. She was very proud of her beautiful 1955 blue and white two-door Chrysler New Yorker. And Carol wasn't bad-looking either. One night we were riding around in her car with another couple in the back seat. People used to ride around a lot back then. I can't remember if we had a destination in mind on our most memorable night, but probably not. We happened to be at the intersection of Greenwood Avenue and Western. As we turned onto Western, I said, "I got my dad's fifty-five Buick to a hundred on this stretch."

Carol stomped hard on the accelerator. As we reached 85 it was obvious I should have kept my mouth shut. I shouted, "Slow down right now! This ends at Glen Flora." She braked hard and just barely stopped in time; she hadn't reached a hundred.

After stopping at the A&W Drive-In for a shake, we continued driving around somewhat aimlessly outside of town. I wasn't paying much attention to where we were. We stopped at a stop sign and turned left. It was a lonely, dark country road. Carol again stood on the gas pedal. As she accelerated, I was trying to orient myself as to exactly where we were. Again I saw the speedometer at 85. She was still hard on it.

Then it hit me. We were on Holdridge Road, and it ended at Green Bay Road, a busy highway that led to Wisconsin. "Slow down," I said. "We have to stop at Green Bay." This time Carol didn't slow. Illinois had a "stop sign ahead" sign before stop signs on highways, a couple hundred yards from the actual stop. I yelled, "'Stop sign ahead' sign!" and she started to brake.

I knew about brake fade from the magazines but had never experienced it. We went through the stop sign and out onto Green Bay Road at about 40. A truck T-boned us on the driver side. Carol's door flew open at the impact and then slammed shut and jammed. When we finally came to rest in front of a church, Carol climbed over me and out the passenger door.

The man who hit us—who, ironically, was heading home from the Waukegan Speedway where he was a crewman for one of the drivers—had broken his arm. Because the Chrysler was totaled, my father came to pick us up. We weren't hurt much. I had to meet with Carol's insurance agent to discuss the accident. She wanted me to say that the brakes had failed—and in a sense they had. My statement was wishy-washy, and Carol didn't get the result she wanted from her insurance company. The accident pretty much ended our relationship.

When I saw her at our 35th high school reunion, she still blamed me for not telling the insurance agent the brakes failed. By our 50th reunion she had mellowed, maybe because she finally realized that my obsession with speed went beyond the twisted wreckage of her '55 Chrysler. I still feel a little guilty, though, more than 50 years later.

Higher (Speed) Education

My mother and father had college degrees, and there was never a question that Lyman and I would go to college too. My high school grades were not a great foundation for that path, but I applied to Clemson College in South Carolina and they accepted me. I loved coastal South Carolina, where my uncle, also named Lyman, had 11 acres on a salt-water river called the Okatie. He had a dock and a couple small boats, one of which was our water-ski boat. He also had a tractor he bought new in 1946—the first motor vehicle I drove solo. Uncle Lyman's place was only 35 miles from Savannah, so when we were on our twice-yearly trips, that's where we would spend weekends. To me it was the best place on earth. This was not a logical reason for choosing Clemson, which was nowhere near the coast, but my uncle's place had given me good memories of South Carolina, and that's about as much direction as I had on choosing a place to continue my education.

The next stage of my life was beginning, and I was still looking for ways to put racing in my future. With no sponsors, no car, and no race experience, college was as good a next step as any—that and work. On the latter score, one of my grandmother's neighbors, Mr. Kelley, came through with a job at Union Bag paper mill the summer before college. Anyone who has ever visited Savannah has experienced the odor of that paper mill. Although I could remember the pall it cast over the city from the time I was a child, I'd never dreamed I'd have Union Bag on my resume.

Mr. Kelley and his wife used to come over to my grandmother's house and drink martinis in her kitchen. When Mr. Kelley drank, he blinked. The more he drank, the more he blinked. If I was around and the martinis were flowing, he would start repeating himself as to the importance of education until the blinking became almost manic. The Kelleys had two boys about my age who went to the University of Georgia in Athens. I think their father may have overemphasized the benefit of higher education because the last I heard, his sons were still there.

Union Bag was the kind of place that gave blue-collar work a bad name. From the minute you entered the factory, you were assaulted by the incessant din of a hundred throbbing bag-making machines. A device in the parking lot gave each vehicle a quick spray on the way home to wash the contaminants off so the paint wouldn't deteriorate. I never saw anything to protect the employees, however. Perhaps it was because they were unpainted.

The first motor vehicle I ever drove was my Uncle Lyman's 1946 Farmall A. It was a perfect fit if I sat on my friend Pinky's lap. *John Morton Collection*

My brother was also spending his summer in Savannah as well, but not to work. At a track on Tybee Island about 17 miles from Savannah, there were kart races on Wednesday and Saturday nights. The Tybee Light Go Kart Stadium was named for the historic Tybee Lighthouse, built before Georgia was a state to guide ships into the mouth of the Savannah River on their way to the Port of Savannah about 15 miles inland. We borrowed our grandmother's 1954 Mercury to attend the races.

Though the working conditions at the paper mill were a little rough, I was making good money for the day—about $1.80 per hour. That put me in the market for a kart of my own so I could race at Tybee stadium. I bought a used kart for $175 from a fellow I knew who was buying a new one. It was a Kurtis Wildcat with twin West Bend engines, but Lyman and I couldn't let the relatives know I had it, so we kept it in the garage of the parents of a girl we knew. We would borrow grandmother's Mercury every Wednesday and Saturday night, leaving her with the impression that we were race spectators rather than entrants.

This is the official identification card that entitled me to work at the hottest, noisiest, smelliest job I would ever have the opportunity to experience. If there was ever an incentive to get a good education, this was it. *John Morton Collection*

The kart racing not only gave me the ability to partly escape the drudgery and boredom of the paper mill job, it also furnished me with something tangible to look forward to as I ran fantasy races in my head. My kart was obsolete when I bought it, however, because it didn't have a live axle; each engine drove one rear wheel, meaning the inside motor wasn't contributing anything in the corners. I drove in the twin-engine races, and then we took a chain off of one engine and Lyman drove in the single-engine race. The only race I won was one for entrants who had never won a trophy. I treasured that trophy even though when I got it, one of the wheels was broken off on the little kart on top.

The last race of the season was a special Labor Day event with many additional entries from out of town. Instead of a qualifying heat for the feature race, they drew numbers out of a hat for starting positions. To my surprise I drew number one, pole position. We lined up and were given the signal to start engines. One of mine started; the other one didn't. I begged it, "Please start." Just before the start-line officials went to push me aside, the second engine caught and we were off on the pace lap. When the green flag fell, I maintained my position through the first turn and then the first lap. After a couple more laps, I was not only in the lead but pulling away from the field.

I held my lead, on top of the world, when suddenly I heard one of my engines overrevving. I'd lost a chain. I was on one engine and a sitting duck. I started losing positions and any chance of a victory. In my frustration, I spun out on the turn at the end of the front straight

Me, posing with my first-ever winner's trophy. It was 1960 at the Tybee Light Kart Stadium near Savannah, Georgia. This was also the year Carroll Shelby retired from racing. *John Morton Collection*

where the spectators sat. I hit the hay bales, and as I got out of the kart and pulled it out of the straw, I heard the people in the stands laughing. I couldn't understand why it was funny that I'd led the race and then spun. Their laughter seemed almost surreal as I struggled to pull my kart into a safe place off the racetrack.

Afterward, I learned that the joke had nothing to do with my hard-lost lead or my spin-out. In my flailing crash, I must have caught my pants on something. As a result, the whole time I was struggling to extract the Wildcat from the hay bales, I was treating the spectators to a bird's-eye view of my Fruit of the Looms. Honestly, I've never fully gotten over that race.

When the summer of 1960 ended, my parents took me to Clemson for freshman orientation. I was assigned a dorm room and a room-mate, and then I picked my classes and got my required books. I had a vague notion that I was really on my own for the first time in my life.

There were only a couple of nonsoutherners on my hall, and it quickly became obvious that if you were a Yankee, you were somehow a bit tainted. In fact it was obvious that my roommate—who was from Clinton, South Carolina—had visions of becoming quite the big man on campus (at least he struck me that way), so a Yankee roommate just wouldn't do. However, he was gone before I even memorized his name, and I never heard of him again.

So I had the dorm room to myself. Even though Clemson was no longer a military school, gun racks were still in the rooms. Out my window I could see the Calhoun Mansion, home of Andrew Jackson's vice president, which was maintained on the campus by the university. As for myself, I couldn't have cared less about the school's history. I was only there because my uncle had a summer house by the coast.

Within a couple of weeks' time it became obvious to me that this was going to be difficult. Except for my feet and my thumb, I had no means of escape I considered hitchhiking somewhere just to get away for a while. On a weekend only two or three weeks into the school year, I was exploring the tiny downtown when I rounded a corner two blocks from the campus and saw an auto repair garage called Clemson Automotive.

In their lot were three cars with numbers on the side and CARE painted in big letters. I asked the guy working on the '37 Plymouth where they raced. He said they raced on Saturday nights at Seneca Speedway about 10 miles from Clemson. CARE stood for Clemson Auto Racing Enthusiasts—a pretty sophisticated name in light of the cars I was looking at. The guy providing answers was Dan Baker, who was about my age. I told him I'd like to watch them race sometime. He said I could go with them that night if I wanted to. He didn't seem to care that I was a Yankee.

Seneca Speedway, a quarter-mile dirt track with a rudimentary grandstand and dim lighting, provided the only fun I'd had since arriving at school. I asked Dan about racing at 18—did he have to lie about his age? He said they didn't care about age. They didn't care much about crash helmets either, because Dan raced with a football helmet. He rolled the Plymouth in the race that night, but apart from a headache he was fine. The Plymouth wasn't badly damaged either. On the way back to Clemson, I told Dan that I wanted to do this too.

"We'll have to get you a car," he said. "Do you have any money?"

I had an account in the college bank, which was intended for school supplies and entertainment, such as movies. Dan agreed to help me find a car on Monday. I withdrew all the money in my account—$43—and met Dan at Clemson Automotive. We drove to Seneca and scouted out some used car lots, looking for a suitable racer. We found a black 1940 Ford two-door sedan that might have filled the bill, but the salesman was asking $65 for it. Dan wisely did the talking. He was a car-buying fool. At the age of 18, he'd already owned as many cars as I would have in my lifetime. Besides, he was a local boy.

"We have forty-three dollars cash," Dan told the salesman.

"Sold," the man replied.

I drove my new '40 Ford back to Clemson behind Dan as fast as it would run.

I had to leave for a class, but by the time I returned to Clemson Automotive that afternoon, Dan had already cut the fenders off with a torch. The car was almost prepared for the following weekend with the exception of the safety belt installation, which was to come in handy later. Looking at this more than 50 years later, it is sad that we ruined a 1940 Ford two-door sedan, which today, in the condition it was in when we bought it, would be worth several thousand dollars.

Still, if these cars hadn't ended up as racers long ago, the ones left might be worth much less.

The owner of Clemson Automotive was a man named Truman Williams. Truman had quite a nice business repairing cars, some of them students' cars. Being only a block from the campus, Clemson Automotive had a captive clientele. There were things about Truman that I learned gradually, but for now he offered to tow my new race car to the track and take me around a few laps to show me how it was done. He claimed that he was once a race car driver.

Truman drove around the track a few times with me beside him before any so-called official running took place. At Seneca Speedway everything was a little informal. I had seen many dirt track races but had never been on a dirt track before. As Truman accelerated, the car felt faster than it had on the highway and was much noisier with most of the exhaust system removed. Parts of the track were dark because of poor lighting. Truman seemed a little tentative. I'm pretty sure he hadn't really been a race car driver himself.

Truman got out, and I took my first laps on a real racetrack at a real racing event for real cars. The track had been watered down, and on my second lap, I went wide on the exit of the first turn, sliding over the banking. The disaster I thought I was headed for was a nonevent. I didn't hit a tree, and the drop-off was not very steep; I just turned and drove back onto the track. It was embarrassing, but I'm not sure anyone even noticed. Running off the track shook me up a little. I was going to have to get into the turns a little harder to keep it from running wide, but I think I was faster than Truman right away.

All I remember about the actual race was that I managed to keep it on the track and I got a little faster. I wore an industrial hardhat I'd gotten from a friend's dad who worked in a steel mill.

My stock '40 Ford wasn't fast enough to challenge for a win, but it did provide a chance to do some good racing. To the detriment of my enthusiasm for school, I started spending too much time at Truman Williams's establishment. To be honest, looking back on this time, two things are obvious: I was too immature for college, and maturity isn't really a requirement for racing, at least not the same kind of maturity.

Dan was a good mechanic for his age, and he could weld too. He was a high school dropout, but after quitting at 16, Dan had second thoughts. He told the principal he'd seen the light and asked if he could return. Naturally the principal said, "Yes, of course you can come back to school." Dan asked if he could speak at an assembly and advise students to remain in school and not make the mistake that he had made. The principal agreed, and Dan gave his testimonial before the student body. Two weeks later, Dan Baker dropped out of school for good.

After my classes, I would often go over to Clemson Automotive and help work on the race cars. Dan was making a new exhaust system for his Plymouth. I helped him by holding the tubes in place as he welded. He used coat hangers for welding rods because they were cheaper than the real thing. Actually, they were free. The coat hangers sparked like crazy as Dan welded. Sometimes they would start a fire. Once they started a fire at the gas tank, but we put it out with a rag. This was truly entry-level hillbilly racing at its finest.

We ran several races at Seneca Speedway that fall: Dan in the Plymouth, Hubert McAlister in the '50 Ford, and me in the '40. The driver who usually won was a man named Floyd Holcombe. Floyd drove a white '37 Chevy 6 that was owned by the same man who owned the track. The car was very light because everything that could be removed had been cut out of it. I knew it had no floor because once before the feature race, Floyd stood on the ground inside the car and peed. Even though the pits were across from the grandstand, I guess Floyd felt that being in the car offered some privacy; I don't suppose he was aware of the small stream flowing from under his private Porta-Potty in plain view of the spectators.

One night before the feature race, I was across the track on the spectator side to use the restroom and get a hot dog. Under the grandstand were Floyd and his car owner. They motioned for me to join them for a drink of moonshine they were sharing. One of them said, "Go ahead and have some. It'll make you drive better."

Another night Floyd told us, "I got so goddamn drunk at one race, I had to just drive around the bottom of the track till it was over." The last time I saw Floyd was at Westminster Speedway about 17 miles from Clemson. He drove Dan and me to our car in the parking lot while he explained that he was "just about healed up from being shot in a bar fight." I can't recall if he was actually in the fight or just an innocent bystander. Floyd Holcombe went on to become quite a prominent dirt-track driver in northwestern South Carolina, as did his son Lloyd.

We continued to prepare our race cars at Truman's Clemson Automotive. He was generous because I was never aware of his being reimbursed for the use of his facility. It was comical to watch Truman dealing with the Clemson students as he worked on their cars. When a car was left for repair, Truman would drive it and tell everyone it was his, which was strange because we all knew the car belonged to someone else. It seemed that he lived in some sort of fantasy bubble with no idea that we all knew he was lying. He would remove parts from one customer's car and put them on another, depending on which one needed to be delivered first. Once I even saw him pull an engine out of one car and install it into another.

Truman was illiterate but tried to fake it. He'd say, "Dan, read this for me. I don't have my glasses." Some of the students got upset about their cars not being finished and went to the authorities. One day while I was there, a marshal came. As Truman left with him he said, "Dan, I'm going with this fellow. I'll be back in a little while." I never saw Truman Williams again.

In the last race I ran at Seneca, I rolled my car. After the track was watered, some of the water ran to the inside of the turn, causing the inside to remain muddy. During the race when I went to the very bottom of turn one, my left front tire splashed my windshield with mud. Unable to see, I hit the embankment on the inside of the turn and rolled the car over. I was OK, but because it was the last race of the season, we just left the car at the track and went home.

Two-Wheeled Terrors

A 1950s Indian Warrior motorcycle was among the junk left derelict at Clemson Automotive. No one seemed to know who owned it. I'd always loved motorcycles but had never actually ridden one. After Dan got it running, I learned to ride. One night we took turns tearing down Clemson's main street past the beer bar at 60 miles per hour with a broken headlight. A small crowd of semi-drunk students exited the bar to watch the show. Somehow we got smart enough to wrap things up before the town cop appeared.

Later Dan and I rode the Indian two-up about 85 miles to the Chimney Rock Hillclimb in North Carolina. Chimney Rock was a state park where twice a year the local Sports Car Club of America chapter was allowed to close about 2 miles of the narrow winding mountain road to hold timed runs up the mountain for sports and small formula cars. It was a great weekend, and though the old Indian was hard to start, it never let us down.

Though he was a gifted mechanic, Dan didn't know anything about sports car racing until he met me. I guess he caught some of my enthusiasm because one night he came into my dorm room and dangled a set of keys in front of me as if to say, "Look what I got!"

I asked, "What are they for?"

"I just bought a Triumph TR 3. Show me how to drive it."

I drove Dan's hot little car to a nearby twisty road and ran it as fast as I could, trying to impress him in a "see what I mean about sports cars" manner. It worked. He said later, "I thought Jesus Christ hisself was driving that car."

Dan started working on his cornering technique and two weeks later rolled the car near Cherokee in the North Carolina mountains, about 100 miles from Clemson. He was uninjured but his passenger, a friend named Kenny, was knocked out. I was told Kenny had sustained some minor brain damage, but I knew him both before and after the accident and I couldn't tell much difference.

Campus Hot Shots

Clemson was a football school; football took precedence over all other sports. The Tigers won the national championship one year only to be heavily sanctioned for recruiting violations. Though located in the heart of stock car country, auto racing had no presence in the curriculum (unlike today, when Clemson offers a graduate course in auto racing and sends a number of its graduates straight to NASCAR teams). In 1960, few students shared my interests. Instead of school colors, I wore a white jacket with a small Ferrari patch sown on the front. One day a fellow student asked me why I had that patch on my jacket.

"I just like Ferraris. I don't actually have one," I admitted.

His name was Tommy Thompson and he was a big fan of Formula One and sports car racing. He was a sophomore and so was allowed to have his own car on campus (freshmen were prohibited from having cars). And what a car Tommy had: a Coronado Red 1960 Pontiac Ventura with factory aluminum wheels, Tri-Power 389 V-8, and four-speed transmission. I really wanted to drive it.

We talked a lot about racing and the various drivers. I told him that Stirling Moss, Mike Hawthorn, and Masten Gregory were my three favorite drivers and that when I heard on the radio that Hawthorn was killed in a road accident right after he retired as 1958 World Champion, I was so distraught that I got in my Dodge and drove down a road outside of Waukegan as fast as the car would go. The road had icy spots on it, and I eventually came to my senses and slowed down; perhaps I was taking my hero worship too far. I liked Gregory because he wore glasses just as I did, and people told me I looked like him. Of course I agreed.

There was a third racing enthusiast we spent some time with named Brooks Schwartz. He claimed to know all of the European drivers because he was a military brat who had lived in Wiesbaden,

Germany, which had enabled him to attend the Formula One races. He had some extraordinary stories about people like Gurney, Moss, and Bonnier, with whom he said he had hung out. I didn't believe most of what Brooks said, but I did give him $5.00 for a knockoff wheel nut, a brake balance bar, and some blueprints from BRM, which I still have. Brooks claimed the BRM wheel nut was off of Gurney's car. I'm pretty sure the parts are authentic, so for five bucks it was a good deal.

Tommy and a chemistry-major acquaintance of his had an interesting plan, and they invited me to go along. The acquaintance had swiped something from the chemistry lab that was supposed to explode in water. He also pinched a jug of alcohol. They were going to have a party featuring heavy drinking coupled with some sort of an explosion.

Carroll Shelby's last Riverside race, October 16, 1960. He finished fifth in this Type 61 Birdcage Maserati. His final race was a week later at Laguna Seca. Carroll finished second to Stirling Moss while popping nitroglycerin pills to cope with his angina. *Bob Tronolone*

Tommy drove up to a remote area on the Hartwell Project, the damming of the Savannah River that caused the Seneca River to become a large lake not far from Clemson. We started drinking the pure alcohol, but not being a big drinker, I took it easy. As Tommy and the chemistry major started getting really drunk, it occurred to me that if I stayed sober I'd be the only one able to drive the Pontiac.

I don't remember much about the explosion, which they told me was spectacular, but I vividly recall Tommy's amazing Tri-Power Ventura. It was the first vehicle I'd driven that was still accelerating hard at a hundred. I got the needle to the 115 mark on one stretch of the four-lane back to school.

Tommy learned that Carroll Shelby had just announced his retirement from racing due to a heart problem. We agreed that although Shelby had won Le Mans the year before for Aston Martin, their Formula One car wasn't good enough for him to have been competitive. One thing led to another in our discussion, and it was soon decided that we would go to Sebring in March, as it was within striking distance of Clemson—600 miles.

Among the Stars

I'd never looked so forward to anything as much as our trip to Sebring, except maybe my first car. We drove Tommy's Pontiac to his hometown of Gainesville, Florida, and spent the night with his parents. The next morning we left for Sebring, having exchanged the Pontiac for Tommy's dad's new Falcon station wagon, as it would be easier to sleep in.

When we arrived at the track on Friday, a four-hour race for small GT cars was already underway. We bought a program and checked the numbers. I wanted to know which car Stirling Moss was driving. I'd written him a fan letter when I was in high school, but he didn't answer. That was OK; he was still my favorite driver. I identified him by his number, although I could have spotted him by his white helmet and just the way he looked in the car. He was in an Austin-Healey Sprite. The Sprite wasn't nearly as fast as the Fiat Abarths that eventually won. Harry Washburn finished first.

After the four-hour main event, I got an unexpected treat: a kart race. Sebring was really not an appropriate track for karts—it was too big. Bobby Allen, a 16-year-old, won the race on a Rathmann Exterminator. Named for the 1960 Indy 500 winner, Jim Rathmann, it was an unusual design made from sheet aluminum instead of steel tubing. It was beautifully built with a gold-anodized finish. After he took the checkered flag, I wondered if Bobby Allen would go on to become a race car driver. He did, earning fame and many wins both building and driving sprint cars.

The last race of the day was the Formula Junior race. My favorite cars were the Cooper Forumla Juniors because they looked like a miniature version of the car Jack Brabham had just driven to his second World Championship. The Rodriguez brothers were in the race. Pedro had a Cooper and Ricardo was at the wheel of an uncompetitive front-engine car. Walt Hansgen and Jim Hall were in Coopers, so it was a surprise to see an amateur driver named Charlie Kolb beat them in a car I'd never heard of: a Gemini. One Cooper was entered by Carroll Shelby. Seems he wanted to remain involved in racing even after his retirement.

Tommy and I wandered around the grounds after the races and found the Camoradi and Cunningham teams sharing one of the old World War II–era hangars. Both teams ran Maseratis. Camoradi had a type 61 Birdcage for Moss and Graham Hill and a type 63 rear engine Birdcage for Masten Gregory and team owner Lucky Casner.

The Cunningham team ran two front-engine Birdcages—a type 60 2-liter car for Walt Hansgen and Briggs Cunningham, and a 2.8-liter type 61 for John Fitch and Dick Thompson. They also had a type 63 Birdcage for Walt Hansgen and Bruce McLaren. The Ferrari teams were not working at the track, so we didn't run into Phil Hill, Olivier Gendebien, Wolfgang von Trips, Richie Ginther, or the Rodriguez brothers. Ricardo and Pedro were driving for the North American Racing Team, which was almost like a factory Ferrari team.

I stood right next to my hero Gregory, but he was talking to someone so I didn't want to bother him for his autograph. This had been a very good day and tomorrow would be even better.

Tommy and I spent the night in the Falcon out in the spectator area. We were awakened by the sound of the Ferraris as their mechanics drove them back to the track from the garage in town, where they had been readied for the 12 grueling hours ahead. What a fabulous alarm clock was the shrill sound of these spectacular cars as the lucky mechanics got to test them over the 5 miles from town. The question for us was this: How the hell were we going to get into the pits?

We stood in the spectator area across from the pits watching the cars being lined up for the Le Mans start. The Camoradi team push-started Moss's Birdcage to warm it up the few minutes before the start. Tommy and I moved to a position past where the last of the competitors were lined up and waited for the national anthem. As the "Star-Spangled Banner" drew everyone's attention to the flag, Tommy and I scrambled over the fence and sprinted across the track into the pits.

Not only did we now have access to the pits and paddock, but we could see a lot of the action on the track as well. Although the Le Mans start looked like chaos, all the cars seemed to get away OK—that is, except for the one Stirling Moss was driving. I had read that Moss was almost always first away in a Le Mans start, but not today; his battery was dead. The crew had to jump-start the Maserati. When they push-started the car to warm it up, we wondered if it was pushed to save the battery.

Gregory led a few laps in the rear-engine Birdcage. The Rodriguez Ferrari got by and ran in the lead for quite a while. When the pit stops began, we lost track of positions. The pits at Sebring were little cement cubicles where the race teams kept their equipment—tools, wheels, and tires—during the race. It was also where the crews and drivers gathered before a pit stop. As I walked by one of the Ferrari cubicles, I saw Phil Hill. I walked in and very tentatively asked him what was probably a stupid question, which I can't remember. He answered and we started a conversation—I was shocked. I couldn't have imagined that a two-time Sebring winner, a Le Mans winner, and the winner of the first sports car race I'd ever seen could have been this approachable. As one of the Ferraris made a pit stop in the pit next to where we were standing, he said, "Look at what bunglers these Ferrari crews are. You'd think they would notice the headrest is backwards." This careless crew had for some reason removed the rear deck cover, which incorporated the headrest fairing. In their haste they were trying to install it backward.

Then I remembered something my friend Ryser Ericson had told me several years before. He was contrasting Phil Hill and Carroll Shelby, America's two best sports car drivers. He said Shelby was very smart and Hill operated more on a big ego and wasn't very smart. The Phil Hill I had just met didn't fit that description. I'd have to wait a while to see about Shelby.

I saw Dan Gurney standing in another pit. His Porsche RS 61, which he was sharing with Joakim Bonnier, was stationary on pit road. A mechanic said, "It's ready to go."

Gurney seemed to know that something was still wrong with the car and said, "It's not fixed. You fix it and I'll drive it."

Someone handed him a sandwich, but before he had time to eat it the mechanic said, "Now it's ready to go." Gurney got in the car. Holding the sandwich in his mouth, he started the engine and put the Porsche in gear. I took his picture.

We left the pit area and walked around the track to view from different vantage points. Ginther in the rear-engine Ferrari looked scary in the turn they called Big Bend. He was so fast; he used every inch of the road—another few inches and he would have been in the grass and it would have been a big crash. He was teamed with Wolfgang von Trips, who we spotted crossing a walk bridge in the spectator area with a camera around his neck. We thought it was cool that a great driver who was still in the race was out taking pictures like a common spectator.

The Rodriguez brothers were also driving very hard. When it was the driver wearing a yellow helmet, I always felt a little envy as he went by because I knew it was Ricardo. Though he was a little older than I was, it was only by three days. He was born on Valentine's Day 1942.

Dan Gurney co-drove his factory Porsche RS 61 with Jo Bonnier at Sebring in 1961. I stood beside Gurney as he ate a sandwich while his crew worked on the car during a pit stop. When the car was ready, Dan hadn't finished his sandwich so he took it with him. I snapped this picture, and if you look closely, you'll see the sandwich in his mouth. *John Morton*

As darkness closed around the track, it became hard to identify the cars, but in a way it was even more spectacular. Headlights and exhaust flames were all that was clearly visible as the ghostly image of a car flashed by. Sound took over from sight as the dominant sense. I'd never seen or heard anything like this before.

Moss and Gregory were never in contention in their Birdcage Maseratis. Both fell by the wayside early with mechanical problems. My new favorite driver, Phil Hill, won the race for the third time.

I had wanted to see this important international race for a long time. In 1960 I listened to the race on the radio in Waukegan as Porsche took its first big overall victory. Actually seeing it was not a disappointment. What was a disappointment was that we were heading back to school with no more racing activity to look forward to until summer vacation, when I planned to resume kart racing.

Kart Attack

Back in Illinois, my brother, who had graduated from high school, got a brand new Go Kart 800 and was already racing when I got home in June. I was having my old kart shipped by rail from Savannah, which took quite a long time. Kart races usually used the motocross scoring system to determine final standings: three heat races for each class, with the final positions determined by total points from all three races. A perfect score of 1,200 was possible if one kart won all three races.

Our parents took us to a track in Wisconsin called Milton Junction, a simple triangular course. Lyman was going to let me run the middle heat. We arrived late and had no time to practice. Lyman had raced there before and did very well, winning the first heat. I started from the pole position in the second heat. I felt awkward on the pace lap, never having been on this track or in this kart before. When the race started, people began passing me by the first corner. On the second lap, I ran off the track and was disqualified. If all four wheels went off course, you were out of the race. I ruined Lyman's chance for a win and felt awful about that, but even worse about my poor performance.

As our father drove the 80 miles home, he said something I've never forgotten. He said, "Lyman, you're very good but, John, you just don't have it. You screw yourself up into a ball." I hadn't had a fair chance and my confidence was already so low that his comments were devastating. The ball comment referred to my leaning over too far as I entered the corners. Maybe he was right about that part, but his comments were not constructive criticism.

That summer, I got a job at Anchor Coupling, a company that made oil and hydraulic lines for trucks, tractors, and other heavy equipment. I was one of the two forklift drivers. Sometimes we would race around the inside of the factory building. We would go in opposite directions so nobody would know there was a race going on. The first one back to the start won. It was better than the Union Bag job and provided me with kart-racing money.

When my hopelessly obsolete kart arrived from Georgia, I traded it in for a new Dart Kart A Bone with a McCulloch MC 6 engine. Several tracks were within driving distance from Waukegan, so Lyman and I did quite a lot of racing that summer. Sometimes I would enter as Masten Gregory and Lyman, Tazio Morton. Two friends also had aliases: Don Stranberg was Wolfgang von Stranberg and Johnny

I got this topless shot of Stirling Moss after both of the Maseratis he drove broke. The front engine Type 61 and the rear engine Type 63 were entered by Camoradi, the team Carroll Shelby drove for the year before. *John Morton*

Opitz was Augie Opitz. It was funny to hear the announcer, who had no idea who these people were.

Lyman and I both won some races that summer. We seemed just about equal in ability, yet he didn't take it as seriously as I did. He was lackadaisical about preparation and often wasn't quite ready when we had to leave for the tracks.

We were to be roommates at Clemson for the 1961–1962 school year. I wasn't officially a sophomore yet due to substandard grades, so I couldn't yet have a car on campus. We talked our father into towing our MG behind the family car and dropping it by Clemson on his Christmas trip to Savannah. We kept it off campus at a friend's house within walking distance of the school.

The '40 Returns

I resumed my friendship with Dan Baker, and he made me a proposal. We would go over to Seneca Speedway, retrieve my derelict '40 Ford, fix it up, and he would build a good engine. We would take turns driving it. I agreed, so we set the plan in motion. I mentioned that sports cars and karts had very quick steering ratios. Maybe we should modify ours to make it quicker.

Dan shortened the steering arms and lengthened the Pitman arm, giving us one and a quarter turns, lock to lock. The modification made it very hard to turn the steering wheel—a classic case of a little knowledge being dangerous. We decided not to undo it, though. It would build up our arm muscles. We installed a World War II–surplus aluminum airplane seat, strapped a 5-gallon jerry can to the back for a gas tank, and painted the Ford red. We towed it back to the Seneca Speedway to test it.

Other cars were running too. The track wasn't watered so there was a persistent red-clay fog hovering above the track. Visibility was poor, to say the least. And conditions were not ideal for breaking in our fresh engine, considering we had no air cleaner. Other than the heavy steering, however, the car seemed pretty good—much better than it was the previous year. Dan and I took turns driving until it finally developed a rod knock. We took it back to Dan's house for another bottom-end rebuild.

We raced the car at Westminster Speedway on Saturday nights. Dan would run the heat race one night and I would run the feature; the next week, we'd switch. I think our class was called jalopy, but whatever they named it, it was the secondary class to the faster sportsman or limited sportsman lineup. These were the nicer cars. They all had flathead Ford V-8s with a maximum 0.080 overbore. One of the best drivers was a kid named Buck Simmons. He was 15 years old.

Once we towed the Ford all the way to Greenwood, South Carolina, to a nicer facility that had been a paved track but was reverted to dirt, as that was more popular at the time. By our main event, huge potholes had developed where the dirt was displaced down to the original paved surface. That made it hard to hold on to the steering wheel because of all the feedback through our ridiculous sports car steering. We took home $15.00, though, which more than covered expenses.

Our last race was back at Westminster Speedway. It was Dan's turn to drive the main event after I did the heat. Dan tended to drive over his head, and this night was no exception. He was starting to get pretty aggressive. As we watched him go down the back straight, Lyman said, "He's gonna crash!" When Dan attempted to pass a car on the outside going into the turn, he made Lyman right. He flew over the outer embankment as the car went end over end. Dan was OK, but our revamped car was finished and so were our jalopy careers, at least for 1961.

I was not taking my higher education seriously and felt I was wasting my time at school. When I told my parents I didn't want to return for the second semester, my father practically begged me to stick out the year. I think he was mostly concerned that it would look bad for his son to drop out midyear; he also thought I'd get over racing. I reluctantly returned.

Lyman, Tommy Thompson, and I went to the 1962 Daytona Continental, the first of the Daytona sports car races that morphed into the 24-hour five years later. Again we made a stealthy pit/paddock entrance while parachutists came down during the prerace ceremonies. This time, facing a much higher fence, we suffered a small amount of clothing damage as we topped the chain link. A few years later, Tommy went to jail for pulling the same stunt.

Dan Gurney won in a Lotus 19 that was the class of the field. The race was a three-hour timed event but just before the finish, Gurney's Coventry Climax engine blew. He had the presence of mind to stop his car on the banking a few feet short of the finish line and wait for the time to expire before coasting down the slope to cross the line and win. Phil Hill, sharing a Ferrari with Ricardo Rodriguez, was second with Jim Hall third in his Chaparral. Moss was fourth, winning the GT class in a Ferrari.

The Daytona Continental was the first time Americans got to see our newly crowned World Champion Phil Hill race since his tumultuous 1961 season. That was the first year of the new Formula One regulations limiting engine size to one-and-a-half liters with no supercharging. Ferrari had the best of these smaller engines, and although their chassis was not as good as the British cars, they were favored to win the World Championship.

I followed the season as well as I could through newspapers and magazines. I knew it was a close fight between Ferrari teammates Phil Hill and Wolfgang von Trips. I was pulling for Hill, who made a big late-race mistake in the French Grand Prix by spinning out with a sure win in sight and blowing his points advantage. The Italian Grand Prix was the next weekend. I was in my bedroom in Savannah shortly before returning to Clemson when I heard a news flash that said, "Championship hope ends in tragedy," and then went to commercial. I clearly remember saying to myself, *Please don't let it be Phil Hill.* When the news came back on and it was von Trips, I felt relieved but still very sad and a little selfish that I'd favored the man who spoke to me in the pits.

In March we again traveled to Sebring with similar accommodations to 1961. This time the little GT race was shortened to three hours. It was wet for a while so Stirling Moss led until the track dried. Then the faster Abarths took over with Bruce McLaren winning, Walt Hansgen second, and Moss in the Sprite third.

In the 12-hour event, Phil Hill and Olivier Gendebien were second overall and first in class in a Ferrari GTO. Lucian Bianchi and Joakim Bonnier won in a factory Ferrari.

Danger at the End of the Road

There were only two months of school left, and it was time to make some serious plans regarding my future in racing. I had tentatively planned to buy a race car with the money that was originally set aside for college and was leaning toward a Lotus or Cooper Formula Junior. In the meantime I would try to hone my driving skills with our MG TD. Lyman and I practiced our cornering speeds on some of the twisty roads in the vicinity of Clemson.

My brother and I had two friends, Joe Richardson and Fred Pearman, who were also very interested in racing. They were freshmen at Clemson and had grown up in the area. I had demonstrated my driving skills for Joe on a road near Anderson, South Carolina, 17 miles from Clemson. He directed me to White City Park Road, which dead-ended into a body of water resulting from the Hartwell Dam project. It offered about a mile of very nice, fairly high-speed curves before it sank into the lake. If you drove to the water to verify that no cars were on the road and then went back a mile and turned around, you had your own private race strip. Joe and Fred had used the road in their own cars many times. After I learned the road, Joe had an idea.

"Let's go get Fred and have him follow us out here in his car. We'll tell him you want to see our private road and you want him to talk you through the turns as you drive. Then you go as fast as you can and scare the hell out of him."

It was early evening when we met Fred as he came out of church, of all places. He had a girl with him named Connie Mulinax. Fred agreed to Joe's plan. He parked his Corvair and got in the TD. I took off with him attempting to direct me. Soon he was silently squeezing the crab bar on the dash. Joe's trick was a great success. Fred said he couldn't believe how fast I was.

It was dark when I asked Connie if she would like a ride. The last turn before the water was a right-hander. Joe and Fred stood on the outside of the turn to watch. As I started to make my run with Connie, I stopped to have her fasten her safety belt and then proceeded. On the final turn with Joe and Fred watching, things went terribly wrong.

"Oh shit!" The car started to spin. The rear wheels slid off the pavement and into a drainage ditch, the running board digging into the dirt. The car flipped over and skidded upside down, sparks flying in the darkness. It came to rest in the middle of the road, wheels up.

Fred and Joe ran to us, pulling us out from under the wrecked MG. I had hit my head pretty hard and had no memory. Connie for some reason was OK. After they put us in the Corvair to drive Connie home, my memory slowly started to return. I don't know how we both survived, turning over and sliding upside down on pavement in an

MG TD with no top and no roll bar. Even the two humps on the cowl behind the windshield were flattened.

All I had was a nasty scrape on my head and a torn sweater. Joe and I hitchhiked back to Clemson. We both checked into the school infirmary and spent the night. I was pretty much OK but didn't want to face Lyman. Joe was even better, but had an unfinished term paper due the next day, so he decided he'd been in the accident too.

Lyman wasn't happy, but I told him he could have my half of the car if it was repairable and could use it for a trade in; he wanted a Triumph TR 4. The wreckage was taken to a body shop in Seneca. We told the owner we needed it to be finished so we could drive it home to Illinois when school was out in about a month. He said he could do it. Lyman and I intended to drive the car to Indiana in time to see the Indianapolis 500 on Memorial Day, Wednesday, May 30.

By the time the car was ready to go it was late afternoon on Tuesday, May 29. They had done a pretty good job on the car considering the extent of the damage. The beautiful little MG we both loved was now a Bondo barge under the new green paint. Unfortunately the wiring hadn't been sorted out and was hanging from under the dash. We used masking tape to identify the two dangling wires that when connected would make the headlights go on.

We had nearly 600 miles to drive by race time the next morning. Things went pretty well until the mountains of Tennessee, when the headlights started to dim and the engine began missing. With the lights off it ran better. I was driving while Lyman was in charge of touching the wires together for a few seconds so I could see in the mountain blackness. Finally the car would go no more so we pulled off the highway to plan our next move.

We considered spending the night in the car but I heard what I thought was a wild animal. Lyman laughed at me. We tried to flag down a semi to no avail. We pushed the car back on the highway and tried a push start; it caught so we followed a car, using his lights, to a rural gas station, which was only about a mile up the road. They charged the battery, and we were on our way as the sun started to brighten the night sky, allowing us to see well enough to drive without headlights.

We missed the start but got to Indy in time to see most of the race. Rodger Ward won his second 500.

The New School
My top priority was deciding how to prepare for the driving career

I was hoping to pursue. I had read that the Cooper Car Company, which manufactured race cars along with the race team, also had a driving school. Starting in England seemed to make the most sense, so I had my mother type a letter requesting information on the Cooper Driving School. In the meantime, I got an Anchor Coupling job again and bought a '56 Rambler station wagon to haul our karts to the races. Lyman traded the TD on a new Triumph TR 4. He seemed a little reluctant about letting me drive it.

After eagerly waiting to hear from the Cooper School, I finally got a letter informing me that the Cooper School was no longer in operation. They were kind enough to suggest that I might contact the Jim Russell School and provided their address. Another letter and another wait. In the meantime, Lyman and I were doing well with the kart racing running three times a week.

A good friend came over to our house one afternoon while we were preparing to load our karts. He had his girlfriend with him, and she was a knockout, about 5 foot 2 with green eyes, dark brown, almost black hair, and a nearly perfect figure. She was the prettiest girl I had ever seen in person. I'd never met her before, although he'd gone with her for a while and she lived less than a block from us. He took her to watch us race, and she must have enjoyed it because she called me and asked if she could go with Lyman and me next time we raced. It was fine with me but apparently not so fine with her boyfriend. He went to her father and told him that he shouldn't have allowed his daughter to go with me because I was a wild driver and she could be in danger. I felt this was an unfair evaluation but understood his possessiveness regarding his girlfriend; I would have been jealous with her too. He needn't have worried, though, as I had no dishonorable intentions.

It was a night race so when we got back to Waukegan it was quite late. Because she was only 17 and knew she was probably going to be in trouble if her father was awake, she asked me to be as quiet as possible. She very gently closed the car door and walked toward her house as I drove away. Unfortunately Lyman's kart fell out the back of the Rambler with a loud crash. She got in trouble.

The Jim Russell School never answered, but I read a magazine story about a new school in California: the Carroll Shelby School of High Performance Driving. School was held at Riverside Raceway. A student had the option of using his own car for $500 or the school car for $1,000. I wrote them, and they gave me an appointment in September. I had a starting point. The Rambler was traded for a very used 1959 Jaguar XK150 coupe. I thought it might make a suitable

Lyman and me (left) posing with our karts in the summer of 1961. We often raced three times a week through the summers of '61 and '62. I won more often than he did because my kart was more reliable. His driving was at least as good as mine, but he lacked ambition in general. *John Morton Collection*

school car and would probably make a better road car than the wagon.

The magazine also said that Carroll Shelby was building a new sports car based on the British AC chassis with a small Ford V-8 engine. My tentative plan was to return to Waukegan after the driving school unless I were to find some sort of job related to racing in California, maybe even at Shelby's sports car factory.

I loaded the Jaguar for the trip, not sure if I was packing for a couple of weeks or the rest of my life. I'll confess that this was the first time that heading to school at the end of summer was anything other than depressing. I received the obligatory advice from my parents: don't drive too fast, don't pick up hitchhikers, and be careful. Then I was off to Riverside.

CHAPTER TWO

Racing from the Wrong End of a Broom

It was exciting being on the road alone, being in places I'd never been before on my way to somewhere I'd only read about in magazines. I did drive pretty fast, covering 860 miles the first day, much of which was on two-lane roads. The Will Rogers Turnpike and the Turner Turnpike were beautiful roads but a little boring. I stopped in Oklahoma City for the night.

The next morning as I was leaving town, I spotted a hitchhiker. He was a young, clean-cut-looking guy wearing a nice light-colored jacket.

What the hell. I stopped and he got in.

"Where are you going?" I asked.

"San Francisco," he answered. "I just graduated from college and I'm going out there to work."

"Where did you go to school?" I asked.

"Clemson," he said. "It's a school in South Carolina."

"You're not going to believe this," I told him. "I didn't graduate, but I just left Clemson in June."

I thought this sort of thing only happened in the movies. I drove another 800 miles, and we stayed the night in Flagstaff. We split up the next day as he headed north and I headed south. I had told him I was going to California to be a race car driver. As he left he said, "I'll look for your name in the papers in a few years." Never heard if he found it.

On Track

Arriving in Riverside I pulled into a small motel called La Casa Contenta. There seemed to be quite a bit of Spanish influence in California. I checked in and then went out to the track. As I wandered around, a man rode up on a small motorcycle, a Honda 50, and asked why I was there. I told him I had an appointment to attend the Carroll Shelby Driving School the next week. He wore a baseball cap and looked as though he might be in the military.

"I'm going to be your instructor," he stated. "My name's Pete Brock."

I was disappointed because I thought Carroll Shelby was to be my instructor. Mr. Brock explained that Carroll was too busy getting his Cobra operation going to teach right then. "You're early," he added. "You don't start until next Monday."

"I know," I said, "but I'll just hang around if it's OK."

Brock said, "I've got a three-day student starting tomorrow. You can watch if you like."

The next day the student pulled into the pit area towing his red MGA inside a U-Haul stake-bed trailer. He was a restaurant owner from Salt Lake City, probably around 50 years old. His name was O. L. Beaney. He was a very nice man, but his car ran so poorly that he spent most of the three days trying to learn how to heel and toe downshift. Under the conditions, I don't think he was able to learn much.

I decided to use the school car because the Jaguar didn't have suitable tires or a roll bar. It was a good decision because the school car was

the very first Cobra prototype. It was pearl yellow, and I had seen it in magazine tests. It wasn't as meaningful then because it was the first of only two or three Cobras that existed. Still, it was amazing for me to be driving the same car I'd read about in *Road and Track*.

There was only one other student booked at the school for my week. He had his own Corvette, a '61 or '62. Pete would watch us in a turn and then give us pointers. He had a 1955 Chevy called a panel delivery—sort of a station wagon without side windows that was very starkly appointed. Pete's was white with blue racing stripes up the middle, his tribute to Briggs Cunningham's team. He would demonstrate the line through Riverside's corners with his Chevy before he turned us loose in our school cars.

The esses at Riverside were treacherous back then because there was a steep drop-off on the outside. If a car left the track, it was likely

Cobra Number one, CSX 2000, was my Shelby racing school car, and it was different from all of the ensuing cars. The fuel filler was on the left side of the rear deck whereas the rest were in the center. This picture reveals the inboard rear brakes exclusive to this car. It made the cover of *Road & Track*, September 1962. *William Motta, Road & Track*

Carroll Shelby won the April 1960 Los Angeles Examiner Grand Prix at Riverside driving a Camoradi-entered Type 61 Birdcage Maserati. His last win was in Colorado on June 26, 1960, driving one of the Meister Brau Scarabs at Continental Divide Raceway. *Bob Tronolone*

to flip at a very high speed, as Count Pedro von Dory's Porsche Spyder had when he lost his life during Carroll Shelby's last Riverside victory as a driver. To emphasize the danger, Pete, with the student in the Chevy, would suddenly drive off the track and go crashing down the embankment. It was pretty brutal on the poor suspension and not always so easy on the student.

Pete lived a stone's throw from the racetrack, and each day he would take the Cobra home. I followed him in the Chevy. As I was slowly driving behind Pete that short distance, the front suspension on the Chevy collapsed, jamming the tire into the fender. Pete turned around, surveyed the damage, and said, "What the hell did you do?"

"I didn't do anything," I replied, thinking it a little weird that he would blame me when his off-track demonstrations were the obvious reason for the suspension failure. This was my first experience with Pete's quick temper. The second was the next day in turn eight.

Turn eight was a decreasing-radius right-hander with a fast entry and slow exit. A crossover road allowed us to cut out the rest of the track and take turn eight over and over. It was one of the most difficult turns on the course, and I was getting faster and faster until I finally spun the Cobra. Pete yelled, "Park it!" which I did. I was getting a little over my head, I guess.

One morning in the middle of the week, a blue and white transporter pulled into the pit area. It was a large enclosed van with a Scarab emblem painted on the side. Two men unloaded the rear-engine Scarab, the last car in the line of very successful as well as very unsuccessful race cars. The car was warmed up when Lance Reventlow, the Scarab team owner, approached, ready to drive.

The engine was the little aluminum Buick V-8. Reventlow climbed into the car, started the engine, and, for what reason I'll never know, spun several NASCAR-style donuts before accelerating out of the pits and around turn one. A minute later he returned to the pits from the wrong direction, shut the engine off, and said it had a miss. The crew lifted the tail to discover a rod sticking out of the block. I was no expert but I felt Reventlow had shown a serious lack of mechanical sensitivity.

After the Scarab test was aborted, it was lunchtime, and Pete invited me to eat with him and Reventlow. I remember being impressed with Reventlow's knowledge. He seemed to be a very intelligent man as he discussed details of his Scarab team. He seemed to know a lot of the inner workings at General Motors too. All but his team's Formula One cars utilized GM engines. I felt very privileged to have attended this lunch because the front-engine Scarab sports cars were my all-time favorite race cars and Reventlow was the reason they existed.

The next day our lessons were again interrupted because the second—and only other—Cobra was brought to Riverside for a test. This was a very significant test because it was the first time that a Cobra, as a race car, would turn a wheel on a racetrack. The dark red car was transported to the track on an open trailer towed behind a pickup truck driven by project leader Phil Remington and engine builder Bill Likes. They unloaded the car and waited for the rest of the group to arrive. Likes made reference to Billie Sol coming soon. The only Billie Sol I knew of was Billie Sol Estes, the alligator-shoe-wearing Texas flimflam man whose bait-and-switch scheme to cheat the government was beginning to unravel. I asked Pete, "Who is Billie Sol?"

With a chuckle he said, "Shelby." I didn't get the connection.

The others soon arrived, Carroll Shelby, Warren Olson, and driver Billy Krause. Krause, who'd won the Los Angeles Times Grand Prix in 1960, was even shorter than I was but far more muscular. He reminded me of a professional prizefighter; there was something about him that said, "I'm tough and don't you forget it."

Though the Cobras looked similar, this car was a different animal from the prototype I'd been driving for four days. It was obviously much more powerful but shared a tendency to overheat, the only obvious flaw that had to be addressed before the car was ready to compete. The group seemed very encouraged about the car's potential. I wasn't familiar with Riverside lap times but the car looked very fast and much more agile than my classmate's cumbersome Corvette.

Pete sensed that I wanted to meet Mr. Shelby and that I was too shy to introduce myself, so he was kind enough to do it for me. I was very nervous but mustered the courage to ask if he might have a job for me in his new Cobra factory.

He said, "We might be able to find something. Come and see me Monday."

I was thrilled. Maybe I wouldn't have to turn around and head back to Illinois after all.

There was another day of school left, and the poor Cobra seemed to be on its last legs. Each time I parked while the other student took his turn at a corner, the Cobra would lose much of its water. It must have had a blown head gasket. When we finished the last day—we had been working on turn six—Pete said, "Take it back to the pits," which I did as fast as I could make the car go. I'm afraid that sort of finished it off, but the week was over anyway. The car had been wounded for at least a couple of days, maybe longer. It had had a hard life with the magazine tests and then the school and deserved a rest.

Reflecting on my week at the school, it has since occurred to me that those days had a significance that couldn't be known at the time. They encompassed both the end and the beginning of two American sports car icons. The Scarab team was, for all practical purposes, finished, and the Shelby era had begun.

A Broom with a View

I had an aunt and uncle who I hadn't seen since I was 13 years old. They lived in Oxnard, about a 130 miles from Riverside. I figured that was a good place to spend the weekend while nervously anticipating my meeting with Mr. Shelby Monday morning. He didn't know it, and probably wouldn't have cared if he did, but his decision was going to affect the course of my life dramatically.

I found the address: 1042 Princeton Drive, Venice, California. There was a sign painted on the front door: Shelby American Inc.

I was shown upstairs to Mr. Shelby's office. He spoke rather loudly in a strong Texas accent; he was a little intimidating. "Follow me downstairs. I'll show you what I want you to do."

He led me to where the brooms and mops were kept and then with a sweeping gesture said, "I want these things painted and the floors and bathrooms kept clean. I want the floors swept every morning, huh?" He had a way of saying "huh?" after he'd made a statement as if he hadn't heard himself. Actually what "huh" meant was, "Do you understand and do you agree with me?"

He showed me around the building and introduced me to Phil Remington, who would be my boss. Actually Phil was everybody's boss—everybody except Carroll Shelby.

The Shelby American building had been the Reventlow Automobile Incorporated—RAI—building, with some of the key employees staying on to work for Carroll Shelby. The general manager, Warren Olson, had owned a foreign car service in Los Angeles, where the first of the Scarabs were born. Warren remained the RAI team manager until he became the general manager at Shelby American. His wife, Simone, became Shelby

If Carroll Shelby had the dream, this is the man who made his dream reality. Phil Remington at 24 (above) and in 1947 at El Mirage dry lake, ready to make a speed run in his flathead Ford V-8-powered Model A Ford-based racer. *Phil Remington Collection*

American's controller. RAI's parts manager, Gordon Goring, kept the job at Shelby's. Phil Remington said he came with the building, but he was far more important in the success of the Cobra than any building.

I phoned my parents to tell them I wasn't coming home and that Carroll Shelby hired me. I thought that being hired by Shelby might impress them somewhat. My mother was never one to mince words or sugarcoat anything. She asked, "Hired you to do what? Drive race cars?"

"No, of course not. I can't even get a license yet."

"Then are you a mechanic?" she asked.

"No. I have to keep the shop clean and do odd jobs if someone asks."

"So you're the janitor," she said.

"I guess, kind of."

I felt lucky she didn't give me a lecture on a college education, although she'd never done that. She seemed to accept my ambitions better than my father did.

That's the Ticket

That evening I found a studio apartment on Inglewood Boulevard about 2 miles from work. It was a pretty nice place and was only $55 a month. That night, feeling like quite the adult with a new job and new apartment, I drove the Jaguar to the McDonald's on Lincoln Boulevard near Washington, just a few blocks from Shelby's. After a delicious dinner, I left for the 2-mile ride home when a sailor in a 1957 Chevy pulled up alongside and, as Jan and Dean would later sing, challenged me then and there to a drag.

We accelerated east on Washington, but I missed the shift into second and he pulled away. At the next light I was determined to do better. The Chevy was a little faster, but I stayed on it until he lifted so I won. We probably never got to more than 65 or 70. I think the speed limit was 35. After I slowed I saw a flashing red light but assumed it wasn't for us because it was so far back. It seemed smart to get off of Washington anyway, just in case.

I turned left and drove around for a few blocks with my lights off. I didn't know exactly where I was, having only lived in the area for about two hours. I stopped at what turned out to be Venice Boulevard and turned my lights back on. So did the cop sitting behind me.

He directed me back to the spot where another cop had stopped the sailor. Needless to say we both received pretty ugly tickets. My ticket said something like "Speed contest" or "Exhibition of speed"—I can't remember exactly—but it made my first night as an adult a lot less satisfying.

The Kindhearted Cynic

On the day Mr. Shelby showed me the shop and explained my duties, I saw a Japanese employee and thought he might be Chicky Hiroshima, the famous Indy car mechanic. He wasn't; his name was Garry Koike, but everyone mispronounced his name as Garry Quicky. When I first talked to him several days after going to work I said, "When I first saw you, I thought you were Chicky Hiroshima." He told me, "When I saw you walking around with Shelby, I thought you were a caterpillar." I had worn a yellow-and-black-striped shirt that first day. I later found out that Chicky and Garry had something in common besides racing. They had both been in Manzanar, the Japanese internment camp in the Owens Valley—Chicky as a man and Garry as a child.

I told Garry that I had been a student at the Shelby driving school at Riverside and drove the Cobra. I was a little taken aback when he answered, "So you're the dumb son-of-a-bitch who burned up that engine. Don Pike and I had to pull it out of the car yesterday and it reeked of burned oil. I said to Don, 'What asshole did this?'"

I tried to explain that it had had a problem with overheating the whole week of the school, that I guessed it had been parked while the other student was driving his car and lost all its water as it sat, and that when I drove it back to the pits on the last day, that must have finished it off.

I didn't know if Garry was teasing me or not. Anyway, we became good friends. He was different from other car people I'd known in that he was very intellectual, very well read, and very cynical. He told me that all drivers were assholes, but I was never sure if it was make-believe cynicism or real. Some of both, I guess. He eventually was given the nickname Foreign Intrigue. No one was ever immune to Garry's cutting appraisal as I received a dissertation on each new employee. Evaluations often started with "Look at that poor bastard," but his caustic facade hid the fact that he was really a very kind person. He just didn't want to act like one. Garry drove a faded blue VW Bug full of clutter. He was not interested in any sort of pretense. As Phil Remington recalled, at lunch Garry almost always peeled and ate a hardboiled egg. As he ate, the egg got blacker and blacker because Garry didn't bother to wash his hands before lunch.

Where Legends Drop By

Lance Reventlow kept a small portion of the shop and a skeleton crew to prepare and maintain the rear-engine Scarab that I saw at Riverside. The crew of two were Paul Camano, the painter who had mixed the color of the beautiful metallic blue Scarabs, and Frank Schmidt, mechanic and engine man, though all of the Scarab's engines had been built by Chuck Daigh or Jim Travers and Frank Coons of Traco Engineering. Both Schmidt and Camano were eventually absorbed into Shelby American.

A rudimentary production line was underway but the shop's main thrust was readying the Riverside test Cobra for a three-hour production car race the day before the 1962 Los Angeles Times Grand Prix on October 14. It would be the first race for the new Cobra—and also the first race for the all-new Corvette Stingray. The number-one priority was to deal with the Cobra's overheating problem. Phil Remington was in charge, with Don Pike his main assistant.

Phil had louvers punched into the back of the hood to allow better airflow through the aluminum Corvette radiator. I can't remember if the Corvette radiator had been installed for the Riverside test I'd witnessed.

If Carroll Shelby was the head man, Joan was the head woman. She was very business-like and seemed to be running the show at least as much as Mr. Shelby was. In fact she was referred to as Mrs. Shelby, but word around the shop was that they were not really married even though they lived together in Playa del Rey. People tended to be more prudish about unconventional relationships in 1962. Joan was quite beautiful.

A few days prior to the Los Angeles Times Grand Prix, Mr. Shelby offered his shop facilities to two of his race driver friends from his racing days. One was Bruce McLaren, who brought his works Cooper Monaco powered by a 2.7-liter Coventry Climax engine. The other was Jack Brabham with a Lotus 23 powered by a Holbay-modified four-cylinder pushrod English Ford engine, which he would run in the under-2-liter class.

It was amazing to me that two of the world's most famous race drivers were working as their own mechanics, especially Jack Brabham, who was twice world champion as well as having brought the rear-engine revolution to Indianapolis in 1961 in a modified F1 Cooper. After receiving the car from customs, Brabham and his F1 mechanic, Tim Wall, worked into the night so it could be taken to Riverside the next day. Everyone in the shop had gone home except for Brabham, Wall, and me. I watched them work aligning the suspension, changing gear ratios, and attending to other details. Brabham was still in his street clothes. He was very focused in his work, showing nothing beyond cold professionalism.

It was getting late. I asked, "Are you guys hungry?" They answered yes, apparently having forgotten that they hadn't eaten.

"Would you like a hamburger and milk shake?"

"Yes."

"What kind of shake?"

"Chocolate."

I went to Friar's, three blocks away, and returned with the food. "Thank you," they said. They weren't into small talk. Brabham offered to reimburse me, but I wouldn't accept it; I was proud to have bought my hero dinner. The next day I drove with Tim Wall to Riverside towing the 23 behind a pickup truck. During the race weekend, I slept on the floor in the motel room shared by Phil Remington and Don Pike.

Bill Krause discusses the Cobra's handling with Carroll Shelby during practice for the three-hour production car race at Riverside in 1962. The Stingray of Dave MacDonald is behind them. This was the first race ever for both the Cobra and the Corvette Stingray. *Dave Friedman*

Sign of the Snake

There were four Corvette Stingrays entered in the three-hour race, driven by some of the best Corvette drivers in the country. The Stingray and the Cobra were classified XP, for experimental, because they hadn't yet been classified by the SCCA. They used a Le Mans start on the back straight, out of view from the pits. Dave MacDonald appeared first in the white Stingray with a big lead over Krause in the Cobra. Krause reeled MacDonald in and passed him. Dave put on a fight, but the Cobra pulled out a huge lead until the left rear stub-axle broke coming out of turn nine onto the pit straight, sending the wheel into the air. I was standing next to Joan as she yelled, "Goddamn son of a bitch!"

I'd never heard a pretty girl talk like that before. I think she was venting for the entire Shelby team. Doug Hooper eventually won the race in Mickey Thompson's Stingray, as all the other Stingrays broke. The handwriting was on the wall, however. A hastily prepared car with a tiny crew had shown superior potential over the best that General Motors had to offer.

Early race shop photo. This was taken shortly after the No. 98 car had made the Cobra's racing debut at Riverside with Billy Krause behind the wheel. Phil Remington (back to camera) is showing something to George Boskoff. Red Rose is just a blur in the background. The white car will be the second team car when it's finished. *Dave Friedman*

The Los Angeles Times Grand Prix was won by Roger Penske in his *Zerex Special*, a thinly disguised Formula One Cooper. Dan Gurney in the Lotus 19 was the only one who was competitive against Penske, but he had a problem early in the race.

The next race for Krause and the Cobra was going to be the Nassau Speed Weeks in December. Phil had some new stub-axles forged and machined to withstand the power of the 260-cubic-inch Ford. Most of the problems with the AC chassis stemmed from the fact that it was essentially designed to handle a 2-liter engine of well less than 200 horsepower. Another factor was the antiquated transverse leaf suspension, front and rear, designed in 1950.

Now in the shop there were two racing Cobras being prepared for the Nassau race, the Krause car and a customer car for a young man named Jon Everly. Everly helped with the preparation, which took a matter of several weeks because this was only the second race car built at Shelby's. During this time the first production Cobra was also being readied for delivery. I remember the owners waiting around for

Bill Krause at Nassau December 1962 for his second and last race for Shelby American. Here he confers with Don Pike. The other Cobra is Jon Everly's, the second race car built and the first customer race car. *Dave Friedman*

a number of days as their car was slowly prepared for them. They were something of an odd couple: a short small man and his big, tall wife. They didn't have far to drive each day that they watched and waited because they lived in Malibu. They never seemed upset and finally drove away, happy in the first Cobra delivered in California.

Remington, Pike, and Shelby went to Nassau to take care of the Cobra. Again the car showed great promise but suffered a steering failure in one race and ran out of gas in another. Shelby took the blame for the fueling mistake. John Everly finished one race and failed in another.

I had to appear in the matter of my own speed contest, the one against the sailor in his '57 Chevy. I sat nervously awaiting my turn before the judge. The sailor was called up first. I had called the court the day after receiving the ticket to see if I could find out how much my fine would be. Based on my violation the lady said $110 for the speed contest and something for each mile over the limit. Was I going to be short on my first rent payment?

Robert and Sylvia Neville taking the keys for the first Cobra street car built and delivered in California. This is a staged shot because I know they hung around the shop a day or two waiting for the car. Actually the first several Cobras were assembled and delivered in Pittsburg by Ed Hugus because Shelby's facility wasn't set up yet. *Dave Friedman*

I listened intently as the judge read the sailor's charges: "Speeding and trying to evade a police officer." He got one year of probation and a $15 fine. I was so relieved. The judge asked me if I had a job. I told him yes, at Shelby American, but I'm sure that meant nothing except that I was working. I got probation for one year and no fine. Wow, was I lucky.

Meanwhile major changes were taking place at Shelby's. Mickey Thompson offered Billy Krause a deal to drive for Chevrolet in 1963. The offer included not just sports car racing but also the Indy 500. Krause left Shelby and signed with Thompson but very soon thereafter, General Motors pulled the plug on racing and Krause was left with only Indy. The Thompson Indy cars were very unorthodox and Krause didn't qualify. Krause today still regrets that he nipped his promising career in the bud by leaving.

Make Mine a "Super"

One of my janitorial duties was emptying the wastebasket and vacuuming the carpet in Mr. Shelby's office. One day as I was attending to my duties, he was talking to someone on the phone offering the person a job. It was Dave MacDonald on the other end, whom Shelby had called to offer the Cobra ride that Billy Krause had abandoned.

A few days later MacDonald came by the shop to take the race car to Riverside and get used to driving a Cobra. Dave and Wally Peat left the shop in the pickup towing the car. Late that afternoon when they returned, Wally and Dave acted a little sheepish. The Cobra had a damaged front fender. Their story was that the fire extinguisher had come loose while Dave was negotiating Riverside's tricky high-speed esses and gotten under his feet, causing him to hit one of the half-buried tires that line the inside of the track in that area.

I remember thinking, *Did you two guys practice telling that story all the way home?*

I'd been planning for years to have a race car by the time I was 21, and that time was getting close. I went down to see Bob Challman, the Lotus dealer in Manhattan Beach about 5 miles from work. There was a new Lotus Formula Junior on the showroom floor. I told Mr. Challman that I had been to the Carroll Shelby driving school and was now working for Shelby in Venice. I explained that I planned to be a professional race car driver and wanted to buy a Lotus Formula Junior to start when I turned 21 in February. I remember clearly what he said: "I won't sell you a Formula Junior. You'd be dead in three months. What you need is a Lotus 7 America."

I thought that sounded a little melodramatic. I said, "I would consider a Super 7 but the 7 America has a Sprite engine, and I'm not interested in that." He pushed hard for the 7 America, but I told him either a Super 7 or I'd go somewhere else. He agreed to order a Super 7.

I wasn't from a wealthy family, but my Great Uncle Lyman had contributed to my and my brother's college careers since we were born. When Uncle Lyman died, I inherited about $18,000 in stocks. Eliminating a couple of years of higher education, I was set financially to launch my racing career. When the Lotus arrived, it would set me back around $3,200, and a very used trailer Challman would sell me was going to be $175. He had sold several Lotus 7s, mostly the Sprite-engine variety, whose owners often hung around the dealership in the evenings. I sometimes would join them, although I never felt part of their little Lotus 7 clique. It was not just because mine wasn't to have a Sprite engine. I guess I felt that racing was more serious to me.

While listening to the car radio on one of these early short trips down Sepulveda Boulevard after work to visit Challman's, I heard some terrible news: Ricardo Rodriguez had been killed in a race in Mexico City. I was stunned. How could this be? I'd always felt a connection to Ricardo because we were the same age. In fact, I had envied more than admired him. He had qualified second in the 1961 Italian Grand Prix, but died before he could even buy a beer in the United States. Sometimes I hated racing and thought it was goddamn stupid, but those feelings quickly passed.

Carroll Shelby had the Goodyear racing tire distributorship, and it started out pretty small. It consisted of a double-deck tire rack against the wall just inside of the rollup door where cars entered and exited the building. Near the tire rack there was a manually operated tire-changing machine like the ones found in gas stations of the period. When someone came in to have tires mounted on a car, I was called on to do the job.

I'd never used the machine or any tire-changing machine when a man came in to have Blue Streaks mounted on his 1957 Ferrari Berlinetta with Borrani aluminum-rimmed wire wheels. It's very easy to damage a delicate wheel on a tire-changing machine, so I was extremely nervous. What made it even worse was that he watched the operation and talked the whole time. We had a long time to talk because I was being so careful with his wheels. I mentioned that I was in the process of deciding which race car to start my racing career in.

He said, "I have a race car you might be interested in. It's a 1956 OSCA that used to belong to Tim Considine, the actor who played Spin on the Disney *Spin and Marty* TV serial on the *Mickey Mouse Club*."

I actually went to the Hollywood Hills where he lived and looked at the beautiful little car but decided it was not a practical car for me. I wouldn't cancel my order for the Lotus. Not buying the OSCA was one of my few good career moves.

Later Mr. Shelby hired a man to run the Goodyear business. His name was Paul Anfang, a metal salesman who often came in to take orders for the company he worked for, Ducommun Metals Company. He was a big, gregarious bullshit artist, and Mr. Shelby thought he would be perfect to run the tire business.

The Roach Coach

The number of people in the shop was increasing rapidly in late '62 and early '63. New faces included George Boskoff, Ole Olsen, Bruce Burness, Cecil Bowman, Red Rose, Mahlon Lamoreaux and Allen Grant. Except for Burness and Grant, they were much older than I was and so consequently had gained wisdom that they often shared with me, usually over our "roach coach" lunches in the back area of the shop.

Ole Olsen, one of the main race engine builders, suggested that I should use the money I'd planned to buy the race car with to get myself a new Corvette and get laid instead. Ole drove to work in a yellow 1954 Buick Special that had seven of its eight cylinders firing. A Corvette must have seemed extra special to Ole, whose wife later worked in the office upstairs. George Boskoff, on the other hand, had a longer-range plan for my money. He said I should use it as a down payment on a house and that I should plan for the future more wisely. This advice was from a 38-year-old man who drove a 1949 Ford pickup and lived with his parents.

It seems like the youngest guy in any group is always the one who is the brunt of the jokes or the teasing, and I was no exception. I was asked about my living arrangements. I told them I had a bachelor apartment on Inglewood Boulevard. My landlady was an older woman who, feeling sorry for me, I guess, had me over to watch television with her sometimes. They asked her age.

"About forty-five," I guessed.

"Is she married?" they wondered.

"Yes, to an older man who is an invalid, I think, because I never see him."

"You could be living rent free," they responded.

I can't remember who first brought this subject up, but there was a consensus for sure. I laughed it off, but they persisted day after day until I was finally almost convinced. I felt I at least owed it a try if for no other reason than just to change the lunchtime conversation.

The landlady asked me over, and as we watched TV, I slowly moved in. I got closer and closer until I had my arm behind her. She finally realized that I was "on the move," so to speak, and she said, "Johnny, you're so close."

I sensed this was not what she'd had in mind, so I sat quietly and just watched TV. The verdict at lunch was that I hadn't tried hard enough, but at least it did change the subject.

Mahlon Lamoreaux was a fabulous machinist with a devilish sense of humor, but he didn't lunch with the rest of us. He ate the lunch he'd brought from home, complete with a small bottle of wine to wash it down, in his blue VW Kombi pickup in the parking lot behind the building. He always smiled as he returned to the machine shop.

Once when Lamoreaux was punching out washers on a punch press, I asked him, "What are those for?"

Mahlon answered, "They're assholes for hobby horses."

Much like Garry Koike, Mahlon would size people up and fill some of us in on his evaluations. He recognized that one of the women in the office that dealt with petty cash seemed overly stingy, so he took a quarter and epoxied it to the floor in the women's bathroom. Sometime later the woman came to Mahlon—the machine shop was near the bathroom—and borrowed a screwdriver.

An early shot of the production line that shared the building with the race shop. These cars all had 260-cubic-inch engines and the problematic worm and sector steering. The first few cars arrived from England in wooden crates. *Dave Friedman*

Cranking Out Cobras

The pace at Shelby American had increased dramatically as more cars arrived from AC. Assembly of the production cars was being streamlined so they could be turned out much faster. Leonard Parsons was in charge of the production line, which consisted of a couple of wooden platforms with ramps for the cars to be pushed into position to allow them to be worked on from above and below. This operation at Shelby American was still in the building with the racing division. In the early stages, some of the same people were utilized in both areas.

A number of race cars were being prepared for an ambitious 1963 season. Preparing the cars for racing was a tremendous job in comparison to what it took to finish a street car for delivery. The engines were modified, dyno-tested, and tuned in the engine shop. They received a racing oil pan, special valve covers, and headers. The cars' front and rear fenders had to be reworked to accept wider wheels and tires; larger brakes were added, as was a roll bar for driver protection, and suspension modifications to improve handling. An aluminum Harrison radiator to improve engine cooling was installed. Each race car required a couple of weeks to finish. Two new race cars were being readied for a club race at Riverside in early February.

We had a man who was the designated parts chaser, named Joe Washington. Joe carried a small bottle with him at all times, and once in a while he could be seen taking a swig from it. When I asked Joe what was in the bottle, he said it was cough syrup that he needed to relieve a chronic condition he had in his lungs. I never knew who made the decision to terminate his driving, but it seemed obvious he had something in the bottle other than cough syrup.

Someone decided that Joe and I should trade jobs. I would drive the Corvair Greenbrier and chase parts, and Joe would be the janitor. I think it was a good call because Phil Remington never seemed satisfied with my janitorial skills, once stating that I wasn't worth "a pinch of shit." I'm sure Joe was a better janitor than I was. I'm not sure how our driving compared.

The smog was so bad in Los Angeles in 1963 that each parts run that took me near downtown would bring on a headache. Other than that it was fun learning the area. In early December just a few days before the 405 Freeway opened, allowing freeway access to the San Fernando Valley (now the busiest highway in America), Shelby Sales Manager Fred Gamble and I took a new Cobra out onto the empty highway in the Sepulveda Pass to take pictures for a brochure. Fred,

Shelby watches as engine man Bill Likes tests the Hill floatless carburetor on the dynomometer. The engine shop was always searching for more power, but this particular experiment didn't find any. *Dave Friedman*

a seldom-mentioned early employee, had been a race driver for Camoradi with such notable teammates as Stirling Moss and Carroll Shelby. Gamble went on to work for Goodyear's racing-tire division, eventually serving as their director of European racing.

Another newcomer to the shop was Leo Ortega, a captain with the Beverly Hills Fire Department. He moonlighted as a carpenter at Shelby's, making wooden boxes to carry equipment and spare parts to the races and performing other needed woodworking.

One morning Joan came down to the shop and told Leo, "Get John and some of your carpentry tools and follow me."

We got in the truck and followed Joan to the apartment in Playa del Rey that she shared with Mr. Shelby. As we entered, it became apparent that the front door was off its hinges. Leo and I were to do the repair. I can't recall which of us asked Joan what had happened, but she said she and Mr. Shelby had had some sort of argument and when she locked him out, he came in anyway.

We were there for a while so I took a couple of minutes to look around, curious about how one of my heroes lived. There was nothing very out of the ordinary except for a large number of alligator shoes in the closet. It reminded me of Bill Likes referring to Shelby that day at Riverside as Billie Sol.

Room for Appreciation

If there were no parts to pick up, I would work with Garry, who was in charge of making some of the smaller parts used on the production cars as well as the race cars. There were so many talented people around that you couldn't help learning something. Most of the highly skilled people were very generous with their knowledge, especially George Boskoff. George seemed eager to help the less experienced guys learn how to do the difficult things he was so good at. Bruce Burness was one of George's protégés, as I was to a lesser extent, only because I didn't have Bruce's innate ability and my real interest was driving. George was to be very instrumental in any success I would have in the future.

Phil Remington was the best and the fastest worker that there was. To say he was mechanically multifaceted is an understatement, but the one thing he was not good at was teaching. It wasn't that he was possessive of his abilities; he just couldn't slow down enough for anyone to follow.

Many of the workers at Shelby American, though they were very conscientious in their jobs, had very little regard for the production Cobras. They couldn't imagine anyone paying the base price of $5,995 for one. I must say that the day Gary Pike—Don's brother—and I were asked to deliver two brand-new Cobras to Downtown Ford helped convince me to agree with the naysayers.

My car was white and had an optional radio mounted under the dash on the transmission tunnel. I was listening to the radio as Gary and I took turns following one another through the traffic on Washington Boulevard. The radio in a Cobra was not a high-value option, as it could only be heard if it was turned up very loud, and this was not popular back then. After halfway into on our 10- to 12-mile trip, I noticed the radio becoming scratchy and then going silent. I quickly analyzed the problem as water dripping on the radio from under the dash.

We decided to complete the trip and deliver the cars anyway. I never found out what had caused the leak, but the cars tended to overheat very quickly in traffic and maybe a heater hose hadn't been tightened. Gary said it was because I'd downshifted when I stopped at red lights, which had nothing to do with it.

I never worked on the production car assembly line. Yet one day when I was in the parts room looking for something, Gary asked me to find another seat bolt. The seats were removed to facilitate engine/transmission installation and then refitted. I couldn't find the proper 5/16 bolt with the English thread pitch.

I said, "All they have in here is this," showing him an American bolt with different threads.

Gary answered, "Give it to me. I'll tighten the son of a bitch up so it'll never come loose."

I think it is fair to say that if there is a joke here, it is on us because a well-preserved or restored example of these early Cobras is worth high six figures and more, and it is still going to appreciate.

Super 7th Heaven

The week of January 13, I got a call from Bob Challman that my Super 7 had come in and was now ready for delivery. I rushed down right after work. They had already installed racing safety belts and a roll bar. Bob gave me a fatherly lecture on how to learn to drive it and gave me a permit to drive it on the street for one week even though it wasn't going to be registered. The permit was supposed to be for a delivery trip.

As I drove out of the driveway of the dealership and onto Sepulveda Boulevard, I thought, *Holy shit, I'm actually driving my own race car after all these years of dreaming.* Heading into the dense night traffic, I remember thinking, *Wow, it feels awfully small out here, a lot smaller than the TD but so much faster.* Even the Cobra seemed like a big heavy car by comparison.

My plan was to drive to work the next morning and arrive just as the whole shop crew was out on the street at the roach coach. I headed from my apartment and drove very cautiously, being sure not to speed

This is in front of Shelby American. The Lotus dealer gave me a permit so I could drive it on the street for seven days. I was stopped by a cop on my way to work on the first day. *John Morton Collection*

or make much noise. I was furnished with a straight pipe for racing, but it hadn't been installed yet. The car was still pretty healthy sounding even with the muffler. As I turned off Washington onto Stanford only four or five blocks from work, a cop stopped me.

Shit, what did I do?

The cop parked in front of me and got out of his squad car. As he approached, he looked very tall, probably because my ass was so close to the ground. He was black. He stood beside me and said, "You didn't do anything wrong but if you have a minute I'd like to take a look at your machine."

Very relieved, I blurted out, "Sure!"

"What is it?"

"It's a Lotus Super 7."

"Where did you get it?"

"Bob Challman's Ecurie Shirlee down on Sepulveda in Manhattan Beach."

"Can I look under the hood?"

We took the hood off, and then he helped me put it back on.

"How much did it cost?"

"A little over thirty-two hundred," I told him. "I'm on my way to work just a few blocks from here at Shelby American."

"When you leave, could you get on it a little? I'd like to see how it goes."

"Yes, sir." Then I blasted off for 100 feet or so and cruised at a respectable speed to work with the cop following me. So the timing was perfect. I arrived at the coffee truck with a cop on my ass.

I found out later that the cop went down to Challman's and bought a Super 7 of his own. We would run our first race together.

The permit to drive the Lotus on public roads got used to its maximum in that week. I went up to Oxnard to visit my aunt and uncle, a round trip of about 150 miles. On the weekend, Gordon Goring, the parts man, and I decided to drive the Lotus to Riverside to see the first Motor Trend 500 NASCAR race. It was going to be especially interesting because Dan Gurney was driving. I'd only seen one NASCAR race and that was at Greenville Pickens, a half-mile dirt track in Greenville, South Carolina, when I was in school. Junior Johnson won that one in a Pontiac after Joe Weatherly blew a tire near the end of the race. Buck Baker had had a big lead in the early part but blew a clutch in his Chrysler 300. It was going to be interesting to see how a great road racer like Gurney would do against these guys.

Gordon was English and had an early Austin-Healey, so the starkness of the Lotus was not a problem for him. Because there was an enormous crowd, we had to remember exactly where the tiny Lotus was parked to have a chance of finding it among the 30,000 or 40,000 American monsters.

I loved the race because Gurney made the NASCAR drivers look pretty inept, but in fairness to them, this wasn't their biscuits and gravy. As we headed home in the dark on the San Bernadino Freeway, we were feeling pretty smug about how a road racer had prevailed over the best stock car drivers.

The Sunday night traffic was terrible and even worse than normal because of the race. Any smugness I had instantly vanished as the Lotus engine quit running as we approached the Long Beach Freeway intersection. We were in big trouble with only two choices, and we had to make one of them quickly. We could leave the car and run for our lives off of the freeway, the car be damned, or we could seriously risk our lives by pushing the car to safety. We chose the latter and all survived. It didn't seem reasonable, but we were out of gas.

I hiked up the ice-plant-covered embankment, climbed a fence to someone's backyard, and knocked on the front door of the house. A very nice man took me to a filling station with a gas can he had in his garage and then got on the freeway and drove me to the Lotus. Gordon and I were on our way with no further drama. In my defense, Lotus Super 7s don't have gas gauges, and their mileage isn't as good as one might expect for such a small car.

Ken Miles was hired to be our second driver. I'm not sure if he was to be considered second to MacDonald or if the two of them had

The first Cobra victories came at Riverside on February 2 and 3, 1963. This was the first race for both Dave MacDonald (198) and Ken Miles (98). Dave won both days with Ken close behind. In the picture, Paul Reinhart splits the two Cobras with his Stingray. *Dave Friedman*

equal status. Miles had had great success designing, building, and winning races in his own cars as well as those of other owners. He was English. Even though he had lived in the United States for 12 years, he spoke as though he'd just gotten off the boat. Dave, on the other hand, was as American as apple pie. In other words, they were as different as their ages: Dave was 26, and Ken was 44. Both men had mechanical ability and seemed to enjoy being involved with the cars they would drive. Ken brought his personal mechanic, Charlie Agapiou, with whom he'd worked when Ken had his own automotive shop. Charlie was a very skilled mechanic and an excellent comedian.

The first race for our two new drivers was an SCCA Divisional Race at Riverside on February 2 and 3. (Divisionals are now called

National races, even though they are still amateur.) The Cobras were in the A Production class, which included the Corvette Stingray. MacDonald won both the Saturday and the Sunday races, but in the Sunday race the team told Miles to finish behind MacDonald. Partway into the race Miles stopped in the pits to have his tire pressure checked, an obvious charade because the tire was fine. But for the rest of the race all the announcer could talk about was Miles' charge through the field until he was on MacDonald's tail; that's how it ended. Dave drove his red Cobra very hard, and it showed as he slid through Riverside turns five and six where I was standing. Ken didn't look as fast in his white car, but he obviously was because he closed the gap to MacDonald and followed him closely to the finish.

The next race for the Cobras was the following weekend at Daytona. It was exciting to see Dan Gurney in the shop trying on a Cobra for size. His presence seemed to lend a new credibility to the Cobra team. Three cars were entered in the Daytona Continental—the same three-hour race that Gurney won the year before in the Lotus 19. Joining Gurney in Cobras would be Dave MacDonald and Gurney's boyhood friend, Skip Hudson.

While the team was away, I took the opportunity to bring my Lotus into the shop and make a small racing windshield for it with the help of Red Rose. Red was one of the best metal men around. He was about twice my age, but he didn't treat me like a punk kid, which I really was. Red had worked for the Stroppe team when it ran the Lincolns that dominated the Mexican Road Race (the Carrera Panamericana) from 1952 to 1954. Red drove a salmon-colored '53 Lincoln to work, a leftover from the Stroppe team, he said. He worked on his own schedule, arriving for the midmorning coffee break and leaving well after everyone else had gone home.

The Daytona race didn't go well for the Cobras. Dan Gurney started with an experimental aluminum engine of 255 cubic inches, which was destined to power Ford and Lotus's attack on the Indy 500 in May. It had serious problems, and the decision to change it for a conventional cast-iron 260 shortly before race time resulted in Dan starting late. Skip Hudson drove a great race, challenging Pedro Rodriguez for the lead until his crankshaft damper came apart. Somehow, this locked the steering, causing him to crash and break his foot. Sadly, for some reason Skip was never given another chance to drive on the Shelby team. Dave finished fourth after having some problems. It was obvious that the Cobras couldn't match the Ferrari GTO's top speed on longer courses like Daytona because their drag limited them to 160 miles per hour with slightly less than 400 horsepower.

Another new employee was a man recently retired from the Coast Guard. He looked to be around 40 years old. I remember feeling a little sorry for him when I was asked to take him out behind the building and show him how to jack up a Cobra, put it on jack stands, and clean it underneath with a solvent sprayer and a bucket of cleaning solvent. It must have been after the Riverside race because it was MacDonald's red car. I thought it had to be humiliating for him for a 20-year-old kid to teach him to do a very menial job. His name was Al Dowd. I needn't have concerned myself about him because in a very short time he was practically running the show. Al's rapid rise from menial helper to upper management garnered him the nickname of Greasy Slick.

Allen Grant was another ambitious fellow who was at Shelby American because he wanted to be a professional driver. Allen was pretty much in the same boat as I was except for the fact that he was

Skip Hudson drove an excellent race at the 1963 three-hour Daytona Continental until a crankshaft damper exploded locking his steering. The resulting crash into the guardrail broke Skip's foot. The buck for the Daytona Coupe was built on this damaged frame. *Dave Friedman*

very aggressive and intended to reach his goals quickly. Garry Koike nicknamed Allen the Blond Ox because of his hair color and he was a bit like a bull in a china shop.

Allen had been very successful auto-crossing and racing his own AC Bristol and was eager to move up. He was living in an apartment behind a house in Venice, very near Shelby's, that also had access to a garage. He asked me to move in with him and share the rent. I liked where I lived, however. Even though I never got on the free-rent program, my landlady, who managed other apartment complexes, told me she had a tenant—a very nice young girl—in an apartment nearby whom she would introduce me to if I'd like. I'll call her Mary because I can't remember her name. I wanted to check her out.

We had two or three dates and were getting along well. She told me she had had a troubled home life and that her father was in prison. One night after a movie we were having a conversation in a restaurant about people we admired. She said, "The man I admire more than anyone else in history is Joseph."

"Joseph?" I asked.

"Yes."

"Do you mean as in Joseph and Mary?"

"Yes, he was so patient. I really admire him."

That was our last date.

As I mentioned, Allen was aggressive, so I relented and moved in with him. We paid $45 apiece per month. Our landlady, who lived in the main house, was a tight-assed old woman with the unfortunate name of Mrs. Allcock. At least the garage provided a place to keep and work on the Lotus.

Perennial Pupil

I was almost 21, old enough to get an SCCA (Sports Car Club of America) racing license. The rule was that a prospective licensee had to attend what was called an SCCA Drivers School. These schools occurred approximately once a month, usually at Riverside for the Southern California or Club Region of the SCCA. Typically, three schools were required, which would take three months provided you and your car performed up to club standards. Back then no credit was given for having attended a private school like Carroll Shelby's.

As luck would have it, the first driver's school I could attend was at Riverside on my 21st birthday, Sunday, February 17. The instructors at the school were licensed active SCCA drivers, usually the more prominent ones, who volunteered their time. Each instructor had several students. My instructor was Bob Challman, who was given all of the Lotus-driving students. First they had a classroom session where we were shown the proper line around Riverside, as well as some of the track's idiosyncrasies. Then we went into a lead/follow routine with our instructor.

Challman would drive a lap in his Lotus Elite Super 100 while all of us followed. The first student behind Bob would pass after one lap and would be observed for a lap. Then another student would pass until the whole group was cycled through. Bob would then talk to each of us, critiquing our performance, and we would all return to the track to do it again a little faster. His only criticism of me was that I seemed a little out of shape for the speed I was going. I didn't say anything, but if I'd wanted to be a wiseass I'd have observed, "How could you tell that? I was pulling away from you."

At the end of the day when all of the Lotus boys were getting our last evaluations from Mr. Challman, he said two things referring to me. The first was, "Remember this guy's name. You'll be hearing it in the future." That made me pleased. He followed with, "I'd give him his license today—he's that good—but I'm going to make him do all three schools because I don't want it to go to his head." That was a letdown.

I towed the Lotus home behind the Jaguar with my friend Gordon Goring. To celebrate a good day, we went to Friar's bar on the corner of Lincoln and Washington, three blocks from Shelby American. I ordered a beer. The bartender checked my license: "You just made it."

Challman now seemed to take mentoring me more seriously; I think he saw me as more than just another customer. Along with driving pointers, he offered a word of caution: "Do not start trying to rework or modify anything on that car until you get your license. Just drive it as it is."

This really didn't feel like advice as much as an order from above. However, Ole Olsen was generous enough to offer to go through my engine in the Shelby American engine room after working hours. How could I turn down this offer? I have to say that Carroll was generous also in allowing this to take place—that is, if he even knew about it! I pulled the engine out of the Lotus and brought it in, where Ole disassembled it. I took the crankshaft and rods to a company called Metal Improvement to have them shot peened and then to Edelbrock for balancing just like the Shelby race engines.

Ken Miles also seemed to take an interest in my engine when he saw it in the shop. One day he handed me a camshaft and said, "Put this in your engine. It will make your car faster."

I asked, "What is it from?"

Ken said, "It's out of a Dolphin Formula Junior that Kurt Neuman drove."

Ole used Ken's cam when he reassembled my engine. Ken was working in the racing department now, occupying an office right in the race shop that was slightly elevated with large windows, allowing a good view of the action. I think his title may have been competition manager.

A week or two after the drivers' school Bob Challman phoned me at work to tell me he wanted me to run my Lotus in a slalom the next weekend. I was busted.

"I can't," I said.

"Why not?" he responded.

"The engine isn't ready yet," I answered.

He was mad. "I want you there. Get it ready."

"That's impossible. Some of the parts aren't finished for the engine."

He finished by giving me the address where the event was to be held and said, "Run it in your Jaguar if you have to but be there."

Slaloms were usually held in a very large parking lot wherein a tight course was laid out with orange rubber traffic cones. The object was to negotiate the course as fast as possible without hitting any cones—every cone hit was a time penalty. I'd never done this before, and the Jaguar was far from ideal for this type of event because of its size and poor visibility.

Before my first run, I watched intently, trying to learn the complex pattern other drivers were following. My turn finally came. The big Jaguar charged hard

Sebring 1963, before the battle. Left to right: Roger Subith, Joan "Shelby" Sherman, Ole Olsen, and Al Dowd, sporting the poorly regarded Carroll Shelby signature bibbed overalls. How can we know this is before the race? Because the straps are not yet broken. *Dave Friedman*

down the beginning straight section into the tight left turn at the end, then another shorter straight and into a sea of cones. I held my braking until very late but could see no pattern, no obvious path to take, so into the abyss I sailed, orange cones flying, people running for their lives and me looking for a driveway to get the hell out of there.

"Oklahoma!"

The engine shop was very busy preparing the new 289-cubic-inch engine that would replace the original 260s for Sebring in late March. The new engines were to be tested at an SCCA Regional race at Dodger Stadium three weeks before the 12-hour.

There was a little contention in the ranks when someone decided that it would be nice if, at Sebring, the entire Shelby American race crew was dressed in bibbed overalls to replicate the look made famous by Carroll Shelby during his driving career. Some of the guys got a little touchy when the Hollywood costume designer invaded the shop with measuring tape and clipboards to take the vital dimensions of the crewmen to fashion for each of them proper, custom-made bibbed overalls.

Carroll blamed Joan for the idea—some say it was Carroll—but at any rate, no one wanted to take credit. When the costumes arrived, they were issued to the proper crewmembers. The overalls, light blue with white pinstripes, were made of very lightweight material. They looked better suited to a two-and-a-half-hour performance of *Oklahoma!* than 12 hours of racing at Sebring.

The SCCA's Dodger Stadium race was held in the vast parking lot around the baseball park. My roommate, Allen Grant, had some friends come down from his hometown of Modesto, California—two guys and two girls. The guys stayed in the lowbrow Rose Motel on Lincoln; the girls were invited to stay with us in our small apartment. This seemed a little risky to me, as Mrs. Allcock warned us from the start that absolutely no girls were ever to cross our threshold. Allen and I slept on opposite sides of the room in our beds while the girls slept on the floor between us. Although Allen pleaded with one of the girls to join him in bed, it was to no avail. We had to leave early for Dodger Stadium, so the girls were warned to leave very quietly so as not to be discovered by Mrs. Allcock.

The race went well, with Dave winning and Ken finishing a close second. The only trouble came the day before, when the two Cobras flunked the decibel noise test instituted because the race was so close

Dave MacDonald takes a victory lap at Dodger Stadium with his wife, Sherry. Ken Miles was second and Bob Bondurant, who would soon join the team, finished third in a Stingray. The team struggled to get the cars quiet enough to pass the stringent noise requirements, wiring steel wool into the Cobra's exhaust. *Dave Friedman*

to downtown Los Angeles and nearby neighborhoods. By wiring steel wool into the exhaust pipes, the Cobras finally passed the test.

I arrived home after the race first because Allen went back to the shop with the cars. As I walked toward the apartment, Mrs. Allcock emerged from the front house and said, "I know you had girls last night. You are evicted. Get your belongings and get out. And tell Allen too."

She had entered our apartment in the morning after Allen and I left and caught the girls before they had a chance to leave. I intercepted Allen at the shop and told him what had happened.

"Let me handle it," he told me as we returned home for the confrontation. Allen apologized profusely, telling Mrs. Allcock that the girls had nowhere else to stay and that absolutely nothing happened. He said he wanted to attend church with Mrs. Allcock. I stood there dumbfounded as Mrs. Allcock started to cry. What a gift Allen possessed! That was a close one.

It was becoming obvious that my Lotus was not going to be ready for the next drivers school in March. This was going to set my race-license timetable back at least a month. I devised a plan to use the school Cobra instead of my car. My pitch was that I would hand out Cobra brochures to all of the racing-license applicants at the track. Surely some of them would buy a Cobra.

Building up my nerve, I went to Mr. Shelby's office and presented my plan. He wasn't the least bit interested, stating, "I can't let you do that. My insurance won't allow it."

"I guess I won't get my license for a long time then," I said, as I started to turn around.

"Why not?" he shot back.

"Because I have to attend three drivers schools, and I only did one so far and there is just one a month."

"I'll get you your license," he said, somewhat irritated.

"How?" I asked.

"I'll call Charlie Gates." Charlie Gates was in charge of licensing for the Cal Club region; he also raced for Triumph.

I got my SCCA license/log book. Impressive!

After the Dodger Stadium race, there was a tremendous push to get the four Cobras that were scheduled for Sebring ready to leave in just over a week. All of the cars had 289 engines, and the two new black ones used the new rack-and-pinion steering. Cobras had never raced at night, so the mechanics had to install not only high-powered driving lights, but also a means of protecting them from the very destructive Sebring course. The race was run mostly on World War II–era, very abrasive concrete runways with a reputation for assaulting cars with chunks of cement.

I had asked for and been granted permission to ride in the car hauler to and from Sebring with the truck driver, Joe Landaker. He had been Carroll Shelby's mechanic in the mid-1950s when Carroll raced for John Edgar. After the last-minute panic and late-night loading of the Florida-bound race cars and related gear, Joe and I hit the road.

The Secret Tiger
In the midst of the near chaos of the Sebring preparation, an innocuous little white Sunbeam Alpine, which no one seemed to pay much attention to, sat over to one side near the small, elevated office in the race shop. It was destined to play a significant role in Shelby history.

After Joe and I left, George Boskoff slowly walked back into the shop and sat on the steps that led into the little office. Carroll sat down beside him and said, "George, I want you to put one of our engines in this car," gesturing toward the Sunbeam Alpine. The next morning the Sunbeam was pushed into a little room in the back of the shop, and George went to work.

The truck ride to Sebring wasn't as much fun as I'd expected. For starters, Joe's personality left something to be desired. Then there was the radio. Although I loved music, Joe must have had the world's keenest hearing because I could barely hear it. He would tolerate no more volume; I guess Joe didn't know that modern music needs to be sort of loud.

When Gene Pitney's hit "Mecca" came on, I asked, "Can I turn it up a little?"

Joe answered, "That's a Jew song." Apparently Joe wasn't very well versed in middle-eastern religion. Actually the song had nothing to do with religion, but I let it go.

The last drawback to the trip with Joe was that the gasoline-powered Shelby transporter was painfully slow. Crossing the vastness of Texas against a strong headwind, the speedometer never topped 40 miles per hour. We finally arrived at the racetrack, unloaded the cars, and rolled them into one of the old hangars left over from when the Sebring airport was a 1940s training base for B-17 bomber crews. The drivers were Dave MacDonald with Fireball Roberts, Phil Hill with Dan Gurney, and Ken Miles with Lew Spencer. Because there were four cars, the driver assignments would be shuffled during the race. Holman and Moody, the famous stock car team, also entered a Cobra with a stupid-looking roll cage.

I was helping on one of the red cars with Jim Culleton when Phil Hill told us, "Do whatever Gurney's doing on his car. He's pretty smart about this stuff." He was referring to putting more rearward rake in the windshield, which was accomplished by removing one of the two bolts on each side that held it in place, allowing it to freely pivot rearward.

Gurney was sitting over the engine on the black car, tinkering with the throttle linkage on the Weber carburetors. Bruce Burness,

The Dan Gurney No. 15 and the Phil Hill No. 12 were the first two rack-and-pinion-steering-equipped cars. The driver lineups became meaningless as the race progressed because drivers were shuffled around as the cars encountered problems. *Dave Friedman*

Dave MacDonald and Wally Peat during a light moment as the Holman and Moody guys check out No. 14, the car that Dave would share with the great Fireball Roberts. This is the first Cobra race car built, so it lacked the rack-and-pinion steering that would be used on later cars. *Dave Friedman*

the crew chief on the car, said Dan spent a lot of time at night, getting his headlights adjusted just right.

I was present for an interesting conversation about brake wear one night after practice. The English Girling factory representative was predicting the number of laps each of the team cars could run before having to make a brake pad change. Phil Remington, MacDonald, and Shelby were listening intently as he gave the numbers for each car, not knowing who was driving any particular car. They could all go about the same distance except for one car.

The Girling man said something to the effect that "whoever the bloody driver is in this car can't go half the distance of the others." The "bloody driver" was poor Dave. He was embarrassed as Phil and Carroll gave him an accusatory look. The Girling man counseled MacDonald on his braking technique. In fairness to Dave, this was his first long-distance race; all he'd ever known was balls out, all the time.

The race started out very well for the Cobras with Phil Hill leading the first lap, but soon things began to deteriorate when all four of our cars encountered problems. The Oklahoma-style bibbed overall costumes were about as durable as the cars. They became a metaphor for the race cars because when the crew was forced to do repairs, their straps began to break. I remember an oil pump pickup breaking off and dropping into the oil pan. Then one of the older cars with worm and sector steering had a steering failure like the one in the Nassau race with Billy Krause.

One of the later black cars finished 11th overall and first in some obscure class for larger GT cars. Phil Hill was in the highest-placing Cobra along with Lew Spencer and Ken Miles. I wondered if Phil contrasted this race with 1958, 1959, and 1961 when he was the overall winner in a Ferrari. This year's winner was Ferrari again with John Surtees and Lodovico Scarfiotti. The Shelby American team had work to do if they intended to be competitive in the endurance races—and they did intend to be competitive.

By the time we got back from Sebring, George Boskoff had made quite a bit of progress on the Sunbeam Alpine. He had had the pleasure of working on the car by himself—George liked to work alone—because the race shop was pretty much vacant while most of the team was at Sebring. We soon realized that this was a secret project, as the large door separating George's room from the rest of the shop was closed. George was a perfectionist to a fault, and the Sunbeam was no exception. He couldn't work without agonizing over each move, never totally confident that he had made the right decision.

Ken Miles had been asked to do a similar project, installing the 260 in another Alpine, this one with an automatic transmission. Ken already had a connection with the Rootes Group, builders of the Sunbeam

Ken Miles pulled off halfway around the 5.20-mile track to see "what was going on under there." He was driving one of the early cars, so it was likely a steering problem. *Dave Friedman*

Phil Hill got a great start at Sebring in 1963, leading the first lap. He drove with Lew Spencer to win the over-4-liter GT class, finishing 11th overall despite many setbacks. *Dave Friedman*

Alpine, because he had raced a Sunbeam Alpine in SCCA races and had been on the Rootes factory team at Sebring in 1962. The job was not done at Shelby American nor was it done with the care and craftsmanship that was going into George's Shelby car. In fact it was what would be described as "quick and dirty." The engine was too far forward for proper handling, and it didn't look like a very practical conversion.

Ken drove the car to Shelby's one day to show it, knowing that a similar project was underway. When George looked at Miles's maroon car, he knew it was not a practical solution. It wasn't going to be that easy. He intended that his white Alpine—when finished—would be as nearly perfect as possible.

The inspiration for this project was the performance of the Cobra when it ran its first race at Riverside in October 1962 with Billy Krause at the wheel. Ian Garrad, the West Coast Rootes representative, thought if this conversion of an AC chassis could be this good, why not a Sunbeam Alpine? Garrad, John Panks—who was head of North American operations for Rootes—along with Brian Rootes—the son of the company head, Lord Rootes in England—conspired on this project without the Rootes factory's blessing or knowledge. Their hopes were that if they could pull it off in secret and make the car good enough, the factory might be inspired to put it into production.

George stayed sequestered in his secret room for five or six weeks, slowly but surely tackling each problem that confronted him on this little car. I visited George's cubbyhole every day, which made him a little uncomfortable because to a large degree he was responsible for maintaining the secrecy. Though we had become good friends, one day he bodily threw me out of his special place. As testament to the level of secrecy George maintained, Dave Friedman—the team photographer, who took pictures of everything that was ever done at Shelby American in triplicate—didn't know until decades later that this effort took place right under his nose. There are no pictures that I know of taken of this project as it was being done.

The biggest hurdle that had to be overcome if this was to be a practical car was that the Ford V-8 had to be moved back several inches. This would give the car a more acceptable weight distribution, which was especially critical because the Alpine had a very short wheelbase. The standard steering arrangement made it impossible to do this, requiring a total revamp of the steering system.

Leroy Pike, Don and Gary Pike's father, was now the parts-chaser-in-chief at Shelby American. He was an excellent scavenger, becoming a great asset to George's Sunbeam project. Well-known race mechanic and race car builder Doane Spencer had a large collection of British car parts. George asked Leroy to bring him as many different rack-and-pinion steering units as he could find. After Leroy came back with several, George chose one from an MG that he felt he could adapt to the Alpine.

When everything was finally in place, it became obvious that the links from the rack to the steering arms required more angularity than the ball joints in the rack could accommodate. George modified the ball joints, but the required angularity was still inadequate. The only solution seemed to be to bend the links, a solution that George was inclined to reject as half-assed because a straight link is always stronger and wouldn't deflect under load. Also a bent link would complicate steering adjustment. Many in the shop, as well as Carroll, knew of George's dilemma as he agonized over having to bend the links.

Finally in a moment of desperation to move the project forward, Carroll came charging down from his office, almost shouting as he ran: "George, I've made the decision. Go ahead and bend the links."

Leroy's parts scavenging came in handy again as he got several exhaust manifolds from a Ford parts manager he knew, enabling George to choose one to adapt to the tight quarters of the Alpine's engine compartment. Roger Subith, a friend of Dave MacDonald who owned a radiator shop, made a special radiator for the car. The pulleys on the front of the engine had to be modified to accommodate the radiator because of the engine's length. The car was nearly finished, but the time was running out. George had been under pressure for several days as the April 20 delivery date approached. On April 19 in the afternoon, there were still a number of small details to finish before the car was ready to be delivered to the Rootes representatives.

Phil Remington sensed that George had reached his limit, as he sent him home, saying that he would finish up the few details left and see George in the morning. When George got to work the next day, the Alpine was finished and poised pointing toward the shop's overhead door, awaiting its maiden voyage. Phil waited until George's arrival, so George could share the first ride in the car he had built with John Panks from Rootes. The car performed perfectly as Mr. Panks drove and George rode. Afterward Carroll drove it with Mr. Garrad. This was the last I saw of this car, but the story continues.

After quite a few miles were put on the car, it was shipped to England in July. Ian Garrad's father, Norman, was the competition manager at Rootes and was aware of the stealth project. When Ian drove to the factory to show the car to the assistant chief engineer, a Mr. Peter Ware, Ware said he didn't have time to look at it. Perhaps his assistant Peter Wilson could take a look. Ian drove the car to Mr. Wilson's office. Wilson could spare them five minutes. Mr. Wilson was so impressed that he contacted his boss (Mr. Ware), saying he'd better take a look for himself. Mr. Ware drove the car and deemed it fantastic.

Arrangements were made for Lord Rootes to view the little Ford-powered Alpine. His Lordship arrived in a chauffeur-driven Humber and asked to drive the car; the chauffeur would follow. The chauffeur didn't follow for long because Lord Rootes in the little white Alpine quickly disappeared. He was gone long enough that there was some concern for his well-being. Eventually he returned intact, went to his office, and said to his secretary, "Get me Henry Ford in Detroit."

Mr. Ford was vacationing in the south of France, currently on his yacht in the Mediterranean. He was reached by radio, and Lord Rootes put in an order for some five thousand Ford 260-cubic-inch V-8s. I understand that it was Lord Rootes who suggested calling the new car "Tiger" after the 1925 Sunbeam Tiger that Sir Henry Segrave broke the land-speed record with in 1926.

The Tiger debuted in April 1964 at the New York Auto Show. It was close to a carbon copy of the Shelby car that George Boskoff prepared a year earlier, right down to the bent steering links. The fact that the day the Sunbeam Alpine with its new 260-cubic-inch Ford engine left Shelby American was April 20 has no significance whatsoever, except to me. That was also the day I ran in my first sports car race.

4/20/63
I'd been planning for this day since 1957, when I saw Phil Hill and Carroll Shelby at Elkhart Lake and thought *This is what I'm going to do*. April 20, 1963, was the day I started doing it.

Allen Grant, my roommate, had a friend from San Francisco named Don Wixcel, who came down to visit (and this time Allen's guest didn't upset Mrs. Allcock) at a very opportune time for me. Don raced a Triumph Spitfire up north and was generous enough to tow my trailer to Pomona behind his station wagon. The SCCA had reclassified the Lotus Super 7 for the 1963 season by moving it from C Production to B Production. If that had happened before I bought it, it would not have been my choice because now the tiny Lotus was in the same class as the pre-1963 Corvettes. I thought I'd wasted my money.

The cop who'd stopped me on my way to work to look at my car was also going to run his new Lotus in this race. His name was Bill Jones. I'll have to admit that the first practice session scared the hell out of me. As I was feeling my way around trying to learn the track, I remember Ronnie Bucknum, one of the best West Coast drivers, passing me sideways in a fast left turn in his Hollywood Sports Cars' MGB as though I were standing still. I remember thinking, *You love this. What's the problem? You're not supposed to be scared.*

I felt better by race time. My ancient logbook says I was 14th and 4th in class on Saturday and DNF, did not finish, on Sunday. I can't remember why I didn't finish, but the car tended to overheat so that's likely why. Bill the cop didn't finish either, and I do remember *his* problem: his water pump fell off. The aluminum casting broke and the pump just fell off. I don't remember much about the race itself, except that when I passed Bill the cop in the last turn, which was in the drag strip staging area, I almost slid into him and thought, *Shit, I can't hit the only guy here I know!* My aunt and uncle came from Oxnard to see my first race and seemed to enjoy it. I don't think they expected much from me, but I did. It was a start, if not much else.

The following weekend there was a race at Del Mar put on by the San Diego region of the SCCA. For this race I had three helpers. They were my friend Gordon Goring, Paul Anfang, the Goodyear race tire

The cop who stopped me on the way to work in my new Lotus was Bill Jones. Inspired by my car, he bought one of his own. Here he loses control of it at Pomona. *Allen Kuhn*

guy, and Anfang's young helper, Dan Doniack. Not one of them was a mechanic, so it wouldn't be right to call them my crew—more appropriately, my company.

When we arrived at the track, which was really just a parking lot with a course defined mostly by hay bales, I discovered that because of my lack of experience, I had to run in the novice race. This hadn't applied in the Pomona race because the rules can vary from one SCCA region to the next. Pomona was in the Cal Club region.

Shelby American had entered a Cobra for Dave MacDonald. It wasn't a Sebring- or Daytona-type effort, with lots of cars and parts and people, just Dave and Wally Peat with a pickup and an open trailer. They had not much more than my little team, which was comprised of a parts man, a tire changer, a bullshit artist, and a novice driver.

During our practice session I got a pretty good feel for the course. It was relatively tight, so I expected it would be good for a car like mine. We lined up for our race. Looking around, it was amazing what a motley group we were. All the production classes were represented and some modifieds because the only criteria was that the drivers were inexperienced. There were several Porsches, Triumphs, Alfas,

Sprites, Morgans, Austin-Healeys, a Sunbeam Alpine, a Corvette, and a Devin Special.

All races then had standing starts. I quickly got into the lead and pulled away. The race lasted only 15 minutes, but I got such a lead, I started showing off, sliding my car through the tight turns at an exaggerated angle and thinking, *I sure look good. I hope someone's watching*. I won by a large margin. It felt wonderful, and I was as excited as my friends. In fact, Anfang, the bullshitter, proclaimed: "We're gonna celebrate. We're gonna take you to Tijuana tonight and get you laid!"

At first I thought he was kidding, but when we left for Mexico, I wasn't so sure. We ate in Tijuana, and then Anfang took us to a bar where we sat near the stage and watched a girl dance as she removed a good deal of her clothes. She reached down and took off my glasses, and as she danced, she put them in places where glasses had no business being. When the music ended, she retreated behind a curtain. I wondered if she forgot to give me back my glasses. I would need them for the race tomorrow. The music started again and she eventually returned the glasses.

Anfang kept saying, "Don't worry. I know my way around here."

The next place was downstairs in a large dark area where we ordered beer as the four of us sat in a booth. An attractive young girl made a suggestive comment, and Anfang pointed to me, at which time she took me into a private corner and asked if I wanted her. I kind of did, but I was trying to be business-like. We had just about struck a bargain when Anfang pulled me away saying, "This is not the place." It seemed as good as any to me, but he insisted, "I know what I'm doing."

As we left, he engaged a cab driver who took us into a back alley and let us out at the side entrance of a pretty awful hotel. The cabby took the four of us to a room. Soon a number of not very good-looking women invaded the room; they were quite aggressive. One grabbed me, another grabbed Dan, who was 17, I think, and they whisked us away to have their way with us for a grand total of $17. I felt Anfang could have done better, but at least he made good, or good enough, on his promise. Winning the race was much better—and likely much safer!

There are very few race drivers who can say that their first race victory and their first sex occurred on the same day. It's a shame a guy had to wait until he was 21 to race in America.

We were a little slow getting to the track Sunday. As we arrived the novice race was already lining up. I guess I was still feeling a little weird about the previous night as I ran to get my racing stuff on. I made it to my pole position on time and as the race started, immediately pulled away from the field. Well into the race with another easy victory in sight, my water pump fell off, ending my heroic drive. I couldn't help wondering if God might have been punishing me for misusing my own water pump the night before. I wasn't very religious back then, but my mother had tried to raise me as a Catholic.

Later in the day, we witnessed an historic race—somewhat obscure, but historic nevertheless. Dave MacDonald in a Shelby American team Cobra was convincingly defeated by a Corvette Stingray, driven by Bill Sherwood. It would never happen again. The race was fabulous to watch. Dave, as always, gave his best as he tried to get by Sherwood, power sliding through the turns and clipping hay bales in a desperate but vain effort to best the Stingray. Sherwood responded to the attack by driving smoothly and steadily, never making an obvious mistake during his impressive drive. Bill Sherwood was a very good driver but Dave MacDonald was a great driver. The difference that day on this Mickey Mouse track was in the cars. The power-to-weight ratio was better on the much lighter Cobra, but the Stingray had a more modern suspension. The transverse leaf spring suspension front and rear on the Cobra was a near exact copy of the 1936 Fiat 500 Topolino front suspension—a very long way from state-of-the-art.

Though I started the Sunday novice race at Del Mar from pole position because I had won on Saturday, I was foiled by a faulty water pump. Kirby Avant, a pretty little tomboy who also worked at Shelby American, won the ladies race. *Allen Kuhn*

Dave MacDonald started from pole at Del Mar on April 28, but was passed early in the race by Bill Sherwood's Stingray. Dave gave it his all but could not get by Sherwood. It was a great race to watch, and the only time I know of that a Stingray beat a Shelby Team Cobra, fair and square. *Allen Kuhn*

Dave MacDonald's Cobra leads Bill Sherwood's Corvette Stingray early in their epic race at Del Mar. Here Sherwood makes his move on the inside of Dave. By the end of the race there was hay all over the track. *Allen Kuhn*

I made plans to travel back home to Waukegan to see my parents and brother and to race on the tracks that fostered my interest in sports car racing in the first place. It seemed that now was a good time because it was early enough in the 1963 racing season to do a lot of racing and then return to California in the fall.

One thing that bothered me about California was that it wasn't very green. The two tracks I'd raced on were in nondescript gray parking lots. Even the worst tracks in the Midwest were at least green. I hadn't really felt as though I had much of a chance of getting on the Shelby team as a driver, but if I was going to get anywhere, I first needed experience, and the experience might as well be on tracks I loved.

I asked for a leave of absence for the summer and a job when I returned, both of which were agreed to. I picked up my aunt in Oxnard, loaded the Lotus on my crummy little trailer, hitched it to my Jaguar, and left for Waukegan.

CHAPTER THREE

Midwest Racer

My goal as I headed home was to run as many races as possible. I especially wanted to run at Meadowdale and Elkhart Lake. There was certainly some risk in leaving California for the summer because if I had a serious problem with the Lotus or even crashed it, the people I knew who could help me get going again, Ole Olson and George Boskoff, were 2,000 miles away. I had just left what was becoming one of the best road racing teams in the country to race on tracks that I had a romantic attachment to. Perhaps I should have recognized that I had a capacity for making somewhat irrational decisions. I guess I was a little homesick too.

Two organizations ran sports car races in the Midwest—SCCA and the Midwestern Council of Sports Car Clubs (MWCSCC). Neither had rules that prevented a driver from competing in the other's events, so I planned to enter every race I could.

The living arrangements were as though I'd never left. My mother seemed OK with my situation, but my father couldn't quite grasp the notion that what I was trying to do could be considered any sort of profession. He believed that I would eventually have some kind of epiphany and go back to school so I could be something.

I got myself on the mailing list for both race clubs so I wouldn't miss any of the entry forms. Entering races was very inexpensive; the entry fees were in the $10–$15 range with a top of $25.

The first race was in mid-May at the Milwaukee fairgrounds track, where I saw my first big car race in 1949 at age seven. The dirt track was paved in 1954, but racing had taken place there since 1903. It was and is the oldest permanent racing facility in the world. This was a Midwestern Council race that utilized most of the 1-mile oval track in addition to an infield course.

My brother and my high school friend Johnny Opitz were my helpers. Another friend came to watch with his girlfriend, the same girl who went to the kart races the summer before, and they brought another friend, a girl I'd had a couple of dates with after high school. The girlfriend's name was Jan and the other girl's name was Joanne. For some strange reason Joanne put a tiny Bible in my driver's suit pocket just before the race. I thought that was a little creepy, but I guess it made her feel good. The race didn't go too well. My car overheated again and I don't know where I finished. In practice I hit a hay bale, and though it did very little damage, it bothered me just the same.

The next race on the schedule was another Midwestern Council race on the weekend before Memorial Day. I was really looking forward to racing at Meadowdale. I sort of considered it a home track because I'd seen so many races there, including the track's first race in 1958.

I hadn't actually been on Meadowdale since the day Lyman and I ran our MG TD there while we were in high school. This very high-speed track shouldn't have been good for a Lotus Super 7, especially against Corvettes, my main competition. The Monza Wall, a steeply banked bumpy 180-degree turn that preceded an almost mile-long straight, much of it downhill, was pretty intimidating. It must have been more intimidating for others than for me, because I could usually make up ground on faster cars there. Then came a fast downhill, a banked right-hander with a steel guardrail around the outside, and a no-escape road called Greg's Corkscrew. There were numerous elevation changes at Meadowdale with challenging combinations of fast- to medium-speed turns.

The crew was again my friend Johnny Opitz and my brother. Unfortunately the overheating returned and I finished third in class.

My brother and I drove to Indianapolis to watch the 500, which was on Thursday, May 30. We had high hopes for Dan Gurney and Jim Clark, who in their Lotuses were using a refined version of the 255-cubic-inch pushrod Ford V-8 that was tried in Gurney's Cobra in February at the Daytona Continental. I was partial toward Lotus too; my nickname at Shelby's was Lotus John. Actually I was Lotus John II because another Shelby employee who also raced a Lotus, John Timanus, was the original Lotus John.

At the 500

Parnelli Jones was fastest qualifier, driving an Offy-powered Watson roadster. There were four rear-engine cars in the race: the Lotus Fords of Gurney and Clark, and the Chevrolet-powered Mickey Thompson cars of Duane Carter and Al Miller. The rest of the field were roadsters—three powered by Novi V-8s and the rest by Offys.

The race was pretty dramatic. Although the powerful Novi of Jim Hurtubise passed Parnelli, it led for only one lap. Parnelli dominated the race, but the less-fuel-efficient Offy roadsters required at least two fuel and tire stops, whereas the Lotuses needed only one. Late in the race, Parnelli's car developed an oil leak. You could see the oil streaks on the oil tank, which sat outside of the body between the front and rear wheels. Eddie Sachs spun, likely in the oil, bringing a caution period. Indy used to have a goofy system of lights that were supposed to keep drivers maintaining whatever their gap from other cars was until the green flag ended the caution laps. Clark had gotten to within four seconds of Parnelli before the spin, but his unfamiliarity with the pacer light system caused him to lose ground, and he finished second. Gurney had problems that dropped him to seventh. It was an epic Indy 500, and I was glad I got to see Parnelli win.

June was going to be a busy month of racing, with two more events at Meadowdale on the 9th and the 30th. The overheating had been a consistent problem, and it had to be fixed if I was to have any real success with this car. The SCCA sent me a drawing of a club-legal cooling system modification called a swirl pot. They also sent a drawing of a frame modification that they deemed legal, which consisted of a couple additional diagonal tubes in the front section of the frame. A welder in Waukegan that my dad knew did the work in time for the next race.

That event, another Council race hosted by the Chicagoland Sports Car Club, was to be run on a slightly different configuration that shortened the course from 3.27 miles to 2.25 miles. It would be better for my car because it shortened the long straight by about half. It was a shame, driving wise, because it cut out a very nice section.

Before practice started, a real dilemma confronted me. My best helper, Johnny, who'd assisted me at each race since I arrived from California, said, "Let me take the car out for a couple of laps in the first practice."

I said, "I can't do that. They'd take my license if they found out."

"I can wear your suit and helmet, and they would never know."

"You don't know the track and never drove the car," I answered.

"Please, just one lap and I'll come in."

"OK, but just one lap and go very slow."

Johnny put my suit and helmet on and went out. Unfortunately he was lined up first. After one lap he was still first and he didn't come in. I was very pissed off. Next lap he went by again. No one had passed him yet.

"That son of a bitch," I said to Lyman. Johnny came in on the third lap.

"Goddamn it, you said one lap."

"I couldn't stop," he said. "There were too many cars behind me." I felt like I'd dodged a bullet. It took a while for it to sink in, but after it did, it was funny as hell.

I started the race toward the front among several Corvettes, including the black one driven by Ralph Webb, who won most of the B Production class races. I led the first lap and gradually extended my lead to the end. Lyman said he was shocked when I came around first on the first lap. So was I. It was a very satisfying day, the kind of day you can only expect once in a while. The cooling system modification seemed to have cured the overheating problem.

Most of the car's maintenance I tried to do myself. I changed the rod bearings and kept the valves adjusted. If I needed something like wheel balancing, I'd drive the car down the alley to the gas station a block away. Derry May, one of Ryser's old friends who worked as a mechanic at Renick's service station, would do the work.

Mom's First Look
The June 30 race at Meadowdale was an SCCA Divisional, which

Forty-nine years after this accident at Meadowdale in Illinois, I was thumbing through a book on the track's history when I came upon these two pictures. The caption indicated that the author didn't know the race or the date on which it occurred. I did. As I looked at the people in the stands, to my shock, there was my mother, hands covering her face at the end of the first lap of the first race she ever saw me drive in, just as she had described to me on June 30, 1963. *Philip Aleo*

made it somewhat more important than the Midwestern Council races, even though many of the same people participated. This time my mother came along. She had never seen me race anything except a kart, a bicycle, and a soapbox derby car.

The event used the full-length 3.27-mile Meadowdale course. There was a very nice blue 1961 B Production Corvette that was running most of the races, driven by Dave Ott. I didn't know him when he approached me and said, "I went to Carroll Shelby's School of High Performance Driving. Pete Brock was my instructor."

I told him, "I went to Shelby's school too, and Pete Brock was my instructor."

"I know you did," he said. "I got a letter from Pete telling me to watch out for a kid with a Lotus Super 7. 'He's coming back there and he's in your class.'"

The notorious Monza Wall at Meadowdale was intimidating to drivers and brutal on cars. It was fast, bumpy, and unforgiving. Here I'm stalking Dave Ott in his B Production Corvette who I passed to win my first SCCA Divisional race June 30, 1963. *John Morton Collection*

I was very flattered that Pete said that because he'd never indicated to me that he thought my driving was anything very special.

Mom sat in the stands across from the pits right where the Monza Wall ended and the long main straight began. She was pretty nervous. The race began with a standing start. There were Stingrays in front. I was somewhere between fourth and sixth as we entered the Monza Wall near the end of the first lap, maybe three or four seconds behind the leading car. As the leaders exited the Wall, a Stingray Coupe spun and was crashed into by a Stingray Roadster, tearing off the rear section of the Coupe, which burst into a huge fireball. Mother stood in horror as she watched the carnage just beneath her. They red-flagged (stopped) the race while they cleaned up the mess.

Fortunately no one was seriously hurt. We re-formed on the grid and waited for about half an hour to restart. To my surprise the corner speed of my Lotus more than negated the Corvette's straight-line speed. I won B Production. Dick Lang in a Stingray won A Production. My mother wasn't the hysterical type, even though the first lap she ever saw me race didn't end well. She covered her face so she couldn't see the chaos in front of her and peeked through her fingers until she saw me pass. I took her on the victory lap and she held the flag. She never tried to get me to quit.

Jan the Race Queen

I think my friend and his beautiful girlfriend may have been having trouble because she called me one day and asked if I could pick her up and take her for a ride. I still had the Jaguar. We went to a place called Petrified Springs near Kenosha, Wisconsin, and walked to the toboggan track. We sat and talked. To make a long story short, she let me know she would be my girlfriend if I was interested. Of course I was and had been since the first time I saw her. She would have to take care of the details involving her current relationship. I felt some guilt because her boyfriend had been a good friend since grade school. I knew this would be very painful for him as it would have been for me if the roles had been reversed. I let her know from the start how important racing was to me. She seemed to understand. She was 18 years old.

There were three weeks before the Wilmot races. I spent most of my free time—that's time not working on my race car—doing things with my new girlfriend. Waukegan is one of those places where, if you had a choice, you would only live there for maybe five months out of a year. But the late spring, summer, and early fall were great.

My brother Lyman sitting in my car wearing my driver's suit before taking a highly illegal practice lap during official practice for the SCCA Divisional at Wilmot Hills, Wisconsin, on July 21, 1963. If our ruse had been discovered, I would have been in big trouble. *John Morton Collection*

At any rate, Jan and I got along well and spent most of our time together. She was from a religious family, but she was pretty hit and miss about that. I was mostly miss, yet before every race I would say a little prayer. I would ask for everyone in the race to be safe and for me to do well. I never asked to win because I didn't have enough ego to think I deserved to win any more than anyone else. Besides it seemed selfish. I outgrew the prayer part.

Wilmot Hills was a ski area 25 miles from Waukegan with a short (less than a mile) road course built around the ski lodge. They called the ski slope Wilmot Mountain, which is like calling its road course the Nürburgring. The mountain is 230 feet tall, and the five-turn race course, built in 1953, is one of the earliest permanent courses in America. In high school, I slipped onto the track one winter in my '54 Dodge when hardly anyone was around. I'd forgotten I had an empty Pepsi six-pack on the floor in the back and the bottles were crashing around as I slid through the corners. I wouldn't stop, though, because I was afraid I'd be kicked off soon.

The crew problem I'd had with Johnny at Meadowdale raised its ugly head again at Wilmot, this time with Lyman. He felt that if I let Johnny drive at a racing event, he should certainly be given the same opportunity; after all, he was my brother. I couldn't deny him, so we pulled the same stunt and again got away with it. Lyman was much more obedient than Johnny had been.

I had brake problems in the race. My car was a 1962, just before Lotus put disc brakes on the front. Every time I pushed the pedal, I got a bad vibration plus erratic locking of the front wheels. The brake drums had gone out of round and would have to be turned before the next race. I finished only fourth in class—very disappointing. Another Super 7 won B Production driven by a guy named Glen Lyall. At least it wasn't a Corvette.

Two of the three Shelby American cars at Kent, Washington, for the July 1963 USRRC. They arrived from California behind three pickup trucks, driven by crewmembers Garry Koike, Ted Sutton, and Jim Culleton. The drivers were Dave MacDonald, Ken Miles, and Bob Holbert. They finished one, two, and three, in that order. I was racing at Wilmot, Wisconsin, that weekend. *Ted Sutton*

Garry Koike waits with his rig for the other crew members to arrive for breakfast at Kent, Washington. The year 1963 would be the last that the Shelby American team would travel like common club racers. *Ted Sutton*

Lunchtime at the food stand as Cobra team members choose their poison—Garry Koike on the left with Cobra jacket; Al Dowd, also in Cobra jacket; Miles who has his hand on his hip; Dave MacDonald, brown sweater; and Bob Holbert, gray sweater. Is this a big-time race team or what! *Ted Sutton*

July 21, 1963, USRRC at Kent, Washington. Leaning on Miles' car from left to right are Garry Koike, Al Dowd, Ken Miles, and Jim Culleton. You only have to look at the pants to see who does the dirty work. Check out the fake Cobra on the hood. There was a real one back at the shop, Al Dowd's pet. *Ted Sutton*

Mike Gammino (center) of Providence, Rhode Island, with his crew and his Ferrari GTO in Kent, Washington. Mike was a consistent competitor for the Cobras. Although he never won a USRRC, it wasn't for lack of trying. *Ted Sutton*

After Wilmot, I read in the newspaper that the Shelby team had made a clean sweep of the United States Road Racing Championship (USRRC) at Kent, Washington.

The next race for me was the following weekend at a new track called Mid-Ohio. It opened in 1962 and was reported to be a very nice course. Johnny had a white 1959 Chevrolet Impala two-door hardtop with a 348-cubic-inch engine and stick shift. It made a better tow car than the Jaguar for the 400-mile trip to Ohio. We were not very good at estimating travel time, so by driving all night, we arrived at the track a few minutes before the gates were opened to let the participants enter the facility.

After my first lap of practice I had the sinking feeling that I would never learn this track. Although it was only 2.4 miles long, it seemed to go on forever. There were 15 turns, many of them blind because of all the hills. It was hardly level anywhere. After a few laps though, I was learning it and loved it.

In the Saturday qualifying race I was second to Glen Lyall, the winner at Wilmot. My only excuse was that he had Dunlop R6 tires and I had Goodyear T4s. I don't remember why I never had Dunlops. Shelby sold Goodyears and I may have gotten a deal on them. On Sunday it rained, and the Goodyears were very poor in the rain; the Dunlops had an even bigger advantage. My car was sliding all over the place while Lyall was building up a nice lead before he had a problem. It was almost 50 years ago, but I think it was a flat. I inherited the lead, pulled away from the Corvettes and even started enjoying the slick conditions, reminding myself of driving in the snow back in high school. I won despite my tires.

We left for home as soon as we got the car loaded, then took turns as we drove through the night. I was asleep in the passenger seat when something that wasn't quite normal woke me up. I looked over at the speedometer, which showed a bit over 100 miles per hour. I yelled, "What the hell are you doing?"

Johnny said, "I just want to get home."

"Yeah, me too," I answered, "and it would be nice if the race car and trailer made it with us." Johnny let up. I still had the same two-wheel, suspension-less $175 trailer I bought from Bob Challman, which I was pretty sure had never seen 100 miles per hour and hopefully never would again.

The Indy cars were running at Milwaukee on August 18 with Jim Clark and Dan Gurney in their Indy Lotus 29s. The two hadn't run a USAC (United States Auto Club) Indy car race since the Indianapolis 500 because they had full schedules in Europe driving on the Formula One circuit. Clark won the World Championship for Lotus and Gurney drove for and with Jack Brabham.

The last race I had seen run on this 1-mile oval was in 1949 when it was dirt. The world had changed a lot since then, and today the racing world was about to shift on its axis. I remember the announcer's words when Gurney was next up to qualify. He said, "This is what we've been waiting for. Now we're going to see what it's all about." And we did see, as Dan obliterated the track record by a second, then Clark bested Dan's time by over a tenth of a second.

Clark led every lap of the race and then sat behind second place A. J. Foyt for several laps, choosing not to lap him, either not wanting to humiliate the volatile Foyt or maybe just playing it safe. Gurney was third with carburetion problems. It was the second historic Indy car race I'd seen this year. I felt fortunate to have observed them in person.

I read later that at Continental Divide on that weekend, Shelby's new driver, Bob Bondurant, won the USRRC in a Cobra.

Dave MacDonald drove this hardtop-equipped car in the USRRC event at Continental Divide Raceway on August 28, 1963. The extra weight caused the rear tires to rub the fenders, and it was never used again. Bob Bondurant won the GT class in his first race for Shelby American. The crewman by the right front fender is Louie Unser, Al and Bobby's brother. *Ted Sutton*

I got an entry form in the mail for a race at a brand-new track not far from Milwaukee and less than 50 miles from Waukegan. It was called Lynndale Farms. I sent in my entry and asked Jan if she would like to go. I would bring her home on Saturday night and pick her up early Sunday morning. We arrived Saturday, and Johnny, Lyman, Jan, and I went to registration to sign our lives away and get our passes. When Jan stepped up to the table to sign in, the nice lady asked, "How old are you, dear?"

Jan responded, "Eighteen."

The woman got all huffy and said, "You can't be in here under twenty-one." She turned to me and said to take her out, right now. I felt bad for Jan because the woman made a small spectacle of the eviction. As I walked her to the exit, I showed her the place at the fence where I would give her my pass, which would allow her in. Afterward no one would be checking. This trick was pulled many times for many years, but it still worked.

It was only a Midwestern Council race but because this was the first race on this new track, they had imported Stirling Moss to be the grand marshal and drive the pace car, a Cobra, of all things. Lynndale was a fabulous little track running up and down through rolling hills with a nice variety of fast and slow turns. It was perfect for spectators because there was an amphitheater-like view allowing them to see most of the track from a single vantage point.

On Sunday we did the pit-pass trick again. Though the Lotus Super 7 was a production car with a passenger seat, I had to take it out before I raced because it was just a padded piece of plywood, which at high speed would be sucked up and try to leave the car. They used to allow a passenger to ride holding the checkered flag on a victory lap, so I told Jan to take the seat to the finish line if I won and I would ride her around with the flag. I did win the B Production class. A driver named Scott Beckett won the overall victory in a Birdcage Maserati with a 289 Ford engine.

During the brief ceremony for Beckett, a newspaper reporter spotted my very pretty girlfriend holding the little seat as she waited for her ride. He grabbed Jan and turned my underage pit violator into the impromptu race queen when he asked her to kiss Beckett. We drove all the way to Milwaukee on Monday to find the picture of her in the Milwaukee paper. We never did.

Soon after this race, Jan had to leave for college in St. Paul, Minnesota. I'd spent so much time with her that summer, it was going to be hard being without her. I promised to visit before going back to California. It seemed that life had been pretty nearly perfect for the past three months, as much because of having her as it was for the racing success.

The Unnamed Champ

The next SCCA Divisional was at Waterford Hills near Detroit on September 1. It was another long tow, about 350 miles. I had decided earlier in the summer that I would make a goal of winning the Central Divisional Championship in B Production. If I won here I would be well ahead in points. On Saturday I finished second in class, having some electrical problem that affected the way the engine ran. The problem was related to the electric tachometer, which was a mystery to me. The MG TD I had in high school as well as my Jaguar XK150 had had electrical troubles and now the Lotus. Could it be that British cars were prone to electrical problems?

I had met a race driver and mechanic who lived near Waukegan and worked at a foreign car dealership in nearby Lake Forest. His name was Horst Kwech, and it was my good fortune that he was racing an Alfa Romeo that weekend at Waterford because he fixed my car. I won my class on Sunday, giving me an insurmountable lead in my quest for the Central Division B Production championship. This wasn't a big deal in the eyes of the racing world but it was at least a goal set and then met, which bolstered my somewhat tenuous confidence.

The week after Waterford Hills there was to be a 200-mile production car race at Elkhart Lake, Wisconsin. They were calling it the Badger 200—a Saturday preliminary to the Road America 500, the race that cemented my future back in 1957. The Shelby team would be there to run the 500 on Sunday. This year the Road America 500 was part of the United States Road Racing Championship, which the Shelby team had been contesting and dominating in the GT class with their unbeatable Cobras.

It almost seemed foolhardy to try to run a 200-mile race in a Lotus Super 7, especially on a track as long and fast as Road America. Our top speed was low due to very high aerodynamic drag, coupled with relatively low horsepower. The advantage of lightness and high cornering speeds would be more than negated by three very high-speed straights. But this was the greatest sports car track in the country, and it was a thrill to be racing there. Dave Ott, whose nemesis I had been, said before the race, "I think I've got you here," counting on the advantage his 1961 Corvette would have on this track. I had to agree with him.

A pit stop was going to be necessary to make 200 miles. I don't remember if it was mandatory for everyone. A field of more than 50 cars started; most had never run a race this long—50 laps around the 4-mile track. I tried to conserve my car by shifting at a lower RPM than I would have in a typical half-hour race.

After about an hour and 20 minutes, I made my pit stop for fuel. It was a rule that during the refueling process, the driver had to be out of the car. The fuel was added by dumping it from cans into a funnel. We had planned for Lyman to put the funnel into the tank then Johnny and I would pour the gas. When I pulled to a stop and exited the car, Lyman, the funnel man, forgot where the funnel was. Lyman always meant well, but tended not to think on his feet or plan ahead very well. Finally the funnel was located and the pit stop resumed.

I don't recall how much time was lost but not too much, I suppose, because not long before the end of the race, Ott's B Production–leading Corvette came into sight. Even though I didn't really know our relative positions at the time, I felt I had to get past him—which I did in Canada Corner. I had won the class, with Dave second. We were sixth overall and with a little better pit stop we might have finished higher, but we still did better than expected.

Dave Ott and I skirmish at Canada Corner at Road America in the Badger 200 B Production race on September 7, 1963. I won after a couple of wild laps late in the race, and Ott finished second. *John McCollister*

We stayed to watch the 500 on Sunday. Lyman and Johnny had seen Cobras race before but never the Shelby team. Miles drove with Bob Holbert, finishing second overall. They had been entered as an over-2-liter modified and won that class. The overall winner was an under-2-liter Elva Porsche driven by Augie Pabst and Bill Wuesthoff. Dave MacDonald and Bob Bondurant won the GT class, with Lew Spencer and Bob Johnson second in GT. Holbert, Bondurant, and Johnson had joined the team after I'd left for the summer.

At Elkhart Lake there were flyers posted encouraging racers to enter a divisional race at a new track in Iowa called Greenwood Roadway. I felt I needed to enter to protect my lead in the championship. The race was just two weeks after the Badger 200, so I would have to do some maintenance on the Lotus. We changed the rod bearings and checked the valve clearances. It was surprising that the Lotus engine had so far been as reliable as it had. It was a 1,340cc English Ford engine with only three main bearings, a cast-iron crankshaft, and stock connecting rods and pistons. Ole Olsen had done a very good job in preparing it because it had raced 11 weekends, including the two 200-mile race at Road America, and hadn't had any major problems.

For some reason Johnny and I had underestimated the distance to Greenwood Roadway. We figured it to be a little more than 200 miles to Des Moines, Iowa. The track was actually just outside of Indianola, but Des Moines was the nearest big town. Lyman had gone back to Clemson, so it was just Johnny and me. We left in the early evening and drove all night. The next morning we thought we were nearly there but upon asking found we had more than 100 miles to go. We asked several times at gas stations and every time Johnny would say, "How much farther to Des Moines." He would pronounce the "s" at the end of Des and Moines no matter how many times I told him they were silent. Having misjudged the trip's distance and being tired made me a little testy, I guess, but he was driving me crazy with his ignorance. The closer we got the worse it became because now everyone he asked must have thought we were really stupid.

When we finally arrived we were not disappointed, just tired. The track looked challenging as its 3 miles wound up and down through the Iowa farmland. There were spots on the outside of a couple of very fast turns that looked like places you really didn't want to go off. I usually didn't inspect these spots very closely because if they presented serious consequences for a mistake, I didn't want it to have an effect on my speed in that area. It was my ignorance-is-bliss theory.

I got enough practice on Saturday to learn which way the track went, and then we checked into the cheapest motel we could find and got a good night's rest. Sunday we were informed that this race was in the Midwest Division, not the Central Division as we'd thought. Thus any points we might get here would have no bearing on my championship effort. I was only slightly disappointed because I thought I had already won the championship, and besides, this was a really good track.

I had a pretty good starting position behind a couple of Stingrays and a Cobra, all A Production cars, so a B Production win should be easy barring any problems. I got by the Stingrays after a couple of laps, which put me in second with only George Montgomery's Cobra ahead. I was pleasantly surprised to be gaining on him. One of the Stingrays running behind us left the road on one of those fast turns that I chose not to worry about and rolled. The driver wasn't hurt. After pestering the Cobra for a number of laps, I finally got by for a very satisfying overall win.

At the SCCA races I would have my logbook signed, the one Carroll Shelby arranged, by the chief steward, sort of the boss of the race, to indicate that the race had been successful. After six successful races, not necessarily wins, the logbook holder could apply for a National license. The chief steward at this race was Bud Seavrens, who was also the regional executive of the Chicago region of the SCCA. I was flattered that when he signed my log for this race he also wrote "Excellent." The trip home was much easier.

The following week I got to see my first mention in a major national racing publication, *Competition Press*:

> In the semi-windup for the division points in A-D production, John Morton, Waukegan, Ill., West Coast trained driver and not yet a national license holder, came out of the blue in his well-prepared Lotus Super 7 to beat George Montgomery's Cobra to the checker. (*Competition Press*, September 28, 1963, page 5.)

The next week, September 28 and 29, we raced at Lynndale Farms again. This time the race was an SCCA Regional, one notch below the Divisionals, but usually with many of the same competitors. The organizers mixed A, B, and C Production cars together, which was common practice. There were two very good Corvette Stingrays entered, driven by nationally prominent drivers, Dick Lang and Ralph Salyer. Salyer often raced a Cheetah in the big modified class. He called his modified cars Cro-Sal Specials, the *Sal* being for Salyer and the *Cro* for Gene Crow, his very fine mechanic and crew chief.

Bud Gates from Indianapolis won the big modified class in his Genie Chevrolet, followed by Augie Pabst in a Ferrari GTO. Pabst was a source of inspiration for me because he won many races behind the wheel of the Scarabs. Third in the modifieds was Ernie Erickson in an Elva Porsche. Erickson was well-known in the Midwest for driving Porsche Spyders and had raced in the 24 Hours of Le Mans.

My race went well, as I finished third overall behind Lang and Salyer and first in B Production, ahead of fourth-place Ott in his Corvette. Another Super 7 was fifth, driven by Dudley Davis. This was the sixth win in a row, which I was glad I could share with my parents, who both came to watch. My parents sometimes attended the close-to-home races. I was proud to be able to take my mother on a victory lap at Meadowdale while she held the checkered flag. I think she was proud, too, and perhaps a little brave even to be here after witnessing what she thought was my near-death experience at her first race. The only thing missing at Lynndale Farms was my race queen.

In the 1963 Saturday preliminary to the Los Angeles Times Grand Prix, at Riverside, winner Bob Bondurant is ready for the start beside fastest qualifier Dan Gurney. My old roommate, Allen Grant, finished a fine second in a privately owned Cobra. *Allen Kuhn*

Allen Grant on a victory lap at Santa Barbara after winning his race. The car, owned by Coventry Motors and prepared by Ole Olsen, was even better than the team cars. His performance at Riverside got him a ride on the Shelby American team. *Allen Kuhn*

There was just one more race on the schedule before I returned to California and resumed my employment at Shelby American. Johnny and I would run the last SCCA Divisional of the season at Indianapolis Raceway Park (IRP) on October 13. It was an easier trip than our other away races, less than 250 miles. The track was 2.5 miles in length with 15 turns. The layout was good but completely flat, unlike most of the tracks we'd raced on this summer, and had a sterile feel about it. I wouldn't rate it as a difficult track, yet I just wasn't getting the speed I usually had. The car didn't seem as fast as usual; I hoped it wasn't me.

There was a driver I'd met before but didn't really know very well who became involved in a protest at technical inspection. His name was Chuck Cantwell, a very competitive driver who raced a dark red MGB. It seems that Chuck had modified his accelerator pedal to make it easier for him to heel and toe as he downshifted—no big deal. The protesting driver said the modification made it too easy for Chuck to heel and toe. This had to be the most chickenshit protest in the history of racing.

The protester was a jerk who raced a Triumph TR 4 in the same class as the MGB. His name was Jim Spencer. He won a lot of races, but his ego was even bigger than his bank account. He was obviously

Carroll Shelby, Dave MacDonald, and Bob Holbert in discussion after practice for the Los Angeles Times Grand Prix at Riverside. Dave Peat listens in over Carroll's shoulder. *Allen Kuhn*

worried that Chuck might beat him; unfortunately he didn't. I didn't do well either, third in class and sixth overall. But I'd had a very successful summer, so although I was disappointed at the race, I had nothing to complain about.

I read in *Competition Press* that Dave MacDonald had won the Los Angeles Times Grand Prix in a Cooper Monaco that the Shelby team had installed a 289 Ford in and called a King Cobra. It was the same day as my IRP race. He won the Pacific Grand Prix at Laguna Seca a week later. These were the two most important races in the country after Sebring. Soon I was going to leave home again for California. In a way, I couldn't wait to get back there.

I received a very troubling newsletter from the SCCA, which listed all of the class champions in the Central Division. My name was nowhere on the list. I called the Regional Executive for the Chicago region, Bud Seavrens, and asked why I wasn't shown as B Production Champion—in fact, wasn't shown at all. He checked, then told me that my home region was the Cal Club region in Southern California, which was in the Pacific Division, so any points I accumulated here wouldn't count. He asked if I'd made the change and it got lost in the shuffle. I hadn't because I didn't know the regulation, which was my fault.

Bud said, "Your Regional Executive for the Cal Club is Otto Zipper. Write him and tell him the circumstances and ask him to send me a letter saying you changed your affiliation to the Chicago region when you left California in early May. Tell him it's OK with me. If he does that, you'll get the championship."

I had my mother type a nice letter to Mr. Zipper. He never answered. Oh well, at least I got a lot of good experience and would have run those races anyway. Besides, in a couple of years no one would remember who won that damned championship anyway.

All I had left to do before heading back to California was replace the Jaguar with a more suitable tow car and then drive to Saint Paul, Minnesota, to visit Jan at school for two or three days. Johnny had a girlfriend, Charlotte, who was going to the same school, so we made the trip together. The school was Bethel College, which was a religious school of the Baptist persuasion, a perfect fit for Charlotte—for Jan, not so perfect. I didn't expect her to be very happy there. It wasn't that she was bad; she just wasn't obsessed enough with being good.

Arrangements had been made for Johnny and me to stay with an older student who lived off campus. Jan didn't seem to have much of a connection with her classmates so we went our separate way, thank God. We spent a lot of time talking and making plans, maybe with a little desperation because we were soon to be apart for at least a few months. I don't remember the plans very well but I do remember we talked about getting married sometime in the not-too-distant future.

Jan decided to write a letter to her parents explaining her feelings and our ultimate intentions. It was a bit of a touchy situation because her parents knew I was not quite up to their spiritual standards. She thought it would be best if I hand-delivered it when I went back. Everyone gets a little nervous before a race, but delivering this letter would be much worse. We arrived back in Waukegan in the evening, but I was to report to Jan's parents immediately to tell them about the trip and how their daughter was doing.

We talked for a long time. It was getting late when I finally built up the nerve to say, "Jan wrote this letter and I have to give it to you or I'll blow my brains out." I'd read the letter and knew it would have an impact. Jan's dad, Mr. Dayton, read the letter and then gave it to his wife. He said, "Well, I can see you two are serious."

I nervously answered, "Yes, we are." Then, as I should have guessed, he brought out a Bible and started reading what he thought were appropriate passages. I pretended to be interested; it turned out to be not as bad as I'd feared.

The 1963 Los Angeles Times Grand Prix at Riverside is the race that lifted Dave MacDonald's reputation from talented production car driver to international star. Dave lapped the field in this King Cobra, his first race in a rear-engine car. *Bob Tronolone*

Bob Holbert, Wally Peat, and engine man Cecil Bowman (wearing hat) stare at the King Cobra's engine as if asking, "Why did you overheat?" *Allen Kuhn*

Later, when Mr. Dayton had his little Bible talk with his daughter, he used the passage that said unlike oxen should not be yoked together. We were pretty small for oxen. My mother also counseled against burdening myself with so much responsibility at my age if I wanted to reach my lofty goals.

A few days later, I loaded the Lotus and hitched the trailer to my new tow car, a white six-cylinder 1961 Ford four-door sedan, and headed west.

CHAPTER FOUR

Cobra Pilot

Upon arriving in Venice, I made sure I could have my job back and then rented a nice bachelor apartment a mile or two from the shop for $62 a month. A lot had happened in the six months since I'd been gone. The majority of the production car work had been moved to a building on Carter Street that was first used to prepare preproduction Fords for commercials—a side job that helped Ford as well as generated some extra money.

The two buildings were about 100 yards apart. In the race shop were the two Cooper Ford King Cobras, one of which Dave MacDonald used to win both the Los Angeles Times Grand Prix and the Pacific Grand Prix. The other one had been driven by Bob Holbert. Holbert had led at Laguna Seca until he was forced to pit because of overheating caused by body damage to the radiator inlet.

When I saw Dave, I congratulated him on his victories. He congratulated me on my success in the Midwest, which shocked me that he even knew about it. I was pretty humbled by that.

There was a project going on that I'd heard nothing about, sort of a skunk works operation to build a streamlined body on a Cobra chassis. The goal was to negate the top speed disadvantage that the Cobras had relative to the Ferrari GTOs on high-speed tracks. Pete Brock had designed the car while Ken Miles and others worked on chassis modifications to both stiffen the standard Cobra frame structure and accommodate the new bodywork. The people I remember doing most of the work on the project were Pete, Ken, John Ohlsen, Donn Allen, and John Collins. Aside from Pete and Ken, all of these people were new to me.

There seemed to be some dissention surrounding the coupe project. There was a kind of "us and them" atmosphere in the shop among the coupe people and the rest of the team. Phil Remington didn't seem to have a lot of faith in it; consequently many others didn't either. I think they looked at it as Pete's Folly.

The team was much larger than it was when I left. Sadly, George Boskoff was gone, but I was determined to stay in touch with him.

I was given a job as a fabricator working in the little corner of the shop managed by Garry Koike. We made small parts for the race cars, such as throttle linkages, water and fuel logs, etc., in addition to production Cobra pieces. A couple of my co-workers were Earl Jones and Jeff Schoolfield, both of whom became close friends.

Allen Grant, my old roommate, had talked a Cobra dealer, Coventry Motors, into buying one of the ex-Sebring team cars and allowing Allen to prepare and drive it. He got Ole Olsen to build the engine, and they nearly beat all of the factory Cobras at Riverside in the support race for the 1963 Los Angeles Times Grand Prix, proving to everyone that there was more to him than just bluster. Allen might have been on his way had Uncle Sam not intervened to take a six-month chunk out of his life at a most inopportune time.

Sometimes a second chance never presents itself, as it didn't with
Bill Krause.

Darker Side of Sunshine

Within a couple of weeks of my returning to California, the Cal Club
was having an SCCA race at the newly revamped Willow Springs
Raceway, a track 95 miles from Los Angeles in the Mojave Desert. I
sent in my entry. Gordon Goring was going to come along to help. Before I left for the race, Bruce Burness gave me some advice: "Respect
that track. It can hurt you."

Willow Springs was built in 1953, making it one of the earliest
purpose-built road courses in the country. My first impression was
to wonder why anyone would build a racetrack on this barren, ugly
wasteland. My idea of beauty had been formed by tracks like Road
America, Mid-Ohio, and Meadowdale. But in fairness to Willow
Springs, it was a great design; most of the track could be viewed from
the pit and spectator areas. It had significant elevation changes with a
variety of challenging corners.

The term *designed* is used pretty loosely with racetracks.
Supposedly local California racer Bill Pollack and his friend John
Hart (an early Lone Ranger), along with the property owner Harold
Mathewson, designed Willow Springs by driving a truck around the
desert property and pounding stakes to mark where the track should
go. Then they borrowed a road grader and gouged and blasted out the
track. Mid-Ohio was supposedly designed by the cantankerous owner,
Les Griebling, driving a tractor around his property to configure the
course. And one of the best road racing tracks in the country, Virginia
International Raceway—a course I would run on in the future—was
said to be drawn over the rolling hills by its creator tying a bag of lime
to a cow and slapping her on the ass.

Today, racetrack designing is a big, lucrative business. For a track
the size of Willow Springs, Mid-Ohio, and VIR, however, a borrowed
road grader, a tractor, and a cow did just fine, thank you. As long
as we're fast forwarding, I changed my mind years ago—the desert
is beautiful.

The race I was in was for production cars A through E, which
included a Stingray, a Corvette, a Cobra, and Ronnie Bucknum in
the world's fastest MGB. There was enough practice that I learned the
course pretty well. Late in the afternoon, as our race group waited
on the pre-grid, I happened to be standing beside the Cobra driver,
Paul Cunningham. I asked him about his car and told him I worked

at Shelby's. He said Monday he was going to take the car to Doane Spencer and have a number of improvements made. I didn't think of myself as very superstitious, but I didn't like to say I was going to do such-and-such thing sometime in the future just before a race. It's morbid, but when Paul said, "I'm going to take my car to Doane Spencer on Monday," I couldn't help but think, *You can't be sure you'll be alive Monday.*

There was a standing start and as we entered turn one for the first time, I went almost completely blind due to the late afternoon sun directly in my eyes. I assumed everyone else did too. The instantaneous loss of vision was startling and lasted until entering turn two some six or eight seconds later. Things were OK until we entered turn eight and again faced the blinding sun.

I could see dust and a glimpse of a car crashing on the outside of the very fast turn nine. The race was red-flagged. It was too late in the day, so it wasn't restarted. That night in the hotel bar, Gordon and I learned that Cunningham was killed in the accident. I had a feeling of extreme sadness coupled with a sense of guilt for the terrible irony of my thoughts when we spoke just before the race. I had heard someone say the crash was caused by Paul trying too hard and he just ran off the road. Davey Jordan racing a Sunbeam had a clearer view than I had and said Paul went too wide as he entered turn nine. I'm sure that was true, but I felt certain the sun was a factor.

The next day the sun wasn't an issue because our race was earlier. Doug Hooper, the driver who won at Riverside in a Corvette Stingray when Krause's Cobra broke a stub-axle, led from the start in his B Production Corvette. This wasn't like the Corvettes I had been racing against in the Central Division. In fact in the Central Division, every B Production race was won by a Lotus Super 7.

Carroll's Promise

I found myself in a very close race with Ronnie Bucknam's MGB, a fact that would have been disappointing if it hadn't been this particular MGB. Hooper's Corvette threw a tread from one of his racing recapped tires, which left the second half of the race to Bucknam and me as we ran nose-to-tail. This was my poor car's 13th race with no major engine work, so it was a little tired. Try as I did, I could never get around Ronnie. We finished first and second. It caused quite a stir because no one in California had even heard my name—that is, except Carroll Shelby, who had happened to be at Willow Springs that day to recruit Ronnie Bucknam for his Cobra team.

Willow Springs, November 16, 1963. Between turns three and four, I attempt to pass Ronnie Bucknum. Carroll Shelby attended this race to recruit Ronnie for the Cobra team. I nearly beat him. If Carroll hadn't been there, I doubt I'd ever have raced a Cobra. *Allen Kuhn*

Carroll was very excited as he shook my hand and said, "We're going to make a shop project of your car and we'll beat Chick Vandergriff." Vandergriff was the owner of Hollywood Sports Cars— and owner of the Bucknum MGB.

He also said, "We'll make you a T5 driver." That sounded good to me, even though I didn't know what a T5 was.

Carroll told me, "Make a list of every part you need to make your car faster and I'll call Colin and order them." He was referring to Colin Chapman, owner and founder of Lotus and Team Lotus, the current Formula One World Champions with Jimmy Clark.

I couldn't have been more thrilled. I felt that I'd just been discovered by the most important person in the world. As Gordon and I drove home, we discussed the parts we should have Carroll order to improve the Lotus's performance. I made my list so I could give it to Carroll Monday morning.

Parts needed for Lotus Super 7:
- Lotus 5-inch magnesium wheels
- Wide rear fenders for the wider wheels
- Disc brakes for front wheels
- Close ratio gears
- Oil cooler

Monday morning I presented my parts list to Carroll. He said, "What's this?"

"The parts you asked me to list for my Lotus."

"Oh yeah." He took the list without looking at it.

At lunch break, I told everyone about my weekend, about Carroll's excitement, about the parts he was ordering and the "We're going to make your car a shop project" comment. Their advice was keep on his ass every day or he'd forget about it. I took the advice.

After about the third day, I saw Carroll in the aisle between the front overhead door and the race shop and asked, "Did you order those parts yet?"

He said, "Goddamn it, John, you're a pain in the ass. I'll go up and call Colin right now."

He turned and headed for his office. I hated being a pain in the ass, but the guys were right. I'm absolutely sure of that.

The next morning, Friday, Jim Culleton came into work late and announced, "Somebody shot Kennedy." I was standing beside the cutoff saw. I didn't notice others' reactions. I don't even clearly remember my own. It seems that when you're completely focused on something so out of the mainstream as racing, you lose perspective on everything else, even things that are far more important.

Rising Commitments

Besides the Coupe project, the team was preparing new roadsters for the 1964 season. All of the race cars to this point had been delivered as standard street cars and were converted to race cars in our shop. This included upgrading suspension components and brakes, changing wheel hubs to accept the knockoff Halibrand magnesium wheels, installing a race engine, flaring the rear fenders, mounting a roll bar and racing seat, and numerous other details. The paint remained whatever color the car happened to be, but the only colors ever used were red, white, or black.

The 1964 cars would be dedicated race cars from the start and would arrive from AC Cars unpainted except for a yellow protective primer. They were wired by our electrical expert, John Shoup. It still required a week or more to get one ready. The biggest difference visually from the earlier cars was the bulbous rear fenders to accommodate the ever-increasing tire widths. Because these cars were unpainted when they arrived, they inspired the use of a team color, Viking Blue, a Ford truck color. Actually the Cooper Ford King Cobras were the first cars to arrive unpainted and the first to be Viking Blue. No, I'm wrong; the first car to arrive unpainted was the very first Cobra, the one I went to school in. They painted that one yellow.

There was another Dodger Stadium race December 7 and 8. By this time the Shelby American team was so well established that it didn't have to bother with these rinky-dink local Cal Club races anymore. But I did. Jack Hoare, one of the new engine shop employees, and John Collins joined my pickup crew. The course was made up of turns defined by hay bales and cement pylons in the parking lot encircling the stadium.

There were several Stingrays entered but no Cobras this time. Ronnie Bucknum won as usual, beating everyone in sight although the best Stingrays had problems, failing to finish. I won my class after a good race with Lew Spencer's very fast Morgan Super Sport. When a spindle broke, one of Lew's front wheels left his car right in front of me, a common Morgan failure. I was third overall, which was not very gratifying; my engine was definitely getting tired but I was too inexperienced to determine that because it was still running OK.

I'd planned to fly home for Christmas and had bought an engagement ring for Jan at a jewelry store in Santa Monica. Only two or three days before I was to leave, the infamous letter from Uncle Sam arrived in my mailbox. It included a date when I was to report for a preinduction physical examination in downtown Los Angeles. If this wasn't bad enough, the exam was scheduled while I had planned to be in Waukegan for Christmas. I phoned the draft board telling them of my dilemma and to my surprise, they gave me a new exam date after my return to California, which was to be on January 2, 1964.

I can't remember who told me that President Kennedy had signed an executive order before he died, exempting married men between the ages of 19 and 26 from being drafted into the military. Too bad I was only planning to get engaged during my visit home. Maybe we would get married the next summer sometime. The thought crossed my mind, but no, I couldn't ask her to do that. What was so troubling about going into the military was that I felt I might be on the verge of a big break in racing and two years in the army would kill any momentum I might have had.

The Christmas trip was going according to plan; I offered the ring, she accepted, a wedding was tentatively planned for summer. Jan asked if I would agree to meet with her pastor at the church she and her parents attended. I knew it would make things go easier for her at home, so I agreed to meet with Pastor Olsen, knowing this was the work of Jan's parents. The pastor was at his desk when Jan and I entered his office. He was very cordial as he made small talk and asked about my racing and my plans for the future regarding Jan. He finally got around to popping the big question that I knew was coming: "Have you accepted Jesus Christ as your personal savior?"

"No, I really haven't ever done that."

"Would you like to get down on your knees and do it now?"

"You mean like here?"

"Yes, you can kneel down right here beside the desk and accept Jesus Christ."

"I can't do that now. It wouldn't be honest of me. Maybe someday but not right now."

This guy didn't give a shit if it was honest or not; he just wanted me to do it. After we left, I asked Jan if she was disappointed. She answered, "It would have made things easier."

Less than a week before returning to California and my preinduction physical, Jan and I were talking one evening as we sat in my dad's car down by Lake Michigan. In passing I may have mentioned that it was too bad about our timing regarding married men and the draft. She said, "You mean if we were married now, you couldn't be drafted?"

"Yes, that's my understanding."

"Then let's get married now."

"Are you serious?"

"Yes, completely."

"OK," I said. "Wear some nice clothes and your long winter coat so they don't show." It was cold as hell. "And come over in the morning."

We'd always heard that kids went to Wisconsin to elope, so we drove to Kenosha, went to the marriage license place, and were told Jan at 18 would need parental consent if she was not a resident. We checked in Waukegan, but discoverd that all marriage license purchasers were listed in the local paper. So we drove to Woodstock, Illinois, about 40 miles from Waukegan, and got a number for the justice of the peace out of a phone booth phonebook. We were on a mission with the resolve to make this happen.

First we needed a blood test and a marriage license. It was Friday, December 27—we would have to wait until Monday to return to be married by the justice of the peace.

A weekend to step back and reflect on what this life-changing act would mean had no effect. At our ages, I suppose neither one of us was very good at reflecting. There would have to be witnesses. Johnny Opitz, his girlfriend, Charlotte, and Lyman would accompany us.

The J.P.'s office was set up like a small courtroom with a low fence between us and his desk. He'd been talking to a man who looked to be a drunk when we arrived. There were numerous pictures of traffic accidents on the wall. The J.P. told the man, "Sit down. This will just take a few minutes," as we approached the fence. Lyman would act as best man; he was twirling the ring Jan's former boyfriend had given her between his fingers as he nonchalantly leaned on the fence.

The J.P. said, "Be careful with that ring."

Lyman answered, "I will." Then he dropped it.

It would be replaced later with a more appropriate one, but for now it would suffice. The J.P. said some words, we both said "I do," and it was done. Lyman handed me the ring and I put it on Jan's finger. We picked up the marriage certificate and headed for home. As I drove, Jan started singing Lesley Gore's hit "You Don't Own Me," accentuating the lyrics, "Don't tell me what to do and don't tell me what to say." It was very funny under the circumstances.

Johnny and Charlotte were whispering to one another and finally came out with it: "You know, you two aren't really married yet." They were fearful that they would be held culpable for what might transpire that evening. After a short stop at the Waukegan draft board, I dropped the witnesses off then took Jan home. We had a date that night.

On Wednesday night, New Year's Eve, Jan was very upset when she came over to go on our last date before I had to leave for California. Our engagement had been announced in the Waukegen *News Sun* and her mother sort of freaked out at the realization that her daughter was really going to marry a heathen. Jan felt a little torn because she already had.

When I got back to California, there was a letter from the draft board saying to disregard my preinduction physical appointment. I had to tell my parents something, so decided on a heart murmur. I phoned home and my mother answered the phone.

"I won't be drafted because I failed the physical. Heart murmur."

She answered, "Oh, then you didn't have to get married."

"How do you know I'm married?"

"I found a motel receipt in your winter coat pocket. I told your father you were married and showed him the receipt, but he said that doesn't mean he's married. But you are."

"Yes, and I don't have a heart murmur."

Ted Sutton working on exhaust headers after installing the 427 engine in a new Cobra 289 chassis. Ken Miles and Pete Brock (backs turned) discuss the Cobra Coupe's progress. *Dave Friedman*

I can't remember if she was relieved about the absence of a heart murmur or not.

I suppose dodging the draft might seem cowardly to many, but the Vietnam fiasco hadn't really gotten going yet and had absolutely nothing to do with my actions. If it had been a couple of years later, I'm not sure how I'd have handled it. I did burn my draft card in the shop a year later but only as a joke. For some reason I didn't think it was my actual draft card but it was. Oh well, it didn't matter anymore.

Big Snake

At Shelby American, the Coupe was really starting to come together. The body panels that had been formed by California Metal Shaping had been trimmed, fitted, and welded together as the car had literally taken shape. Though not yet fully accepted as the answer to the

The first Cobra Coupe nears completion. Mark Papov-Dodiani, squatting, and John "Granny" Collins, walking away, were on the project from the beginning. *Dave Friedman*

Cobra's high aerodynamic drag problem, the push was on to finish and test the car before the Daytona Continental on February 16.

John Ohlsen, a New Zealander, headed up the construction as he had from the beginning. He had removed the body from the Cobra that Skip Hudson crashed at Daytona in 1963 so that the bare chassis could be used to build the buck for the Coupe. In the early stages, it was Ohlsen, Ted Sutton, John Collins, Donn Allen, and Mark Papov-Dodiani working methodically and quietly with Pete Brock, who often, with pencil in mouth, checked on progress and made detail changes. But now the thrash was on, and almost every available able body was pressed into service.

Another somewhat off-the-wall project was also well underway. Ken Miles is generally credited with the idea of installing a 427 engine in a standard street Cobra to more or less see what would happen—a little like flushing a cherry bomb down a toilet. Ted Sutton was given the job of doing the installation because Ted had impressed Phil Remington with the small-block Ford-powered Austin-Healey he'd built. Ted said, "Shoehorning a 427 block into a space where the tiny 289 was meant to live was a task similar to the Healey/289 switchover I did. Modifying the foot boxes to allow for exhaust pipe clearance and positioning the bell-housing tunnel further aft were the biggest considerations. The rest was standard hot rod work."

The inside and outside perceptions of our operation at Shelby's were quite different at this time. The workers were motivated, Shelby was getting good press, and Ford was excited, but not so much the residents of the trailer court 400 yards from the factory. Tired of screaming engines on dynos and unmuffled race cars being shuttled back and forth, they called the sheriff. A notice appeared by the time clock stating that anyone caught running the dyno or race cars after hours was subject to immediate dismissal.

Ted Sutton remembers: "About two days after that notice, I found myself waiting for mufflers and in need of gas with the tank near empty. What better excuse, I figured, to take a test drive in the first 427 Cobra. Off I went, me and *The Big Snake*! I couldn't help myself, getting on it pretty good and squirting around a corner real hard. I parked it outside the shop when I got back and went inside. Seldom was the shop P.A. system used except for the occasional phone paging. I heard 'Ted Sutton—report to the reception office immediately.' Catcalls went up in the shop. I even waved goodbye to the guys, thinking I was going to be made an example of. The receptionist said Mr. Shelby wanted to talk to me and she would tell him I was waiting.

"Well, the job paid poorly, I thought. The only way you could stand to work there was because of the vast quantities of overtime. I was on the clock thirty-four hours straight once. That's no way to live, I told myself. But I snapped to attention when Ol' Shel came down the steps.

"He had a stern look as he carefully maneuvered his crutches. It seems he had undergone knee surgery a few weeks before but hadn't advertised it. After he took forever getting to the bottom step, he looked me square in the eye and asked, 'How'd it go?'

"'Uh, just fine, sir,' I stammered.

"Then he hobbled out to the car and said, 'Let's take her for a spin.' He handed me the crutches and slowly got into the driver's seat. I could see it hurt, so I asked him if he wanted me to come along. 'Sure. You can sit on the floor, can't you?' was his reply since I'd only put in the driver's seat.

"The next two or three minutes were the most frightening times in an automobile I have ever experienced. We tore around this little tract neighborhood at impossible speeds. The car, straight off the boat when I had started work on it, still had the real skinny two-ply shipping tires to move it from England. Pressure never checked. Those tires were OK for a run to the corner store maybe but not for eighty miles an hour, sliding through ninety degree turns at the end of each street, which is what Shelby was doing. There weren't stop signs, but that wouldn't have made any difference anyway because we flew through every intersection, drifting through bumpy corners with this overnourished, undershod, nose-heavy, hairy-chested beast with some thrill-crazed cripple taking all the world's anger out in a few blocks.

"I know I was trembling when I handed him back his crutches. But his shifts had been smooth. His throttle control was perfect. He was the master of these cars.

"As Shelby extracted himself from the car, he looked at me and said, 'Let's make a race car out of it, huh?' I answered, 'Yes, sir.'"

I sent my entry for an SCCA race at Riverside on February 1 and 2. A young man whose name escapes me came to see Pete Brock about work. Pete told him he would need to get some experience first and suggested he talk to me about helping on my race car. I've never to-tally forgiven Pete for that event, though I'll bet he doesn't even re-member it. The kid drove a jacked-up '54 Chevy and knew even less than I did when I first arrived in California, but he was ready to help so I agreed to let him come along. All of the guys in the shop who'd helped me before were so busy getting ready for Daytona that they didn't have time to take the weekend off. George Boskoff, who I vis-ited often, would come along too.

The Riverside track was familiar to me because of the Shelby driv-ing school I'd attended, but my car was ill-suited because the gearing was too low. Another problem was trying to stretch a 15th race week-end out of a very tired engine.

Pete Brock was in my race in a TVR, an English fiberglass coupe with an MG engine. Pete had raced his own cars, first a Cooper and later a Lotus 11 for several years, but the TVR belonged to a friend of Pete's named Fritz Warren. I remember passing Pete, and I certainly should have because the Lotus was a much better race car than the TVR.

Partway into the Sunday race, my engine overheated very badly because my new helper had checked the water just before the race

Three Shelby employees having at it in Riverside's turn six February 2, 1964: Joe Freitas in the ex–Dave MacDonald Corvette, Pete Brock in the TVR, and me in my Super 7. *Allen Kuhn*

and left the pressure cap loose. I didn't finish and my engine was shot. It had served its purpose admirably and was going to get a well-deserved rebuild, this time by George Boskoff. I would never accuse Pete of saddling me with my new crewmember just so he could beat me at Riverside, but it worked.

As an aside, there was a 90-degree corner where Princeton Drive and Carter Street met only a couple hundred yards from Shelby American. When I first started working there I would slide around that turn as fast as I could in my Jaguar, arriving for work in clear view of the gang at the morning "roach coach." Phil Remington referred to me as the Janitor in the Jag, expecting—not necessarily hoping—to see a crash some morning. It never came.

However, one night after work, I had the Lotus in the race shop to remove the engine so George could rebuild it and was assisted by my new helper. As we got in our cars to leave, I mentioned that the turn down there is fun to take fast. He took off in his jacked-up Chevy as I was just backing into the street. I watched. I clearly remember thinking, *Wow, he's really entering fast!* and then his car started doing a little hop, as jacked-up cars will do. A split second later sparks flew as the Chevy and a telephone pole bit the dust. The kid wasn't hurt physically but his car was history and the telephone pole replacement put a heavy financial strain on his budget. I only saw him once more. He was working in a gas station in Santa Monica and was eager to show me his new car. I don't remember what it was.

Within a day or two of the Riverside race, the Cobra Coupe and the 427 roadster were taken to the track for their first tests. Actually it was the only test either car would have before they actually raced. The Coupe was pretty much finished except for paint and some small details, but the 427 was still in street trim with wire wheels, standard brakes, and its original dark red paint.

Bob Bondurant was to test the 427 and Ken Miles the Coupe. Bondurant had been a very successful Corvette driver and a rival of Dave MacDonald prior to Dave joining the Shelby team. Bob was hired in late 1963. The 427 test was unremarkable and inconclusive because of the street trim. All that was really determined was that it had a hell of a lot of power.

The Coupe was a different story. The doubts about its aerodynamic advantage over the roadster configuration vanished as even Miles questioned the rear-end gear ratio. He had trouble accepting the rpm he was getting in conjunction with the very tall (high) rear-end ratio the car was supposed to have. He had the crew jack the car up, turn the rear wheels one turn, and count the driveshaft revolutions to verify that the crew hadn't accidentally installed a rear end with a lower (shorter) ratio. They hadn't. The car really was in the range of 20 miles per hour faster than the roadster down the 1-mile-plus-long Riverside straight. Pete Brock had been proven right. The entire Coupe crew was gratified. Even the nonbelievers found that the taste of crow was pretty sweet.

After a quick paint job and some small details attended to, the Coupe and three roadsters headed for Daytona. This year, 1964, Daytona was changed from the three-hour race it had been in 1962 and 1963 to a 2,000-kilometer (1,240-mile) race in 1964. Not until 1966 would it become the 24 Hours of Daytona. Also in 1963 and 1964 the race was for GT cars only, no prototypes (purpose-built race cars) as there had been in 1962, and would be from 1965 on. Confusing, isn't it?

I wasn't normally part of the traveling team, so what happened at Daytona in 1964 I learned from the crewmembers that were there. The Coupe with Dave MacDonald and Bob Holbert driving had a spectacular debut, leading from the start, leaving a gaggle of Ferrari GTOs, Cobra roadsters, and Stingrays in its dust. Then, approaching two-thirds distance, the Coupe pitted for fuel. John Ohlsen slid

Passing my driving instructor/co-worker/future boss Pete Brock on the outside of turn seven at Riverside on February 2, 1964. Pete was driving his friend's TVR. The Lotus overheated, so Pete beat me anyway. *Dave Friedman*

under the car to check a suspect rear end, which was running very hot. Fuel spilled, ran under the car, and ignited, engulfing John in flames. He was pulled out and doused with a fire extinguisher. As the flames were extinguished, John's main concern was for his wallet; it takes a while for the damage received from burns to be realized. The car was damaged enough to be withdrawn. John's burns eventually healed, but he was out of action for a while. It was almost a lot worse.

Dan Gurney and Bob Johnson finished fourth in a wounded Cobra roadster. Phil Hill and Pedro Rodriguez, Ricardo's older brother, won in a GTO Ferrari followed by two more GTOs. Aside from the rear end overheating at Daytona, the biggest problem the Coupe had was the tremendous heat that the drivers were subject to in the cockpit.

Sebring, where Shelby American would run five cars, was just more than a month after Daytona. There were so many different projects going on in the race shop at one time that it was hard to keep track of them all. First there was the Coupe, which needed not only repair from the Daytona damage, but modification to address the hot cockpit problem. There was the Cobra roadster hot rod with the 427 engine, now being made into a race car that was to run at Sebring with the Coupe and three 289 roadsters. Plus, a small group of separatists were building a new Cooper Monaco Ford for Dave MacDonald. The group was comprised of Wally Peat, Joe Freitas—a close friend of MacDonald's when they competed with one another in Corvettes—Dave himself, who was an excellent mechanic, and Craig Lang, the owner/financier of the group. They intended to contest the USRRC Championship as a de facto Shelby American team with Carroll's blessing.

Last and probably least was to be the effort to run a Sunbeam Tiger for Lew Spencer in the SCCA Nationals. A red, engineless Tiger had been delivered to Shelby American and was being race prepared with the 260-cubic-inch Ford engine that powered the early Cobras. It was amazing that in well under a year from the time George Boskoff's Sunbeam Alpine Ford was sent to England, a production version was being prepared for racing. The SCCA class for the car would be B Production. I worked on the Tiger with Ted Sutton after helping with the engine installation in the 427. There was word that after this car was developed, there would be a second Tiger and I would be the driver. I didn't care much for Sunbeams, but that changed things.

The Sunbeam Tiger and the Cobra Coupe were taken to Riverside—the Tiger for its maiden voyage and evaluation by Lew

Spencer; the Coupe to try to get a better idea of the airflow patterns over the body. Pieces of yarn about 4 to 5 inches long were taped to the body every few

The Cobra Coupe heading for a test at Riverside prior to the 1964 Sebring 12-hour. I'm steering while Donn Allen, Jeff Schoolfield, and Al Dowd push. *Dave Friedman* inches. As the car was driven, the yarn would indicate what the air was doing as it flowed over the bodywork. Pete Brock was there to study the flow patterns, hoping to gain more information about his creation. One of the priorities was to learn how to get airflow through the cockpit for the overheated drivers.

Ken Miles drove the Coupe. Charlie Agapiou and John Collins made sure everything ran smoothly. Ken gave me a ride in the Coupe after the testing was over. It was a real eye-opener. I'd never been in an enclosed race car before. It sounded and felt like being trapped inside of a giant drum. I couldn't believe how he got that thing through the Riverside esses so fast. It's a common belief that in a race car, the passenger's seat travels about 20 miles per hour faster than the driver's seat. It was a thrill.

The Big Time

As Sebring approached I started lobbying to be included on the traveling team. Jeff Schoolfield and I let everyone know that we would do almost anything to go. I'd gone in 1961 and 1962 from college and the previous year in the Shelby transporter. A couple of weeks before the race, Jeff and I were called up to the office to see the controller. Our lobbying had worked, sort of anyway. She told us that she had been authorized to give us each $25 if we would drive our own cars to Sebring. We would be night watchmen at the track where our race cars were worked on in a World War II–era hangar. She suggested it would be wise for us to pool our money, taking just one car on the 5,000-mile round trip. Neither Jeff nor I had a car we felt could even make the trip, let alone on $50. We thought of John Shoup and his VW Karmann Ghia, and then asked if we were to find a third person, could we get another $25. She agreed, and so did Shoup. We had a plan.

I called home to tell my parents about our plan, and then called Jan at school in Minnesota, as I did every few days. The phone many of us used was in the hallway near the bathrooms and close to the machine shop. It was a pay phone, but a very special pay phone, which someone had modified so that when quarters were inserted into the coin slot, they would fall through and into the coin return. The person most suspected of having made the modification was machinist Mahlon Lamoreaux, though he never made a confession that I know of. It may not sound like a big deal today what with cell phones and unlimited calling minutes, but in 1964 to be able to make a ten-minute-long distance call and still have your quarter afterward would save a poor, underpaid mechanic several dollars.

My parents, knowing Jan and I were married, offered to bring her to Savannah on her spring break; then my brother would pick her up in Savannah on his way to Sebring from Clemson.

The transporter left with the five Sebring-bound Cobras. The three of us left on the Saturday night, one week before the race. As we loaded ourselves into the black-with-white-top Karmann Ghia coupe, it quickly became obvious that this would not be an easy trip. The car was not designed for a full-size person to ride in the back, so we planned to take turns. One of us would drive, with another in the passenger seat and the third suffering in the rear. We would rotate every fuel stop.

I started out in the back with Jeff driving. Shoup's first stint started somewhere in Arizona in the morning. It soon became apparent that we had a problem. Shoup, after driving only a few minutes, fell asleep at the wheel. We gave him a second chance, and he fell asleep again. He had to be eliminated from the rotation. More bad news: he was too fat to fit in the back, so he had to ride to Florida in the passenger seat while Jeff and I traded positions in the rear torture chamber.

We never stopped to rest, only to eat once in a while. Jeff got a speeding ticket in Florida, only a couple of hours from Sebring. We arrived in town after 54 hours on the road and checked into a cheap upstairs hotel at about 4:00 in the morning.

After only a couple of hours sleep, we awoke to the sound of race cars as they were driven from the track into town for technical inspection. Our room was less than a block from the inspection area. Jeff and I went down to watch the cars being inspected while Shoup stayed in bed, exhausted from sitting on his ass in the passenger seat for 54 hours.

Almost immediately we ran into Ken Miles and Lew Spencer, who were there to oversee the inspection of the Cobras. Ken asked me, "Do you have an FIA license?" An FIA license is an internationally recognized racing license required for important races like Sebring, Le Mans, etc.

I answered, "No."

He said, "Can you get one?"

"I don't see how. All I have is an SCCA amateur logbook and I don't have it here. Why?"

"Because we have five cars entered and only nine drivers. We might need you to drive the 427 with me."

He took out a small pad of paper, scratched out a note, handed it to me, and said, "Take this to race headquarters. See if they'll give you a license."

I read the note. It said, "John Morton is qualified to be issued an FIA license." It was signed "Ken Miles." I took the note to the Kennelworth Hotel, where race headquarters was set up, and handed the note to someone who looked to be an official. After a short time I was given an FIA license. This was the third license to drive I'd received in my life, and the third one I hadn't actually earned.

I was beside myself with excitement, anticipation, and fear. All I'd ever raced was a Lotus Super 7 in amateur races. Now I had tentatively been handed a possible ride in the biggest professional race in America in the most powerful car in that race, one that I had never even driven.

I had no driving gear with me, but I was able to borrow a helmet from a fellow who was running a preliminary motorcycle race on

Ken Miles cuts holes in the nose of the 427 to increase air to the radiator. The openings replicated those used on the Ferrari GTO except were a little cruder. This was done early in practice before the car crashed into a tree. *Dave Friedman*

Friday before the Saturday 12-hour. I bought a gray driving suit from a vendor at the track for $15. I was ready.

The nine assigned drivers on the team were Phil Hill teamed with Jo Schlesser, Dan Gurney with Bob Johnson, Bob Bondurant with Lew Spencer, Dave MacDonald with Bob Holbert in the Cobra Coupe, and Ken Miles with no named co-driver in the 427 roadster.

I did my night watchman duty early because my new wife would arrive in a day or two, and I wanted to get my important duties over with before she arrived. On Thursday I asked Al Dowd, our leader, if I could practice after Ken finished.

He said, "I'm not taking the responsibility of letting you drive until Shelby gets here."

It became a moot point because Ken hit a tree, the only tree it was possible to hit at Sebring. The damage was significant; my chance to drive had vanished, for if the car could be repaired, which was doubtful because even the frame was bent, there would be no time for me to practice. Ken had the nickname Teddy Teabagger, but after the crash he became Teddy Treebagger. Ken was also called Sidebite because he held his mouth to one side when he talked and also for his sideways driving style.

The Sebring 427 sits forlorn where it was deposited by the wrecker after Miles hit the only tree available on the entire course. The car's two occupants may have been tired spectators resting after a busy day at the track. They were not part of our team. *Pete Lyons*

Miles struggles with a Porta Power in an attempt to straighten the car's right side main frame tube. He felt pretty bad about the crash, so he went to work before even taking off his driving suit or getting medical attention for cracked ribs. *Dave Friedman*

Phil Hill made the cruelest dig when he said to Ken, "Looks like you got a little behind in your steering."

The car was taken back to our hangar, where the extent of the damage was assessed. Miles pronounced it fixable. Everyone else had doubts. Ken felt pressure to get the car in the race because as Dr. Frankenstein, he had destroyed his own monster.

The right front suspension was destroyed, the frame was bent, the right front and side of the body were mangled—even the exhaust headers were damaged. If this wasn't enough, Ken had injured some ribs, possibly having cracked them. Without even taking the time to change out of his driving suit, he lit into the massive job of repairing the car. Ken Miles, crew chief Ted Sutton, Jim Culleton, Jeff Schoolfield, Garry Koike, and I worked late into the night. By race time Saturday, the car was more or less ready to go. It even had a fresh Holman and Moody engine installed. There was talk that Jim Clark, who was under contract to Ford and scheduled to drive a Ford Cortina in the race, was offered the drive with Ken. He wisely had declined.

The plan was to have Ken start the race. If one of the other four cars had problems, its co-driver could relieve Ken. It had worked perfectly in 1963 when all of the Cobras had problems and there were soon more drivers than needed.

From the start, the Cobras began building up a commanding lead in the GT category; even the 427 was running well at first. Ken pitted early with brake problems and then continued. As the team cars pitted for fuel and tires, I took the used mounted tires to Goodyear so they could be replaced with new ones. After I finished, I took a break to walk up to turn one with my brother and Jan to watch for a while; all of our cars were still running strong.

I decided to check back in at the pits, curious about how they would deal with the driver shortage if no one had a problem; they couldn't leave Ken out there indefinitely. When I got to our pit, someone said, "Shelby wants to see you."

I went to the house trailer that had been towed into the paddock area behind the pits. Motor homes weren't very common or roomy back then, so the larger teams would have house trailers installed for the race. Shelby normally would have been in the pits the whole race, but he'd had an operation on his knee and was either in a wheelchair or on crutches this weekend. I opened the door and walked in. Carroll was sitting with some Ford people.

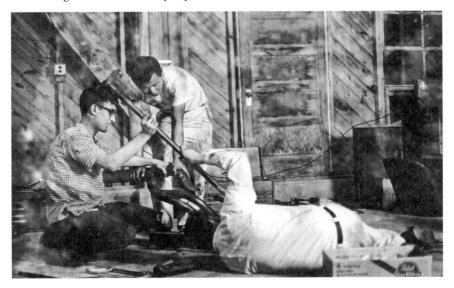

Straightening headers: Garry Koike, crew chief Ted Sutton (lying on the floor), and I work on straightening the damaged headers. When the difficult all-nighter was over and the car appeared to be race ready, the exhausted crew was asked to replace the engine with a fresh Holman and Moody stock car engine. *Dave Friedman*

Ken and I continue to work on straightening the frame while Al Dowd, skepticism written all over his face, looks on. *Dave Friedman*

Ken assesses the frame repair. He seems satisfied with a job well done while Jeff Schoolfield, hammer in hand, and Jim Culleton work on body repair. Garry Koike is behind the door. Schoolfield and I were to be night watchmen; working on the car wasn't in our job description. *Dave Friedman*

He asked, "John, do you know this track?"

"Yes," I answered. "I've been here several times."

I didn't mention it was as a spectator, but he didn't really care about details; he just needed a driver.

He said, "If Miles needs relief when he comes in, you be ready, huh?"

"Yeah. I'll go get ready now."

I put my suit on and got my borrowed black helmet with someone else's name painted on it and waited for Miles's arrival in the pits. He came in, got out of the car as was required during refueling, and walked toward the pit wall where I was standing. I asked very tentatively, "Do you want relief?"

He gave me a strange almost startled look I'll never forget, and then he said, "Yes."

Oh shit. I was afraid he might say that. I got in the car, buckled the belts, and started the engine. As I pushed in the clutch, I noticed my leg was shaking so hard I wasn't sure I could do this. I knew which way the track went from watching races from the spectator areas but it wasn't the same as driving, especially not in that 427 Cobra. The car felt as far removed from my Lotus as a car could be. In a word, it felt like the piece of shit it was after what it had been through this week. I'm sure it would have felt better if it hadn't been wrecked two days before.

There were two turns that weren't visible from the spectator areas. They were simple 90-degree right turns that were defined by hay bales way out on the runway out of sight of everyone. On my first lap, I spun on both of them, but no one knew except me.

This was the race, but it was my first practice session too, so I was still being a little conservative. On the fourth or fifth lap going into the final turn on the track, which followed a very fast straight, I lost my brakes completely. Had I been up to competitive speed I'd surely have crashed, but by downshifting I was able to get the car slowed down enough to make the turn and enter the pit lane.

The crew worked on the brakes and sent me out again, but they failed again and I made it into the pits a second time. The crew was skeptical of my analysis. Ken Miles was still in the pits, so I asked him to take the car out again and see if he could analyze the problem. He took a lap, came in and pronounced that the car had no brakes. The crew got serious.

The problem turned out to be that the shaft that the brake and clutch pedal pivoted on had slid out of position far enough to

With a driving suit I bought at the track and a helmet borrowed from a motorcycle racer ("Henri," it appears), I'm taking over the 427 from Ken Miles. Boy, was I ever scared.
Dave Friedman

disengage the brake pedal, making it inoperable. It was an easy fix once it was discovered, and I was on my way again.

Driving the car started to be fun, as I got more comfortable with it and the track. I even passed Jim Clark in his Lotus Cortina. Actually I had no way of knowing Clark was in the car at the time, but I liked believing that he was. It would have been pretty pathetic if a 427 Cobra couldn't have passed a Cortina, regardless of who was driving.

The Cobra developed a disturbing vibration and I pitted to inform the crew; it would be years before radio communication would be developed between driver and crew. Nothing was obvious, so they told me to keep the revs under 5,000 and sent me back out.

Sometime later, around 4:00 I would guess, the car made a noise as the clutch failed and the engine lost drive to the rear wheels. I coasted to a stop off the track between two 90-degree turns known as the Websters, got out of the car, went over the spectator fence, and started the long walk back to the pits when a man stopped me.

He said, "I'm with Ford and we would really like for that car to finish the race."

I said, "The clutch is gone."

"Is there any way you can get it back to the pits?" he asked.

I said, "I will see if it will move at all."

I got back in the car and started the engine, and to my surprise, it would slowly creep along at 5 or 10 miles per hour. It was a scary 3 miles back to the pits with the healthy cars blasting by, sometimes at 150 miles per hour faster than I was going.

The crew jacked the car up and discovered that the clutch housing had come loose from the flywheel; the bolts had vibrated out. Luckily they were able to reattach the clutch by installing the missing bolts, one at a time, through an access opening at the bottom of the bell housing. The engine was rotated until all of the bolts were replaced and tightened. I rejoined the race to discover the vibration was now so severe that the rearview mirrors were useless. Another stop for instructions.

"Don't go over three thousand five hundred rpm."

One more fuel stop near dusk. The crew took the tape off of the headlights. I'd never raced at night except for my jalopy in South Carolina, so was really looking forward to it. It had looked so spectacular as a spectator.

Going into the esses just before dark, the engine went silent and I almost spun in my own oil as the car slithered off the track. I let it coast to a safe spot in the grass, 20 or 30 feet from the racing surface. The engine had quit so suddenly I thought the problem could have been electrical and the slide in someone else's oil until I opened the hood. I saw engine parts on the outside that were supposed to be on the inside.

Someone on the team told me during one of my many pit stops that if the car breaks down on the course somewhere, don't leave it. I think they explained that it would be disqualified, or was it that after the race, the

427 Pit stop: Garry Koike pours water on the brakes as I try to convince Al Dowd that they actually did fail completely. Lew Spencer is standing on the pit wall waiting to take over from Bob Bondurant. *Dave Friedman*

I drove the resurrected 427 Cobra in the race less than two days after the collision with the tree. The right front fender still shows signs of its ordeal, but it looks damn good for the shape it was in. *Pete Lyons*

spectators would steal parts off of it? For whatever the reason was, I stayed with the car for about two hours.

I was starting to feel like the kid holding the bag on a snipe hunt when in the blackness of the night, the sky in the direction of the pits suddenly was very bright. Something big had happened and it couldn't be good. I left the car and hurried through the spectator area to the pits. The fire was out but it had been caused by a devastating crash when Bob Johnson in the class-leading Cobra he shared with Dan Gurney collided with the Alfa Romeo TZ driven by Italian Consalvo Sanesi.

The sick Alfa was limping along at a very low speed just trying to finish the race, possibly with no taillights, when Bob Johnson, straining to read the pit signal board, ran into the back of it at well in excess of 100 miles per hour. The Alfa burst into flames while Johnson's Cobra tumbled down the track, completely destroying itself. Sanesi was heroically pulled from the burning car by Jocko Maggiacomo, a driver from New York. Although Sanesi was badly burned, he survived.

Bob Johnson sustained a very black eye and a broken nose. He was extremely lucky on one hand and unlucky on the other because he and Gurney had all but won the GT class when the crash occurred. As it turned out, Dave MacDonald and Bob Holbert took their place with a class win and a fourth overall for the first win with the Cobra Coupe, now called the Daytona Coupe. The Gurney-Johnson car was so completely destroyed that when it got home to California, it was cut up and literally put in the garbage.

The Shelby team had had their most important international victory finishing first, second, and third in the important GT class as well as fourth, fifth, and sixth overall behind three Ferrari factory prototypes. It was also Shelby American's most expensive race with the loss of two race cars: the Gurney-Johnson 289 roadster and the 427 prototype, which this day had run its first and last race. It was too damaged to be of any further use and would be discarded.

After the race, I left the track with my brother and my wife to spend a week with her and my parents in Savannah before flying back to California. As we started the drive to Savannah, I felt a little sorry for Jeff, who'd worked so hard to help get the 427 in good enough shape to race, having to drive back to California in the Karmann Ghia alone with Shoup.

The week in Savannah passed quickly, and then it was back to California. As I pulled up to the shop on my first morning back, I noticed that John Shoup's Karmann Ghia had Visqueen (clear plastic film) taped all over the left side. On closer examination it was obvious it had been in an accident.

I went in to ask Jeff, "What the hell happened to Shoup's car?"

Jeff told me that when they left Sebring in the early afternoon the day after the race, he knew he was going to have to do all of the driving. He drove for 15 hours until he was completely used up, and then in desperation asked Shoup if he could drive for just a short while for him to get some rest. They'd gotten into Mississippi. Shoup agreed; Jeff crawled into the back and tried to assume a position that he could rest in. As Shoup drove along the two-lane road in the dark, traveled largely by 18-wheelers at night, Jeff finally fell asleep.

He was soon jarred awake to the sound of crunching metal as the Karmann Ghia spun out of control, finally coming to rest at the side of the road. As Jeff exited the car, still in a bit of a daze, he had trouble accepting what he saw. Shoup had fallen asleep and had a head-on sideswipe of, unbelievably, another Karmann Ghia—possibly the only other Karmann Ghia in Mississippi. It was driven by a couple of college kids on their way to Fort Lauderdale for spring break.

The Karman Ghia's rear suspension was damaged, but with no money for parts, they did a makeshift repair just so they could continue toward California.

I reflected on the events of the last week—the transition from night watchman to Shelby team driver in my first professional race, spending time with my new wife—and on what an exciting future lay ahead. It would be one of the most memorable weeks of my life, and I owe it all to Carroll Shelby and Ken Miles. All three of us had a very exciting two weeks that would never be forgotten.

It's Not Grrreat!
The 1964 USRRC season started at Augusta, Georgia, in early March. Dave MacDonald and Bob Holbert were to contest the driver's championship in King Cobras, while Ken Miles would again be the number one Cobra team driver in the GT category, backed up most often by teammates Bob Johnson and Ed Leslie.

Dave and Ken started off well by winning their respective classes in Augusta, with Dave the overall winner. At the second race, Pensacola, Florida, just two weeks after Sebring, Ken drove the King Cobra, failing to finish. I think that was the only time he raced one.

The weekend of the Pensacola USRRC race in Florida coincided with the competition debut of the Sunbeam Tiger in Tucson, Arizona.

The Daytona Coupe got its first GT win in the hands of Dave MacDonald and Bob Holbert, following the last-hour crash of the Gurney/Johnson Cobra. Here Holbert is in the car.
Dave Friedman

I had worked with Ted Sutton preparing the car and was very eager to see how it performed because I would hopefully be driving the proposed second car when it was finished.

The race was an SCCA Divisional held on a course at the Tucson airport with Lew Spencer as the driver. My first vivid memory of the weekend was when Dave Friedman, the Shelby team photographer who documented just about everything that had ever happened at Shelby American, showed up at the track and asked Ted and me to disconnect the speedometer cable on his rental car. The Tiger program was a low-budget operation for sure.

Lew Spencer was a great guy and a very good driver; however, both of these attributes would be strained this weekend. The main competition in the Tiger's B Production class were the pre-Stingray Corvettes, the best one of these belonging to Joe Freitas, another Shelby employee.

When practice started, it became obvious we had a problem. Lew, who was always smooth, controlled, and fast, looked like an overzealous yahoo in his first race. No fault of Lew, the car handled like shit.

After spinning more times than he'd spun in his life up until this day, Lew just had to back off and hope to finish the race. There were very few significant adjustments available to us at the track, so Lew was forced to get through the weekend as best he could. He did very well under the circumstances, finishing second to Freitas' ex–Dave MacDonald Corvette in B Production.

I really wanted to like the car, knowing I might be driving one soon, but I just couldn't. I even disliked the bland pale yellow it was painted. In an added bit of irony, Earl Jones, another Shelby employee, won the C Production class in the same race—Earl won in the Morgan Super Sport he had recently bought from Lew Spencer.

Diverse Dave

Dave had been offered a ride in the Indianapolis 500 by Mickey Thompson. Carroll agreed to let Dave accept the offer as he had done the year before, when Bill Krause was made the same offer, the difference being that Krause left Shelby permanently to join the Chevrolet-backed Thompson team, whereas Dave was released to run only the Indy 500.

By now MacDonald was a valuable commodity to the Ford Motor Company, so the switch by Thompson from Chevrolet power in '63 to the new Ford four-cam race engine for '64 made borrowing Dave for Indy possible.

MacDonald was an amazingly versatile driver. I'd watched him nearly win the Golden State 400 NASCAR race at Riverside in 1963. He would have won if his transmission hadn't lost half of its gears. Dave had a huge lead over the best drivers in NASCAR and still finished second with only two gears. The painfully overused NASCAR word of today—*awesome*—could have been used very appropriately that day to describe Dave MacDonald.

It was pretty exciting for many of us that Dave was going to run the Indy 500. Several of our best people had been involved with Indianapolis cars, including Phil Remington, George Boskoff, Ole Olsen, and Red Rose. The Thompson car was not one of the better rides to be had; in fact the previous year Krause failed to qualify for the race, although a couple of Thompson's cars did get in.

First, Dave had four races to run in the new Cooper Ford King Cobra owned by Craig Lang, which would forever be known as the Lang Cooper. Its first race was to be at the new Phoenix International Raceway, a combination 1-mile oval with 2.5-mile road course. Allen Grant had returned to Shelby American after his stint in the army and was looking for a ride. I was too, in a halfhearted way—halfhearted because I thought more chances would come with Shelby. Allen and I went to Phoenix to watch Dave's debut in the Lang Cooper and to seek new opportunities to drive.

Allen talked to Allen Green, a Chevrolet dealer from Seattle, about driving his Cheetah. I liked Lotus 23s and had my eye on a white one with a Corvair engine entered for a driver named George Follmer, who I assumed wasn't really serious or he wouldn't have screwed up his car with a Corvair engine. I never built up the nerve to ask him about driving his car for him.

The thrash to get the Lang Cooper ready didn't leave enough time for Wally Peat and his crew to have the car painted, so it was raced in bare aluminum. No matter though; Dave was on pole and won the race easily from Skip Hudson. Skip drove a similar Cooper, but with a Chevrolet engine for the famous Chicago dealer, Nickey Chevrolet. Ken Miles won the GT class.

There was only a week between the Phoenix race and the Riverside USRRC, which was followed by Laguna Seca in another week. The Lang Cooper had assumed its rightful color, bright orange, at Riverside, as Dave took another pole position by a substantial margin and was running away with the race until his clutch failed. Skip Hudson won in the Nickey Cooper Chevy, with Chuck Daigh second in the Arciero Lotus 19 that Dan Gurney made famous when he won the first Daytona Continental with it in '62. Again Ken Miles won the GT race with Ed Leslie second.

Lotus at Laguna

In addition to the USRRC at Laguna Seca, there were to be SCCA Regional races on Saturday. I was entered, but my car, which was at George Boskoff's garage behind his house in Redondo Beach, was running behind schedule. The parts that Carroll had ordered from Colin Chapman had finally come in. Gordon Goring called me into the parts department saying, "Your Lotus parts from Colin Chapman are here."

I excitedly opened a small box that contained a close ratio gear set and an oil cooler.

"Where are the rest of the parts—the wide wheels, fenders, and disc brakes? There must be other boxes?"

Gordon said, "The box says one of one. That means there are no more boxes coming."

Disappointed, I took the parts to George that night. He'd spent weeks preparing my car, which included completely rebuilding the engine. We were down to the wire. It was Thursday night, the car wasn't quite ready, and we had to be in Monterey, 340 miles away, by Friday morning for tech inspection and practice.

Two friends from work offered to come with George and me to help. They were John Collins and Bob Skinner. John, whose nickname was Granny, had been one of the best mechanics on the Daytona Coupe project, as well as a great all around asset to Shelby American. Bob Skinner, along with Mahlon, ran the machine shop. I was very lucky to have such highly skilled friends willing to help me and was a little embarrassed that we were in such a thrash for this race.

As we prepared to load the Lotus on my trailer, George said, "I'm not going."

Shocked, I said, "You have to go. You did all this work. You have to. Come on, go."

John and Bob didn't understand, but I did. George had some things going on inside his head that were hard to identify with. Why he left Shelby's didn't make a lot of sense to his fellow employees. He just had to leave. I'm not sure he understood it himself. We almost pleaded with him to come; he finally gave in.

We hit the road in my 1961 Ford about midnight, all of us already tired from a hard night's work. I drove. As soon as we were on the freeway heading out of town, I was fighting to stay awake with a seven-hour drive ahead. I fought sleep for about four hours, never feeling fully awake on the two-lane road. John Collins offered to drive for a while. I got in the back seat and tried to get some sleep. Almost immediately I noticed that John's driving was a little suspect because he dropped the right wheels onto the shoulder of the road several times. Now I was finally wide awake thinking, *If anybody is going to wreck my car, it ought to be me.*

I asked John to pull over and let me drive again. "I'm fine now," I told him.

We stopped for a quick breakfast and then went to the track. We got through technical inspection OK and then waited for our practice group. George's rebuild made my engine better than it had ever been. The close ratio gears were a huge improvement too. I felt comfortable with the Laguna Seca track pretty quickly, but with some sleep, Saturday would be even better.

We left the track and checked into the Avalon Motel on Fremont Avenue in Seaside. It was a cheap motel, but at this point any place with beds was good enough for all of us. All of us except George, that is. George had asthma so he was sensitive to the musty room.

He opened the windows and door and then gave one of the beds a try, pronouncing it not level. He stepped outside to find a couple of bricks for shims. After adjustments were completed, we went to a bad Mexican restaurant for supper. John Collins, being English, probably wouldn't have liked it if it had been a good Mexican restaurant, so we were even.

The next day we were pretty much recovered from the trip and ready for the race. The Laguna Seca track was short, only 1.9 miles, but was one of the most active tracks in the country. Even though the top speeds were relatively low because there were no long straight sections, the high speed turns, especially turns two and three, were not only challenging but also intimidating—not so bad in a Lotus Super 7, but what must they be like in a King Cobra?

My qualifying speed had been fairly good because I was gridded pretty far up in the field. My good friend from work, Earl Jones, was here with his ex–Lew Spencer Morgan Super Sport. Lew named his Morgans *Baby Doll*. He was up to *Baby Doll V* when he started to work for Shelby. Earl's Morgan was Lew's previous: *Baby Doll IV*.

Earl and I had a lot in common. We were both from Illinois, we both came to California to be race car drivers, and now we both worked for Carroll Shelby.

I got a very good start. My new close ratio gears helped with the standing start, still the standard starting procedure, and by turn three, I challenged a Porsche Carrera for the lead. I got partially alongside him as he turned into the very fast left-hand turn three. We touched, his rear and my front, which

My first race at Laguna Seca. After a first lap spin, I rejoined the race in 15th. Then I drove hard, passing both Earl Jones's Morgan and Mike Watson's leading Super 7 near the end to win. *Dave Friedman* caused me to spin. I had to sit beside the track until I could find an opening because it was the first lap with everyone bunched together.

I rejoined the race way back about 15th. There had been no damage so I started passing the slower cars easily. The closer to the leaders I got, the longer it took to get by. I worked my way through most of the cars, but time was running out. There was my friend Earl Jones in his Morgan up ahead. I caught him and got by with only a few laps to run. Earl had been running second but was challenging Mike Watson for the lead when I passed him. Watson was driving a Lotus Super 7 too, but mine was better. I passed him, and with only two or three laps remaining, I pulled away for a very satisfying victory, both for me and for my friends who had endured a tough few days to help me.

The next morning before going to the track for the USRRC, we had breakfast at a Denny's on Fremont Street. As we walked in, I bought a paper—the *San Francisco Examiner*—and checked out the sports section. To my amazement, they had covered the amateur races. The report of our race stated that it was one of the wildest races in Laguna Seca history and then gave a thorough blow by blow of the whole race.

The GT race was won by Ed Leslie with Miles second and Bob Johnson third. I think the finishing order was prearranged, something

Taking the checkered flag at Laguna after the toughest race I'd run in the Super 7. I traded the trusty Super 7 on a less trustworthy Lotus 23. *Dave Friedman*

the Cobra boys did once in a while with their tremendous advantage over everyone else. Corvette driver Dick Guldstrand walked up once when the Cobra guys were flipping a coin and asked, "What are you guys doing?"

The GT division determined the manufacturer's championship; the purpose-built race cars, called Group 7 cars, like the King Cobras and the Chaparrals, determined the driver's championship. Bob Holbert in the King Cobra was the class of the field in qualifying, getting the pole by over a second on Jim Hall's Chaparral. Dave MacDonald was having problems with the Lang Cooper and only qualified eighth.

At the start, Holbert left the rest of the field in his dust. Bob had always been very fast in his King Cobra, but had never had the success that Dave had. This race was no exception; with a commanding lead, his rear suspension failed. Dave drove an excellent race from his eighth place starting position to finish second to Jim Hall. Roger Penske was third.

Driving home after a race win was so much less stressful than in the other direction. It always is.

Thomson Terror

One week after Laguna Seca, the team of Cobras and King Cobras traveled to Kent, Washington, for another USRRC. Ken Miles, Ed Leslie, and Bob Johnson were in the Cobras again. Holbert would drive the King Cobra with Dave driving the Lang Cooper.

Indianapolis took up nearly the entire month of May with practice and testing preceding the first day of qualifications on May 16. When practice started at Kent, Dave was still in Indianapolis

Ed Leslie in turn six at Riverside driving his own Cobra. Ed's success in this car led to his inclusion on the Shelby American team where he drove Cobras, King Cobras, and the Lang Cooper. *Allen Kuhn* trying to get comfortable in the unorthodox Mickey Thompson car while passing his rookie test. The team wanted to get some laps on the Lang Cooper before Dave arrived, so Bob took the car out to do a few laps to make sure it was OK.

The track was wet, and as Bob exited the last turn onto the front straight, the car broke loose and spun into the pit lane. The result was total bedlam. Bob hit several cars, completely destroying the Lang Cooper, the Nickey Cooper Chevrolet of Skip Hudson, and Trevor Harris's Chevrolet Special, driven by Stan Burnett. Holbert, Hudson's crew chief, Ron Kaplan, and Burnett were injured. Both Kaplan and Burnett sustained head injuries but would eventually recover. Holbert's injuries were less serious.

For the race, MacDonald would drive the Shelby King Cobra, which he qualified third behind the two Chaparrals of Jim Hall and Hap Sharp. Early in the race Dave was running a close second to Hall as he drove the comparatively obsolete Cooper to its limit and slightly beyond, the standard MacDonald style, finally taking the lead. Dave hadn't opened much of a gap before he spun, giving the lead back to Hall. When the Chaparral suffered a minor mechanical problem a few laps from the end, Dave won with Hap Sharp a distant second. Dave Ridenour was third in a Huffaker Genie Ford.

After the race, Joe Freitas, Craig Lang, and Wally Peat drove Dave to the Seattle airport for the trip back to Indianapolis. They discussed plans to build a new Lang Cooper for Dave. He was worn out from the race and the rapid pace his life had assumed, hoping to get a seat on the plane where he could stretch out and sleep. He'd expressed some concerns about the handling of his Mickey Thompson Indy car to Wally.

The following weekend I had an SCCA Divisional race at Del Mar. Only George Boskoff came with me. The track was just like it was the year before when I won the novice race, but for some reason now the

Bob Johnson: Bob Johnson and Ed Leslie earned their positions as Shelby American team drivers with dominant performances in their own Cobras. Here Johnson drives his own car in an SCCA race at Watkins Glen in June 1964. *Road & Track* Collection

car had too much understeer. We tried to cure the problem by changing to different front tires but it didn't help. During the race I was able
to keep Earl Jones and his Morgan in sight but I couldn't catch him,
much less pass, until his left front spindle broke and his wheel went
flying off the track, just like Lew Spencer's had at Dodger Stadium. I
won, but Earl should have; it wasn't a very satisfying victory.

On the way home I discussed my racing future with George,
telling him I was ready for a faster car, one I could compete with in
professional races. When we stopped for supper, I called my parents
on a pay phone and told them my plan. I asked them to sell some
more of the $18,000 in stock I had inherited from my Uncle Lyman;
I needed it quick.

I had heard that Lotus was coming out with a Ford-powered
sports racer to replace the old Lotus 19 Monte Carlo and that Shelby
might be buying some to replace the aging Coopers. They would
be $10,000 with a fuel-injected Ford engine. It sounded like a very
reasonable price. I asked Carroll if he could get me one too. He said
he probably could but sounded a little vague. The car was called the
Lotus 30. For some reason I dropped the idea, one of the few really
good racing decisions I ever made. The car was probably the worst
race car Lotus ever built. Shelby passed on it too and bought new
Coopers instead.

I went back to see Bob Challman, the Lotus dealer, to see about
trading my Super 7 on a new Lotus 23B with an English Ford Twin
Cam engine. He tried selling me a slightly used one that had been
driven by Jim Clark to win the under-2-liter class at the 1963 Los
Angeles Times Grand Prix, but I said, "I want a new one."

It was only $500 more. I don't remember what he gave me for
the Super 7 in trade, but it had been a car that exceeded my most
optimistic expectations and deserved better than just to be cast aside
as a used car. But because I was eager to move up, there wasn't time for
sentimental attachments. Or well-thought-out decisions.

There was a big professional race called the Players 200 at
Mosport in Canada, about 65 miles north of Toronto, on June 6, the
week after Indy. Carroll said I could put my new Lotus in the transporter and Shelby American would enter it as a team car along with
Cobras for Ken Miles and Bob Johnson, as well as a King Cobra for
Dave MacDonald. It was very generous of Carroll to do this and also
to paint my car Viking blue, the team color, in our paint shop.

Dave had qualified for the Indy 500 on the first day of qualifying
at more than 151 miles per hour to put him into the field in 14th

starting position. Most of us in the shop were very interested in keeping tabs on his progress. He was doing well in spite of the car he was in.

I had never driven a rear engine car, so was very eager to drive my new car before it went to Canada. Ken Miles was going to do a test on his Cobra before it left for Canada, so I tagged along to Riverside with the 23.

Very quickly I discovered that a car with the engine in the back felt very different from my Super 7 or the Cobras I had driven at drivers' school and Sebring. I felt that something might be wrong with the suspension and wanted a second opinion. Ken was out of the Cobra for the time being so I asked him if he'd mind taking a couple of laps in my Lotus and give me his impression. He drove two or three laps, came in, and said, "It's fine. Nice little car."

That gave me confidence that the strange feeling was only in my ass. I continued to drive. I was starting to feel pretty good. Then I spun in the very fast turn two. I had bent the rear lower A-arm pickup point when I left the road. The cars were leaving for Mosport that night so I rushed back to the shop to see if a repair could be made in time. Red Rose had it repaired in short order. He even reinforced the pickup; it was better than new. There were some wonderful people at Shelby American.

The four cars were loaded into the semi and Red Pierce and I set out for Canada. Unlike the trip to Sebring in 1963 with Joe Landaker, this tractor had a sleeper cab that I thought would make the grueling 2,700-mile trip more tolerable. I was soon to discover that the sleeper was pretty much off limits to me. Red's theory was if I can't sleep, you can't sleep.

It was still exciting: Traveling across the country in an 18-wheeler with my new race car. Riding with Miles' and Bob Johnson's Cobras and MacDonald's King Cobra. Going to my first professional race, not counting Sebring, of course—but Sebring was a fluke, where this one was planned.

Red was pretty tired when he asked me if I wanted to try to drive the rig. I said, "Sure. I'll give it a try."

The biggest truck I'd ever driven was a pickup. Red pulled to a stop. It was just daybreak. After some instructions, I put the monster in gear, let out the clutch, and we were back on the road. Damn, that thing felt big. It was hard to tell how much of the road I was taking up. After a short while, we came to a Y in the road. One way was a tight left curve; the other way was straight ahead. At the last minute Red

When I went to the Lotus dealer to trade the Super 7 on a Lotus 23, he offered me this used car for a $500 discount. He said it had only one race on it. The user was Jimmy Clark, here winning the class in the 1963 Los Angeles Times Grand Prix. I opted for a new car.
Bob Tronolone

said forcefully, "Go left!" I couldn't. I didn't think I could make the monster turn and went straight. Red yelled at me in disgust. I lost my driving privileges for the remainder of the trip.

Saturday morning we were able to get the Indy 500 broadcast on the radio as we drove. We both felt we had a stake in this 500, not just because we knew Dave; we were also transporting his car to his next race. We knew he didn't have a great chance of doing very well because of the car he was driving, but he could get the most a car had to give and more—like the Pacific Grand Prix he won in the King

Cobra while holding the car in gear with one hand as the transmission tried to jump out into neutral.

After the fanfare, the race started. Jim Clark jumped into the lead from his pole starting spot and started to pull away. There was a crash in turn four on the second lap. The announcer said several cars were involved. He told the names of the drivers that he could see. Dave was one of the drivers who had crashed. The race was stopped. The Indy 500 had never been stopped before because of an accident. It had to be bad.

In a little while Sid Collins reported that Eddie Sachs had been killed. He gave him an impromptu eulogy. Dave was badly injured. You could tell it was bad by the sound of Sid Collins's voice. We stopped and Red left the truck for something. I think it was at a gas station. Sid Collins came back on and said Dave MacDonald had died. When Red climbed back in the cab, I said to him, "Dave died."

Red asked almost rhetorically, "Did Dave die?" He heard me. It was just his way of reacting.

I don't know why Red drove to the speedway that night; maybe he thought it would somehow make it better. We went in. He seemed to know some people. Everyone was sad. After a short stay, we just continued on to Canada.

I think I was tougher then than I am now, writing about it 48 years later. A number of things about Dave's May at the Speedway came out later—later to me anyway. Some things are hearsay; some are fact. It's a fact that they struggled all month with the car's poor handling, not a situation a rookie should have to deal with at that track.

Wally Peat urged Dave to abandon the team. They argued over it. He said Dave had been offered a ride the following year by J. C. Agajanian, a very respected car owner. Wally also said that the story about pole sitter and reigning world champion Jim Clark, who followed Dave in practice, was true. Clark approached Dave and said, "Get out of that, car mate. Just walk away." It was reported that Dave's car carried 80 gallons of gasoline in a possible attempt to run the race without a pit stop. Wally said it carried 75 gallons and Dave had never practiced with that much gas on board.

Dave felt he had made a commitment to Mickey Thompson he had to honor. As a driver myself, I can understand that because I would have done the same thing. The difference is that I think I would have been very careful and just tried to get the day behind me. Dave MacDonald didn't know how to do that, passing five cars on the first lap, but then, I was no Dave MacDonald.

Dave left two children and his beautiful wife, Sherry.

Learning the 23B

When we got to Canada, we unloaded the cars at the Comstock race shop. Comstock was a large commercial contractor that sponsored a Canadian racing team running both a Cobra and a Cooper Ford/King Cobra that they had purchased from Shelby American. Their driver was Canadian Ludwig Heimrath. Paul Cook, a very nice man who ran the Comstock team, was very helpful to us while we were there.

For everyone on the Shelby team, this was going to be a difficult week. We had lost Dave. And then when Dave was killed, Bob Holbert, who'd been injured in Dave's Cooper, decided to retire. The King Cobra had no driver. Ken didn't want to drive it, preferring to stay in the Cobra. I even heard mumbling about possibly putting me in it. I wouldn't turn it down if they asked, but I hoped they wouldn't because I just wasn't ready to make that leap yet, knowing I would be over my head and wouldn't be able to do the car justice.

After working in the Comstock shop for a day, the cars were reloaded onto the transporter for the 40-mile or so trip to the Mosport track. My car was more trouble to load so the Comstock guys offered to take it in their box van, a small, enclosed truck. We loaded the car backward and discovered that there was no easy way to tie it down safely, so it was decided that I should sit in my new Lotus and hold the brakes until we arrived at the track. That didn't sound so bad. I'd always liked sitting in race cars. Sometimes at the shop I would eat my lunch sitting in the Formula One Scarab that Reventlow had left stored there when Shelby took over the building or, later, in one of the King Cobras.

When they shut the back doors, the world turned totally black. I couldn't even see my hand in front of my eyes. It was a strange feeling at first but after rumbling along for a while, it got weirder and weirder until I was almost completely disoriented. It got to the point that I felt the car was rolling so I pressed the brake pedal harder and harder. I didn't get carsick, but when we stopped at the track and the doors were opened, it was a great relief. They were the hardest 40 miles I'd ever driven. And backward too. The car hadn't moved an inch.

The drivers entered in this race were among the best in the world, including World Champion Jim Clark, Formula One drivers Dan Gurney and Bruce McLaren, as well as A. J. Foyt, who, less than a week earlier, had won the tragedy-marred Indy 500 for the second time. Foyt and Augie Pabst were driving for the Mecom team—Foyt in the one and only rear-engine Scarab, which had been purchased from Lance Reventlow, with Pabst in the Lola GT, the forerunner to the Ford GT 40.

Bruce McLaren was driving the ex–Roger Penske *Zerex Special*, now with Oldsmobile V-8 power replacing the Coventry Climax engine. Jim Hall and Roger Penske were in Chaparrals.

Nearly half of the field was made up of under-2-liter cars, many Lotus 23s like mine. Bob McLean and Mike Goth were in 23s. Potentially the fastest under-2-liter cars were the Robert Bosch Special Elva Porsches of Bill Wuesthoff and Joe Buzzetta, and the similar Carl Haas–entered cars for Skip Scott and George Wintersteen.

Mosport was one of the most difficult tracks I'd been on with its preponderance of very high-speed turns, several of them blind and all of them with elevation changes. Even the long back straight wasn't truly straight as you counted the blind hills to know when it was going to end in a very fast 180-degree right-hand curve.

During practice I felt my accelerator pedal suddenly get much easier to press and thought that a throttle return spring might have broken, which would make a stuck throttle more likely. Throttles stuck wide open have caused many serious accidents in racing because by the time a driver realizes what has happened, it is often too late to prevent a crash. I didn't want to lose the practice time, so against my better judgment, I stayed out. As I continued, I started practicing reaching for the ignition switch on the dash, just in case. Then, in the most unforgiving place on the track, coming through a very fast downhill left, approaching the slowest two turns on the track, Moss Corner, the throttle finally did stick. Had I not practiced reaching for the ignition shutoff, which was a conventional ignition key, my shiny new Lotus would have been history. The throttle spring had in fact broken. It was an easy fix, which I'd never put off again.

Augie Pabst in the Mecom Lola blew his Chevrolet engine, making him available to drive our King Cobra.

Qualifying was done oval track style, one car at a time with an out lap, a timed lap, and a cool-off lap. Dan Gurney in a Lotus 19B was on pole with Bruce McLaren second. Pabst qualified sixth.

In the under-2-liter class, Bill Wuesthoff qualified first at a 1:39.7. I was very pleasantly surprised to do 1:39.9 for second place ahead of Joe Buzzetta in third at 1:40.5. (My memory is pretty good; I remembered that I qualified second and that my time was 1:39.9, but I cheated and looked up Wuesthoff's and Buzzetta's times.)

The race was run in two 100-mile heats with about an hour in between. I spun in the first heat, letting Buzzetta by, and finished third. In the second heat I spun again, this time twice in the same lap. I had to take it easier for the rest of the race to keep from making more mistakes. I lost concentration as the race wore on, something I really needed to work on. I still finished third in the under-2-liter class. Late in the second heat, Ken Miles passed me just as a large puff of smoke came from under his Cobra as he slithered down the track in his own oil. He had broken a transmission tail shaft, putting him out of the race and stranding him on the course. Bruce McLaren won both heats as the two Chaparrals and the Scarab had problems. Gurney broke his Lotus' transmission early, and Clark withdrew from the race unhappy with the modified Lotus he was to drive. Augie Pabst finished second in our King Cobra and retrieved Ken on his cool-off lap. Bob Johnson in a Shelby American–entered Cobra won the GT class.

With a race now successfully run since the loss of Dave MacDonald, the pain had subsided to a degree, but it was well understood that Shelby American would never be quite the same again.

Allen Grant had run the Allen Green Cheetah at this race but had little success, as was usually the case for anyone who raced a Cheetah. Ole Olsen had come along to help Allen and was driving back to Los Angeles in a Chevrolet El Camino. I hitched a ride with him. Ole told me that his real passion wasn't race cars but unlimited hydroplanes, and that he would do almost anything to be a crew chief on one. Although he had a great and somewhat wicked sense of humor—he once sprayed an unamused Carroll Shelby with Bullshit Repellant in the engine shop—he never seemed content with his situation. On the way home we stopped in Las Vegas. I'd never been in Las Vegas, so it was exciting to watch Ole shoot craps. He got on a winning streak and was up $260 when he wanted me to roll the dice for him. Ole's hand was trembling, but I didn't want the responsibility. Eventually he lost it all without my help and we went to bed. Maybe it was a good lesson; I've never liked to gamble since.

Short Straight Shot
During a lunch break in early 1964, the group conversation turned to the dragster one of our machinists, Bob Skinner, was building. It was to be an AA Fuel dragster that would compete in the fastest class of drag racing. The car wasn't finished yet, and they hadn't selected a driver. I had never had any interest in drag racing, though I had been exposed to it once in 1956 when my dad took us to Union Grove, Wisconsin.

Bruce Burness piped up and said, "You should have John drive your dragster."

Bob asked, "Do you have fast reactions?"

"I guess I do."

He pulled a bill out of his wallet and asked me to catch it between my fingers as he dropped it just above my hand. I caught it several times. He said, "You're fast enough," and dropped the subject. I didn't think any more about it.

After the car was finished, Bruce and I went to Lions Drag Strip to watch its maiden run. It turned 176 miles per hour. I was amazed at the spectacle and the speed, but had a very passing interest only because someone I knew was involved.

Bob had two partners in the car: Tom Jobe and Jimmy Crosser. They called their team Skinner, Crosser, and Jobe, which was the way teams were often named in those days. Sometimes the car itself carried its own name such as *The Bounty Hunter* or *The Swamp Rat.*

Skinner, Crosser, and Jobe ran nearly every weekend, and on Monday mornings we got a race report, rarely if ever including victory. They seemed to go through a lot of drivers. I was never sure if they were unhappy about the driver or the drivers were unhappy with them. One of their drivers was Mike Sorokin. They liked Mike, but there was a conflict with Crosser over a girl as I recall, so Sorokin had to go. There was Bob Muravez and their latest driver Roy "Goob" Tuller.

In June Bob asked me at work, "Do you still want to drive our car?"

Actually I never did say I wanted to drive their car. I just happened to catch the dollar bill. I said, "Sure."

"Come with us next weekend. We're racing at Pomona. Tuller knows he's out after that race. He'll show you how to pack the chute."

"Why do I have to learn that?"

"Because if it doesn't open, it's not our fault. It's the driver's."

Their race shop was at Skinner's mother's business on Santa Monica Boulevard, the Red Apple Motel. The car was housed and prepared in one of the motel's small garages. That weekend at Pomona, Tuller showed me how to deal with packing the parachute into the small container attached to the back of the car. They had me drive the car back to the pits after Tuller had made a run. It was on straight alcohol on the return road and didn't feel very fast; when they made a pass on the strip, there was a lot of nitro methane in the alcohol, which they said made a very big difference.

We went to Bill Simpson's house, where he started his safety equipment company, stitching the fireproof suits and parachutes himself. He made an asbestos head cover for me. After picking it up, as we drove back to the Red Apple, I wore the headgear and played at scaring people out the window. I had to use glass goggles for racing this car, which were impervious to the nitro methane.

The next week I made a couple of trips to the Red Apple after work just to sit in the dragster and familiarize myself with the controls. There was a gas pedal, a clutch, a handle for the parachute, a fuel shutoff valve, a hand brake, and a cutoff switch for the magneto. I was told the sequence for shutting down after the quarter mile run was over. It seemed easy, but at nearly 200 miles per hour things would need to happen fast.

I sat in the car with my legs over the rear axle housing and the rear end right against my crotch. I had been told how Jack Chrisman, a famous drag racer, was seriously injured when the car he was driving had a failure that caused the rear end to break loose from its mounts and rotate, causing the mutilation of Chrisman's male parts. Bob and Tom assured me that their axle housing was very securely mounted but this story did come to mind when I sat in the car.

Race day arrived. We had breakfast and then drove to Pomona. I'd never even driven down a drag strip in my life and wondered if maybe I'd gotten into something I shouldn't have. I put on my Simpson gear and was strapped into the dragster. In the staging area, the centrifugal force tried to push my foot off the clutch. When I floored the throttle, it was like I stepped on a hand grenade.

My first pass was a single, only me on the strip with a low percentage of nitro. Holy shit, it was fast! I feathered off the throttle for a split second halfway down the run. That pissed me off. The speed was 179. I was mad at myself for easing off and never did it again, but the next run was only 180, so I hadn't let off much.

We didn't win that day but that wasn't unusual for this low-dollar team. The next race was at Lions Drag Strip in Long Beach. The race

The Pomona drag strip, June 1964. This was my first run down a drag strip in my life. Car owners Bob Skinner and Tom Jobe gave me a low dose of Nitro methane (60 percent) for my first pass. It was a little scary. I ran 179.
Charles Strutt

was at night, and we ran a 180-something and again didn't win. The famous guys like Garlits, Kalitta, and Prudhomme were winning.

On the same day I had to leave for the USRRC race at Watkins Glen, I was to drive the dragster at Pomona again, my last drive in it. I would have a week to get to New York, so I planned to spend a day or two in Waukegan to see my mother, father, brother, and wife, whose parents had planned our wedding for the fourth of July. It would be a fake wedding, but they didn't know that. Jan was three and a half months pregnant. They didn't know that either.

We ran an 8.04 ET at 189 miles per hour and still lost. I had committed a cardinal sin for a drag racer; I'd run a quicker ET—elapsed time—and still lost. I felt bad about it; Bob and Tom weren't happy with me. I'm pretty sure they would have given me a chance to redeem myself later, but they wanted to run nearly every week and I couldn't make that commitment. This ended my drag racing career, but it also was the beginning of the end of the losing streak for Skinner, Crosser, and Jobe. They got rid of Jimmy Crosser, reunited with Mike Sorokin, changed their name to the Surfers (although neither one surfed), and went on to become one of the winningest drag racing teams in America.

In 1967 Skinner and Jobe left drag racing to try their hand at road racing, winning Can-Am races with drivers John Cannon and Francois Cevert, as well as the 1970 Formula 5000 Championship with Cannon. Mike Sorokin remained in drag racing and died at Orange County Raceway in 1967 when the clutch on the dragster he was driving disintegrated, cutting the car in half.

Running Around Watkins Glen

I left Pomona about 5:00 p.m. and headed for Waukegan, planning to drive straight through without stopping except for gas and food. My friend Earl Jones had made a similar trip and gave me some pills he had left over that a doctor had given him. They worked pretty well because I got to Waukegan Tuesday morning after 39 and a half hours on the road. I left for New York Wednesday night to connect with the Shelby team at Watkins Glen.

We were staying in a rustic, wooden two-story hotel on a winding road across the lake from the village of Watkins Glen. This little village was the birthplace of modern sports car racing in America, when in 1948, a race was held that ran through the town and over the surrounding rural roads. The race continued on public roads until a permanent course was built in 1956, making it the second-oldest purpose-built road course still operating in America. Willow Springs is the oldest, built in 1953. The first Sebring race was held in 1950, but the course was laid out primarily on the runways of an Army Air Corp training base.

Our cars were being prepared at the Watkins Glen Ford dealership. It seemed that for a dealership to survive in such a small town, nearly everyone in Watkins Glen would have to drive a Ford.

There was to be a new driver in the King Cobra for this race. His name was Skip Scott. I remembered him from Mosport, where he drove an Elva Porsche. Skip seemed to appear from out of nowhere because I followed racing closely and hadn't heard of him until Mosport. The guys on the team thought he must have had connections at Ford or was wealthy enough to pay for his rides. I heard his family owned the Scott Paper Company. I never did find out, even though we became friends. It's hard to ask a friend, "Where the hell does your money come from anyway?"

Ken Miles, Bob Johnson, and Ed Leslie were in the Cobras. Ken was very conscientious about staying in shape, maybe because at 46 he was getting pretty old for a race car driver. He would get up early in the morning on race weekends and run for a couple of miles before the rest of the team was even awake. He invited other team members to join him, but they thought he was nuts. Fitness was not a high priority for most people in the early 1960s. But I liked running when I was in school, so I agreed to join him. At about 6:00 a.m., Ken knocked on my hotel-room door and called, "Wakey, wakey!"

We ran through the woods as I labored to keep up, not having done anything like this since high school. I think we were both trying to avoid showing we were the weaker one. Maybe because I was less than half his age, he had to prove something, and maybe because I was, I had to keep up. We crossed a narrow stream by walking on a small log. Ken slipped and fell. Neither of us said anything as he quickly got up and we continued. It reminded me of an occasion in the shop when someone brought in a skateboard and was riding it around. Miles watched, and then had to try it. I'm pretty sure he'd never ridden a skateboard, so when he did the board went out from under him. His feet were as high as his ass and he came down hard on the cement. He jumped up instantly and pretended it didn't hurt, but I know it had to.

On race day, someone, probably Carroll, arranged for a police escort so we could drive the race cars from the dealership to the track to avoid having to load them into the transporter again.

The first race was the 100-mile GT race, which Ken won with Leslie second and Johnson third. There was about an hour between the GT race and the start of the 200-mile Watkins Glen Grand Prix. Ken decided to run the Grand Prix in the Cobra he'd just won the GT race in. In the hour between the races, the team installed the endurance fuel tank in Ken's car so he didn't have to stop.

The weather was hot; it was a pretty tough race for me. I did finish third in under-2-liter behind two Elva Porsches, driven by Charlie Hayes and Don Wester. Jim Hall and Roger Penske were first and second in Chaparrals with Miles fifth; I was seventh overall. Immediately after the race, the cars pulled into the paddock and the drivers got out of their cars. I was completely spent, but assumed Miles would be near collapse after running both races in a car that was physically much harder to drive than my Lotus 23. I was soaked in sweat when I asked, "You must be really tired, aren't you?"

"No, I feel fine," he answered.

Miles often took the top of his driving suit off when he was out of a race car, revealing a build that looked more like that of a refugee from Dachau than the he-man that he actually was. He also walked like he was a little light in his loafers, which made it even harder to believe that he was the toughest guy on the track.

After the cars were loaded, I left for Waukegan to prepare for my fake wedding. Jan's mother made the clothes for the bridesmaids, accentuating the Fourth of July theme. There was the cake with two plastic people on top. Hardly anyone knew we were already married and even fewer knew Jan was already pregnant. Even though the wedding was something of a charade, it had significance because from then on we could be together.

Jan and I left on our honeymoon to Eagle River, Wisconsin, about 320 miles north. We had until the 17th to get to Greenwood Roadway, site of the next USRRC race near Des Moines, Iowa. After four or five days in Eagle River, we headed back to Waukegan. Listening to the radio as we approached Milwaukee, there was a commercial for a USAC stock car race at the Milwaukee Fairgrounds. I asked Jan if she minded if we went. She said it was OK with her, which I took as a very positive sign. Parnelli Jones won in a Stroppe Mercury; his teammate Rodger Ward was second.

We got back to Waukegan after the Sunday race, which only left three days to get ready to drive to California to start a new chapter in both of our lives. My parents and brother Lyman, along with his girlfriend, followed us as far as the race in Iowa, after which they would return home. While in Iowa, Lyman confessed to me that he too had gotten secretly married, but for a different reason than I had. It seemed his girlfriend Gilda had gotten pregnant, at least that's what she told him, but the truth eventually came out, or I guess more accurately, didn't come out. But the damage had already been done. I could go on about Lyman's unfortunate choices of women but don't feel comfortable throwing stones; I might break something.

Ed Leslie would drive the King Cobra, Ken Miles and Bob Johnson were in Cobras, and again I was in my Lotus. I was starting to be concerned that there was no way I could beat a well-driven Elva Porsche in a Lotus 23, but there wasn't much I could do about it. They had a lot more horsepower, as well as wider wheels and tires than the 23. For this race, the SCCA had combined the GT class with the sports racers.

After the Friday practice, it was decided that loading up the cars to take them into the Ford dealer in the small town of Indianola was too much trouble, so a police escort was arranged for the Shelby team cars to be driven on the highway the 15 miles into town. Wally Peat drove the King Cobra, Tom Greatorex was in a Cobra with Garry Koike as a passenger, while I followed in the Lotus with Jan by my side. For a reason we didn't understand at the time, the cop left us at a curve in the road. As it turned out, he had come to the boundary of his jurisdiction and peeled off, leaving the three race cars to fend for themselves.

Though we didn't take advantage of the loss of our chaperone, as some racers would have, we did pass a few cars. While passing a line of cars, I, being third in line, got back on the right side of the road just slightly after the passing zone ended. There was really nothing to it except one of the cars we passed got upset as we found out later when the police came to the Ford dealership while we were working on the cars and demanded to know who was driving car No. 97. Al Dowd came to me with the news. I'd forgotten my driver's license so they decided to tell the cop that Tom Greatorex had been in old No. 97. Tom and Shelby went to the police station and paid the $15 fine. Case closed.

On the first practice day, Ken Miles was asked if he would go into the station WHOTV for an interview after practice was over. When the time to leave came, Ken decided he didn't want to bother and told his mechanic Charlie Agapiou to go in his place. Charlie protested but Ken said, "I'm your boss; you're going."

Charlie's nickname was Who because his real last name was hard to understand when he said it with his strong English accent. The name on his team uniform was Who?, which fascinated the people at WHOTV. When the interview started, the Midwesterners realized that they couldn't understand a word Charlie said and started laughing. They enjoyed that unintelligible interview so much they had him back the next day for another one.

Greenwood Roadway, which had been so good to me and my Super 7 less than a year earlier, extracted its revenge Saturday during practice when my engine blew. After being towed to the paddock, I lifted the rear body to reveal engine parts scattered on the belly pan; the crankshaft had broken. My dad, ever the optimist, looked at the broken engine and proclaimed, "Well, it looks like you're not going to get killed today."

We stayed to watch Ed Leslie win the race in the King Cobra and Miles win the GT class. When Bob Johnson's Cobra broke down on the course, Charlie Agapiou and Garry Koike jumped on a motor scooter to see if they could get him going again. Garry was riding with Charlie on the back. Garry must not have been a very good rider because he lost control of the scooter and rode over someone's tent. I think the camper was out watching the race so no one was hurt. Johnson's race was finished.

Settling In

Jan and I got to California and rented an upstairs apartment just 2 or 3 miles from Shelby's. A couple of weeks later, an apartment became available in a four-plex even nearer to work. Two of the four units were already occupied by parts man Gordon Goring and his wife, Rita, and Earl Jones and his wife, Connie. These were two of my best friends, so the decision to move was easy. Another factor was a one-car garage for each unit. I'd have a place to work on the Lotus with Earl's Morgan on one side of me and Gordon's Austin-Healey on the other.

As soon as we moved in, Jan and I went to see Mrs. Allcock, Allen Grant's and my old landlady from over a year earlier. I'd left an old rabbit-eared portable TV in her garage and wanted to retrieve it. When Mrs. Allcock came to the door, I introduced her to Jan and told her we would like to get the little TV set if she still had it. Right in front of my new wife, the old lady started ranting again about the girls Allen and I had smuggled in that night over a year earlier. I repeated our true story that nothing untoward had happened, but she was not having any of it. The uptight old bitch charged me $15 storage on the TV just for spite.

Ole Olsen made the generous offer to rebuild my blown engine, much of which had to be replaced. I was hoping to have the car ready for the fall pro races at Riverside and Laguna Seca.

Back at Shelby American the team was preparing for the next USRRC at Meadowdale. There would be a significant change for the Shelby cars as the team color changed from pale metallic Viking Blue to a darker metallic Guardsman Blue. I'm pretty sure the Viking Blue was the same color as our company Ford pickup truck.

Another change for Meadowdale would be the use of American Mag wheels instead of Halibrands. They were lighter and I'm pretty sure were cheaper than the Halibrands.

My hopes of becoming the driver of the second Sunbeam Tiger faded with nearly every race the car ran. It was painfully obvious that this was a very low-priority effort by Shelby American and would likely be terminated before a second car materialized. The T5 that Carroll mentioned to me in his exuberance at Willow Springs after my race with Ronnie Bucknum in his MGB in November of '63 turned out to be the Ford Mustang. When I saw the first one I remember thinking, *This sure doesn't look much like a race car.* Nevertheless, it became a very important project. Ken Miles and Richie Ginther worked on developing the car for competition. Quite a bit of the preliminary testing was carried out at Riverside by Ginther using a modified Ford Falcon as a test bed. One of the early prototype Mustangs that was tested at Riverside had independent rear suspension.

This was the only Mustang I ever got to drive on the track. Ken let me take it out for a few laps, and even with my very limited experience, the car seemed to handle poorly. As it rolled into a corner, I felt the rear trying to steer the car. I'm sure independent rear suspension could have ultimately been an asset, but production costs would have been higher and the advantage perhaps minimal. The idea was quickly scrapped although I never knew the politics behind it. Actually I never knew the politics behind anything that ever happened at Shelby American.

I had picked up at least two of the three Coopers from LAX that were destined to become 1964 King Cobras for the fall pro races at Riverside and Laguna Seca. These new King Cobras would be extensively modified over the two earlier 1963 cars. Their chassis were being reinforced for added stiffness and strength, whereas the bodies were changed to accommodate wider wheels and tires. The radiators were relocated in a horizontal position in an effort to reduce drag, which entailed extensive changes to the car's noses.

Ken Miles, the father of the ill-fated 427 Cobra we shared at Sebring, had decided to double down on the idea by scratch building a new car to accommodate the big-block Ford engine. The project was started in the late summer of 1964. Joe Fukashima and Red Rose did most of the fabrication work. The front and rear body sections would be made to articulate, facilitating working on the chassis and engine components, hence the nickname *Flip Top*. I'm not sure it had an official title, maybe *Super Snake*. The unofficial name was *The Turd*. Although it would be lighter and more powerful than a 289 Cobra race car, it would retain the same antiquated, transverse leaf suspension front and rear. Its intended purpose was to compete with the Corvette Grand Sport—a Corvette look alike that was no more a Corvette than *The Turd* would be a Cobra.

If I hadn't blown my Lotus engine in Iowa, I would have gotten to drive at Meadowdale and Mid-Ohio with the team. At Meadowdale in early August, Miles won the GT class with Bob Johnson second. There wasn't much competition for the Cobras in that class except for other Cobras, and the privateers didn't stand much of a chance against the Shelby American cars. The Stingray contingent had pretty much thrown in the towel. Miles again did double duty, finishing fifth in the modified race in his Cobra, while Ed Leslie broke in the Shelby American King Cobra. Jim Hall won again in his Chaparral.

The American Mag wheels that the team ran at Meadowdale were cracked after the race, so they reverted back to the Halibrands.

With two USRRCs left in the 1964 season, I was told I would be driving a team Cobra in the final race, the Road America 500 at Elkhart Lake, Wisconsin. I should remember who told me something that important, but I don't; it had to be either Carroll, Ken, or Al Dowd. I would be teamed with Skip Scott. Ken accompanied Skip and me to Willow Springs in mid-August so the two of us could get some time in the 289 USRRC Cobra before the race. Skip told me he was going to soon be able to beat Miles. Skip was good, but thinking that he would soon be faster than Ken seemed to be wishful thinking. I think he really believed that though; I wished I'd had that kind of self-confidence.

At Mid-Ohio the Shelby American Cobras were first and second in the GT race, only this time Bob Johnson was first with Miles second. Miles again ran the modified race, finishing fourth behind winner Hap Sharp in a Chaparral, with Hall second and George Wintersteen in his Cooper Chevy, third.

Ed Leslie in the King Cobra qualified well but had transmission problems and dropped out of the race at Meadowdale. Here he gets a little out of shape. *John McCollister*

The Cobra team had breezed to the USRRC Manufacturer's Championship nearly uncontested, but the European Cobra effort had not gone as well. The highlight of the European season was the class victory of Dan Gurney and Bob Bondurant in the second Cobra Daytona Coupe at the 24 Hours of Le Mans. They finished fourth overall and would have finished higher but for a leaking oil cooler.

Ferrari led the FIA Manufacturers' Championship, but Shelby still had a chance when Gurney in a Daytona Coupe won the class in the Tourist Trophy at Goodwood in England on August 29. With the points Bob Bondurant got in hillclimbs in a Cobra Roadster, there was still a chance for a Shelby championship if Cobras won Monza on September 6 and Bridgehampton on September 20.

Ferrari had an ongoing dispute with the FIA over the homologation of the Ferrari rear engine 250 LM. The FIA required 100 cars to have been built before they would be eligible for classification in the GT category, therefore qualifying to earn points toward

Ken Miles won the GT class at the Meadowdale USRRC. Here he is running on the punishing Monza Wall. They decided to try American Mag wheels instead of Halibrands. Miles was lucky because after the race, the wheels were cracked. *John McCollister*

the Manufacturers' World Championship. The number of 250 LMs produced was far less than the required 100 so the FIA denied their homologation. Ferrari had tricked the FIA into homologating their 250 GTO in 1962, but this time the FIA had resolved not to be fooled twice. Ferrari knew that their aging 250 GTO would likely lose to the Daytona Coupe on the very fast Monza circuit, opening the door to a Shelby World Championship if Cobras also won at Bridgehampton, NY, two weeks later.

Ferrari demanded that the FIA allow the 250 LM to enter Monza as a GT car. His demand was rejected so Ferrari pulled strings and had the GT category excluded from the Monza race, which eliminated Shelby American's chance for a World Championship in 1964.

The week after the Monza race in Italy, the USRRC Shelby team was headed for Elkhart Lake, with me included. A Shelby car other than the Cobras was also headed for Wisconsin. The Sunbeam Tiger would be flown to Chicago from LAX to be delivered to a group from

Ohio called Sports Car Forum. Their driver, Don Sesslar, planned to share the car with Ken Miles in the Badger 200, a preliminary race for production cars held on the Saturday before the Sunday Road America 500. Exactly one year prior, I had won my class in this race; my class then was B Production just as the Sunbeam Tiger's was in 1964.

Sesslar was also entered in the 500 in an Elva Porsche, but he crashed in practice, breaking a couple of ribs, and couldn't drive. Ken Miles would have to drive the 200 miles solo, a piece of cake for him.

The cars that were entered in the 500 practiced first on Friday, starting at noon and running until 2:00. Technical inspection was held in a barn about a mile north of the track. In order to pass technical inspection, a car had to be driven about 20 miles per hour and then the brakes were to be locked up and all four wheels had to skid with the driver's hands held in the air to prove he wasn't holding the steering wheel. If the car swerved or didn't lock all four wheels, the car failed inspection and had to try again.

It was very stupid for a number of reasons, but that was standard practice then. The Cobras were having trouble passing the test because with cold brakes, they tended to pull to one side or the other. I was driving when team manager Al Dowd told me to hold the steering wheel with my knees as my hands were raised. It worked and we passed.

Practice went well for the Cobra team, which had entered three 289 roadsters. Bob Johnson and Ed Leslie were in No. 99; Ken and Ronnie Bucknum in No. 98; Skip Scott and I drove No. 97. The Cobra was certainly a different animal from the Lotus Super 7 I'd driven here last year.

Bob Johnson planned to drive his new McKee sports racer in the 500 in addition to driving the Cobra with Leslie. I can't remember who his co-driver was to be in the McKee. Bob seemed very anxious that the car hadn't arrived at the track yet. It was coming from Bob McKee's shop in Palatine, Illinois, about 160 miles from Elkhart Lake. Word finally arrived that Tom Greatorex had attempted a quick shakedown run on the road near the shop before loading the car. He lost control of the very powerful car and crashed it; it wouldn't be coming. Tom wasn't hurt physically, but Johnson's weekend was off to a poor start.

The first practice for the Badger 200 started at 2:10. Ken went out in the Sunbeam Tiger but when he slowed for the tight left-hand turn five on the first lap, the engine moved forward and damaged the radiator. There was no spare, so Ken, Ed Leslie, and I drove to

A few minutes before the start of the race at Road America I received a good luck telegram from a friend in Santa Monica. *John Morton Collection*

My best friend and former race crew Johnny Opitz came from Waukegan to see the race. He looks more stressed than I do. *John Morton Collection*

Sheboygan to find a radiator shop that could do the repair. The only way to fix it was to block off the two damaged tubes. The Sunbeam Tiger was already prone to overheating, so this would have exacerbated the problem. The car's performance in half-hour races had been less than stellar; it was wishful thinking that it could race successfully for two and a half hours.

It was determined that the engine had moved forward enough to damage the radiator because the motor mount bolts had been left loose. Before the car was loaded into the transport plane at LAX, the Tiger mechanics were told to install a new engine while it was waiting at the airport, probably by Carroll Shelby so he could bill Rootes for another engine. In their haste to make the plane, the bolts were neglected.

Qualifying for the 500 was held Saturday. Ken and Ronnie Bucknum started seventh with Johnson and Leslie eighth. Skip and I

Mike Donovan and me, getting ready to put the car on the grid. It was getting pretty nervous around here. *John Morton Collection*

were well behind in 21st, but faster than the privately entered Cobras. We didn't have nearly the experience of the other team members, but it was still a letdown starting so far behind them. Nevertheless the Shelby American team qualified first, second, and third among GT cars.

At 3:30 that afternoon the Badger 200 started. I had a special interest in watching this race, partly because I had worked on the Tiger when it was first prepared and raced by Lew Spencer. Also, this would be its last race as a Shelby American car—the end of the project that I at one time hoped would make me a regular Shelby team driver. Still another reason to watch was that I was curious how long the Sunbeam Tiger would run before it broke.

To my great surprise the damn thing ran strong for the entire 200 miles, Ken easily winning the B Production class and finishing second overall to Dan Gerber in a Cobra. Why didn't it overheat with the makeshift radiator repair? I guess that old man had some kind of magic.

One last cigarette before the start of the 1964 Road America 500. I'm talking to crew chief Mike Donovan. The plan was to share the car with Skip Scott. *John Morton Collection*

I'm out of Road America's turn 14 and up the front straight ahead of Mike Hall in the Elva Porsche. *Tom Schultz*

Skip Scott passing the understeering Chaparral of Gary Wilson. Skip ran the second stint. Miles batted cleanup and brought us home class winner and second overall. *Tom Schultz*

On Sunday, Jan's and my parents as well as my friend and helper from last season, Johnny Opitz, drove up from Waukegan to see the Road America 500. I think they were pretty impressed by the size of the Shelby American Team.

It was decided by someone on the team that I would start the race. I was told to take care of the car and not to worry too much about speed, just drive to finish. I, of course, was obedient and have always regretted it. Dave MacDonald would have busted his ass to go as fast as he possibly could, even if Shelby got pissed off and shook his fist at him during a race. Dave had been a gentle, almost shy man until the green flag dropped, at which time he reverted to a fierce competitor who was anything but gentle and shy. Shelby admired that.

The No. 99 Johnson/Leslie car dropped out on the 42nd lap. I drove 180 miles, or 45 laps on the 4-mile course, moving from 21st up to 7th before pitting to turn the car over to Skip Scott.

Skip must have spun or gone off the road on his third lap because he had a lap time that was about 25 seconds too long. He drove well and his fastest lap was slightly faster than my fastest lap. But on his 11th lap he pitted to reattach his safety belts, which had come loose while he was driving. The crew seemed to lose respect for Skip because he pitted for such a trivial reason. Twenty-three years later as I was exiting the pits at night in the Daytona 24-hour, the same thing happened to me. I drove that one-hour stint in a GTP Jaguar with disconnected belts recalling the Shelby team's reaction to Skip's unscheduled pit stop.

Ronnie Bucknum took over for Miles on lap 62, but 15 laps later pitted again with oil pressure problems. Ken got back in and seven laps later the engine blew. Skip pitted on lap 86 and Miles replaced me for the last 39 laps. Ten laps from the end, Ken passed the Penske/Hap Sharp Chevrolet Grand Sport to finish second overall behind the Walt Hansgen/Augie Pabst Ferrari 250 LM and we won the GT class.

What a thrill it was to have shared the winning car in the Road America 500, the race that in 1957 had such a profound impact on me. I think my parents felt some comfort in seeing that my racing dreams might not be totally unrealistic.

That night I celebrated with the crew in a bar in Sheboygan. I wasn't a big drinker but we were doing shots, something I'd never done before. We had done several when someone had the bartender put vinegar in my shot glass when I wasn't looking. I downed it in a quick gulp before I realized it wasn't whiskey. I laughed too; nothing could have made me mad that night. I still don't mind the taste of vinegar.

The Shelby team went directly from Elkhart Lake to New York because the Bridgehampton Double 500 was just a week after the Road America 500. With the USRRC season over, the Double 500 was the last race of the FIA season for the Shelby team, which started in February at the Daytona Continental. I'd never been to Bridgehampton. I'd never been to New York either. We had a day to kill in New York City, so some of us went to the World Fair. It was big and we did a lot of walking. I'm afraid not much of it stuck in my mind; there was almost too much to see.

The next day we drove to Bridgehampton way out on the end of Long Island; it seemed to take forever to get there. It was a hell of a long way from civilization, that is, if one considers New York City civilization. The team would use a large area in the building that housed the local Ford dealership.

Red Pierce unloaded the three Cobras from the Road America 500. Another open car hauler arrived from California bringing three brand-new competition Cobras and a street car with automatic transmission. The truck driver was Joe Freitas, another alumni of the Carroll Shelby School of High Performance Driving. Joe attended the school more than a year before I did in his own 1961 Corvette, which he had bought from Dave MacDonald when Dave bought a 1962. He was a friend of Dave's and hung around the shop in 1963 when Dave started working and driving for Shelby, eventually getting hired as a truck driver and generic helper with no real job description—such as janitor.

Joe was a Corvette man, as was Dave MacDonald, Wally Peat, and Craig Lang. All four of them had 1963 Stingrays for passenger cars and would park them in formation in front of the Shelby building in a lighthearted act of defiance. Shelby, in an effort to cover his ass lest a picture emerge revealing that his star driver and friends drove Stingrays, instructed them to park behind the building.

The team did the preparation on the three Road America 500 cars, which included engine changes, brake replacement, and general maintenance. We weren't told right away how the cars were going to be assigned to the various drivers, except that Ken Miles always drove his special car, which was No. 98. It was called the Heim joint car because Charlie Agapiou had installed Heim rod ends in the A arms to eliminate the rubber in the standard Cobra suspension and offer some adjustability as well.

Three very happy drivers: Miles, Morton, and Scott. Shelby American general manager, Peyton Cramer, exhaling beside Kerry Agapiou. Pat Rogers is fondling her cobra.
Dave Friedman

Every able-bodied Cobra roadster that we had was being pressed into service, along with all of the best privateers like Lew Florence, Hal Keck, and Chuck Parsons in anticipation of a possible World Championship of Manufacturers' shootout with Ferrari. But that all changed when Ferrari himself had the class eliminated from the Monza race. Nevertheless, the plans had already been made and wouldn't change except for the plan to have Dan Gurney, who'd won this race last year, drive one of the cars. With the championship lost, his services wouldn't be required.

Al Dowd gave Joe and me the news that we would share the new No. 94 car in Gurney's absence. I suppose in a way Joe and I had Enzo Ferrari to thank for this ride.

Joe had never raced anything other than his solid axle Corvette, but he'd won several races in it. The only real competition Cobra he'd ever driven was the first 260 after it was repaired following the Riverside race with Bill Krause in 1962. He was given a few laps in the car at Riverside. This race would be a real trial by fire for Joe, who had lost some of his passion for racing after Dave MacDonald's death. On Memorial Day, he was at Santa Barbara for an SCCA race when Dave died. He just loaded his car and went home, as did some of the other Corvette drivers.

Naturally Joe and I were excited and began adjusting the seating position, belts, etc. It was a new car all right, and it was almost finished. But the first time Joe sat in the car at the dealership, the steering wheel came off in his hands. It seemed obvious it hadn't been tested, or if it had been, someone was very lucky.

The automatic Cobra was to be driven to the track everyday by Joe so it could be displayed; I hitched a ride with him. I'd never been in an automatic Cobra before and never liked automatic transmissions; they took some of the fun out of driving, but this one really hauled ass and did great burnouts. It still seemed to be the waste of a good car, though.

Bridgehampton was not a particularly difficult course, except for the first turn, which was quite intimidating. At the end of the long start/finish straight there was a bridge, which in a Cobra was approached at about 150 miles per hour. Beyond the bridge the track seemed to disappear, leaving only blue sky as a reference point until the beginning of a very fast right hand sweeping turn with nothing on the left but soft sand, daring the driver to go just a little faster next time.

The other Shelby American drivers were Ken Miles, Bob Johnson, Ed Leslie, Ronnie Bucknum, and Charlie Hayes. Charlie was new to the team but not to Bridgehampton. He had raced extensively in the east driving a short wheelbase Berlinetta Ferrari.

Joe and I had to share our car for practice, which cut our time in half—time we both sorely needed. Again Miles was the fastest Cobra with Ronnie Bucknum second. I guess they called the race the Double 500 because both the prototypes and the GT cars were in the same race. The fastest qualifier was the Ferrari 330 of Ludovico Scarfiotti, entered by the North American Racing Team—NART—of Luigi Chinetti. Second was Walt Hansgen in the rear-engine Scarab owned by Mecom Racing, the same car that I saw Lance Reventlow try to test at Riverside during my five days at the Shelby driving school in 1962. This Scarab was built in the same building that we all worked in now. Originally it was powered by a Buick engine, followed by an Oldsmobile engine, but it now had a more powerful Chevy engine.

Dick Guldstrand was the best Southern California Corvette driver not to switch to the Shelby team. Actually, his business was Corvettes, so how could he?
Allen Kuhn

The Cooper Ford driven by Sherman Decker was third and Pedro Rodriguez was fourth in another NART Ferrari. Miles was the first GT qualifier in seventh.

It was left to Joe and me to decide which of us started. We flipped a coin and Joe won. As the cars completed their first lap of the 500-kilometer race, I didn't see Joe. I hoped I'd just missed him in the chaos of the first lap but soon he came limping in, having gone off the road and into a sand bank. Very little damage had been done and he continued without further drama.

I can't remember much about my half of the race except we finished 6th in GT and 11th overall. Scarfiotti had engine problems and Walt Hansgen won with Rodriguez second. Bob Grossman was third in a Ferrari 250 LM and Miles fourth, and first in GT. The only Ferrari in the GT class was the GTO of Mike Gammino, and he had a problem in practice so was a nonstarter. Had Ferrari not had the GT class canceled at Monza, Shelby would likely have won the World Championship.

This race concluded the 1964 racing season except for the fall races at Riverside and Laguna Seca, which I hoped to run in my Lotus 23. It had certainly been an eventful year for me. I won some amateur races, raced three times as a Shelby American Cobra driver, drove an AA fuel dragster, got married, and would in a couple of months become a father. Not sure I was really ready for all of it, but nevertheless it would be a hard year to top.

Shelby Expands

When I returned home from the races in Wisconsin and New York, I'd been gone for about 10 days. Jan wasn't happy that she was left alone for that long. She was six months pregnant, and we hadn't been apart since our fake marriage on July 4. Earl and Connie Jones, as well as Gordon and Rita Goring, were good company, but that didn't seem to be enough. I didn't have much choice; none of the other Shelby drivers brought their wives to the races.

It is difficult, no—impossible—for a man to understand completely what a woman goes through when she's pregnant and even more impossible (if that's possible) if the man is very young and preoccupied with, in this case, racing. I should have recognized my own immaturity and made a better effort to compensate for it.

At work the thrash was on to finish the King Cobras for the Los Angeles Times Grand Prix at Riverside on October 11. Shelby American was entering four of them plus the new Lang Cooper, a Cobra roadster, and my Lotus 23. The King Cobras would be driven by Bob Bondurant, Richie Ginther, and Ronnie Bucknum, with Ed Leslie in the Lang Cooper and Miles in the Cobra roadster. There was some guessing in the shop as to who would drive the fourth King Cobra. I didn't have any expectations that it would be me, but when it was announced that it would be Parnelli Jones, I thought, *What a stupid choice.* To put an Indy car and sprint car driver, as good as he may be, in a road race car of this caliber and in such a competitive race seemed more like a publicity stunt than a rational choice of a driver who would be competitive.

My Lotus would be listed as a Shelby American entry, although it really was never prepared by Shelby American or funded by them aside from entry fees and transportation to the three races I drove in the summer. Ole Olsen was doing the preparation at his home in Panorama City in the San Fernando Valley. Ole's preparation was every bit as meticulous as that being done at the shop on the Coopers.

The way I remember the prize money being distributed to our drivers was that a percentage of all the money that the team won at a race was divided evenly among all the drivers. If one driver or team of drivers won a race and another driver or team of drivers finished further down or even failed to finish, they all got the same money.

Of the three races I drove for Shelby American—Sebring, Road America, and Bridgehampton—each garnered first-place prize money, as well as money for our cars that finished further down. Well after the last race had been run, I hadn't heard anything about prize money, so I decided to ask.

I went upstairs to see the controller. "Have you distributed the prize money checks to the drivers yet?"

"Oh yes, quite a while ago."

"I never got mine," I responded.

"Oh no, we used yours to pay down your account."

"There must be some mistake. I don't have an account."

"Yes, you do."

"An account for what?" I asked. Her answer gave me a "You've got to be kidding" moment.

"For the parts Carroll got you for your Lotus 7."

I already knew that Carroll's words didn't always match his deeds, but wow. I never spoke about it to him.

With the Lotus 23 ready to go again after Ole's engine rebuild and chassis preparation, my seven-months-pregnant wife and I headed for Riverside and the 1964 Los Angeles Times Grand Prix. We towed the Lotus behind our 1961 Ford four-door sedan. This was the first time that my little blue car had the indignity of traveling to a race on a $175, spring-less open trailer rather than luxuriating inside the Shelby transporter, surrounded by factory team Cobras and Coopers.

The Los Angeles Times Grand Prix was the second-most-important sports car race in America, behind only Sebring. The entry for the 1964 race was virtually a who's who of the greatest drivers from the United States and Europe: Jim Clark, Dan Gurney, Bruce McLaren, Jack Brabham, Parnelli Jones, A. J. Foyt, and Roger Penske, to name a few.

Jan and I arrived on Thursday along with Ole, his wife, Helene, who also worked at Shelby American, and their friend Jim Burris, who brought along a Honda 50 as our pit bike.

Jan had never been to Riverside, so I thought she would enjoy a ride around the track on the back of the Honda. Someone with unusual—no, just basic—common sense suggested that it was a little risky, considering Jan's condition, to take her on the motorcycle, but on a Honda 50, what could go wrong?

We left the pits and serenely putted through the esses and around turn six, down the straight and up the hill that preceded the steeply downhill left-hand turn seven. As we entered the turn, the Honda suddenly started to fishtail violently. I couldn't use the brake because I was already struggling to keep the bike from crashing as we continued to careen to the bottom of the hill. It seemed to take forever, but we finally stopped as the track leveled out. The rear tire had blown at a very inopportune time. Fortunately Jan and whoever was inside her dodged a very large bullet that day, no thanks to me.

The entry for the under-2-liter class contained four new Brabham BT 8s with 2-liter Coventry Climax engines producing nearly 200 horsepower, plus several Elva Porsches with 1,800cc engines producing 170-plus horsepower. The twin-cam 1,600cc Lotus Ford engine in my car produced only 140 horsepower as they were delivered in the Lotus 23, many of which were entered here. It was a little discouraging, knowing the 23s wouldn't be able to compete on an even basis with at least eight cars in the under-2-liter class.

After qualifying on Friday there were two qualifying races on Saturday, one for under-2-liter cars and one for over-2-liter cars. The results of these races determined the starting positions for the 200-mile Los Angeles Times Grand Prix on Sunday.

I don't remember where I qualified, but my starting position for the Grand Prix was 25th. The fastest 2-liter car, the Brabham BT 8 driven by Hugh P. K. Dibley and entered by Stirling Moss, had the 18th starting spot.

To my great amazement, Parnelli Jones was the fastest King Cobra driver and third-fastest of all behind Dan Gurney in his Lotus 19 B Ford and Bruce McLaren in the first of a very long and successful line of race cars carrying his name. Based on their results in the qualifying race, McLaren would start from pole with Walt Hansgen second in the Scarab. Jim Clark was third in the uncompetitive Lotus 30; Penske in Jim Hall's Chaparral was starting fourth, with Parnelli fifth. Parnelli spun in the qualifying race, losing positions, but was still the highest Shelby American driver with Ginther seventh and Bucknum eighth.

Bob Bondurant had a small accident in the qualifying race and had to start in the back with Gurney, who had a mechanical problem. Frank Lance, Bondurant's crew chief, explained that Hap Sharp in the second Chaparral, while waiting for the green flag to start the race, held the gas and brake at the same time trying to get a jump with the car's automatic transmission. The flag was delayed and the overheated transmission started spewing fluid. The race started but coming around at the end of the first lap, Bob hit the transmission fluid and spun, ending his chance for a good starting spot in the Grand Prix.

Earl and Connie Jones came out Sunday to lend moral support. What I needed was better luck. Early in the Grand Prix, my generator seized when the field coils came apart and wrapped around the

Nice shot entering Riverside's turn six. It must have been in early practice, as the stands are empty. Dave Friedman used to sell these pictures to us racers for a buck. He still sells them, but the price has gone up.
Dave Friedman

armature. This in turn stopped the water pump and my race. As a small consolation, I got to see the rest of the Grand Prix as a spectator.

A. J. Foyt was amazing in the John Mecom–entered Hussein, a car named in honor of King Hussein of Jordan, a friend of Mecom's family. It was an ill-conceived monster created by mating a 426 Hemi Chrysler engine with a Cooper Monaco chassis. It had a custom aluminum body built by Jack Lane, one of the aluminum-shaping experts who had put the first Cobra Coupe body together at Shelby American. I think it took Foyt to drive that thing because he didn't know any better. The Hussein DNF'd because of a fuel leak, but it was spectacular while it ran.

Several other promising cars dropped out. Dan Gurney's Lotus 19 Ford was making good progress toward the front when he stopped with suspension problems. Front row starters McLaren and Hansgen quit with water and oil leaks, respectively. Miles' Cobra roadster broke an axle, ending his race.

Of the King Cobras, only Ronnie Bucknam's car didn't make it to the finish line. I never asked Ken why he chose to drive a Cobra when, with his position in the company, he certainly could have had a King Cobra.

I'm waiting on the grid for the start of the qualifying race. Beside me is the Elva Porsche of John Cannon. *John Morton Collection*

Ole Olsen, Earl Jones, and my pregnant wife, Jan, waiting for me as I prepare for the 1964 Los Angeles Times Grand Prix. *John Morton Collection*

Turn six with Don Wester No. 60 Genie MK 10 Ford, me, Charles Cox in the ex–Dave MacDonald King Cobra No. 39, and Rick Muther in his Lotus 23 No. 111. *Dave Friedman*

He'd never shied away from fast cars. Maybe he just didn't like the Coopers; he had driven them.

Bob Bondurant did an excellent job of coming from the back, finally passing up-and-coming Indy car driver Bobby Unser to finish fifth. Unser was driving the Frank Arciero–owned Lotus 19 that Dan Gurney had been so dominant in, now with Chevrolet power replacing the 2.5-liter Coventry Climax engine.

Jim Clark took third in the Lotus 30. He may have been the only driver in the world who could have done that well with such a poor car. Roger Penske was second, as he was the previous year behind Dave MacDonald, the only car on the same lap as the winner. But the star was first-place Parnelli Jones, who had shown everyone that he was even better than they thought he was.

Carroll's deal to have Parnelli drive the King Cobra at Riverside almost fell apart over tires. Carroll was a Goodyear distributor. He could get Parnelli any Goodyear tire he wanted. But Parnelli sold Firestones. They made a deal: whichever tire was fastest, Parnelli would run. He tried them both and got a better time with the Firestones, so Firestones it would be for the race.

Yet when he got to the track Sunday morning, Parnelli's car was shod with Goodyears. He told the crew, "If you don't put the Firestones back on, I'm not running." I'm not sure whose bright idea

Ken Miles always tried hard. In the 1964 Los Angeles Times Grand Prix at Riverside, he stood no chance of beating the pure racing cars but he wasn't deterred until a rear hub broke. *Bob Tronolone*

it was to switch the tires, but Parnelli called the bluff and beat the field on his brand.

Hugh Dibley won the under-2-liter class, and, surprisingly, Californian Rick Muther finished second in his Lotus 23.

The following weekend was the Monterey Grand Prix. Most of the same teams that had run Riverside traveled north to Laguna Seca. Ole, Helene, Jan, and I towed the Lotus 23 the 340 miles from Los Angeles, hoping to improve on the poor performance and bad luck we'd had at Riverside. The Shelby team entered just three King Cobras and the Lang Cooper for this race. Richie Ginther had either quit or been fired over a temper tantrum at Riverside during or immediately after the race. His '64 King Cobra was given to Ronnie Bucknum, and the '63 ex-Holbert car Ronnie ran at Riverside was parked.

This race was to be run in two heats of 100 miles each with roughly two hours between them. It became obvious pretty early that it was not going to be easy even to make the race for an under-2-liter car. I was trying to monitor my competitors' practice times. Jan, who was now carrying her excess baggage prominently out front, had learned to use a stopwatch. I was doing something on the car, which was jacked up in the pit lane. I saw Charlie Hayes in his Elva Porsche exiting turn nine, heading for the start-finish line. I yelled to Jan, "Quick, time Hayes!"

She ran to get a better view of the track, tripped over the jack handle and fell face and stomach down on the asphalt. She seemed to be all right, just a little skinned up, but what about the baby? Jan believed she hadn't done any real damage but we couldn't be sure. This was the second near disaster in just over a week. Fortunately there were no more races before Jan's due date in December.

I wasn't able to find enough speed to make the race, so I had to run the consolation with several other under-2-liter cars and a few over-2-liter cars. I don't remember how many cars from the consolation race would transfer to the Grand Prix. I do remember that I was trying very hard when I overshot the braking point into the corkscrew turn, skidded across the track, and planted myself deeply into the hay bales that lined the outside of the left-hand turn. I destroyed the nose of my car, ending my race and my season on a very low note.

Roger Penske in the Chaparral was on the pole with Dan Gurney second and the amazing Parnelli Jones third, again the fastest King Cobra driver in spite of the fact that this was only his second sports car race. I wondered how Bondurant and Bucknum dealt with this, but that is a question you can't even ask a friend.

At the start, Penske took the lead with Gurney second and Jones third. After a few laps, Jones spun on someone's oil, losing lots of positions. He was quickly moving up through the field and had passed his teammates when he crashed in turn two. Apparently there was some kind of mechanical problem as he entered the very fast turn, crashing into the hay bales that lined the outside. The car burned, igniting the hay bales, which smoldered for a very long time. Parnelli escaped unharmed.

Roger Penske won both heats with Gurney second. Bob Bondurant was third and Ronnie Bucknum fourth. This race marked the conclusion of the Shelby American King Cobra/ Cooper program. The

My first racing crash occurred at Laguna Seca after braking too late at the corkscrew. It made the paper but not in the way I would have liked. *John Morton Collection*

team had, in 1963, taken a nearly obsolete Cooper Monaco, installed a 289 Ford V-8 engine, and beaten the fastest sports racers of the period three out of four times in the two most lucrative sports car races in the world: the Los Angeles Times Grand Prix and the Monterey Grand Prix.

Although the Shelby-modified Cooper Monacos arguably represented the last time Cooper Cars were dominant in a major race series, they did win a couple of Formula One races afterward, one in 1966 and one in 1967. But the impact that Cooper had on auto racing can't be overstated. Shortly after World War II, Charles Cooper and his son John began constructing race cars in Charles' gas station garage. Because of the scarcity of money and the lack of any sort of race car industry in England right after the war, the resourceful Coopers built their cars using front suspensions salvaged from the 1930s-designed Fiat Topolino at both ends of their minimal little open-wheel racer. They powered the cars with 500cc motorcycle engines installed behind the driver. The cars became so popular that most of the best postwar British drivers honed their skills in these rudimentary racers.

When Cooper started building full-scale race cars in the mid-1950s, they didn't follow other race car manufacturers. The Coopers employed a designer named Owen Maddox, a trained engineer and part-time jazz musician. Maddox' designs, maintaining the rear-mounted engine layout of the original 500cc motorcycle-engined cars, dominated Formula One in 1959 and 1960, making Jack Brabham World Champion in those years.

Parnelli Jones at Laguna Seca one week after winning the Los Angeles Times Grand Prix at Riverside. He was running a strong third ahead of his teammates when he crashed in turn two from an undetermined cause. The car was so destroyed that it was thrown away. *Bob Tronolone*

In 1961 Brabham brought a modified version of the Maddox-designed championship-winning T 53 Cooper Formula One car to Indianapolis. Brabham finished ninth in the vastly underpowered car, setting the stage for a complete revision in Indy car design philosophy.

Quickly other British teams followed Cooper's lead and built rear-engine Formula One cars. Designers like Colin Chapman (Lotus), Eric Broadly (Lola), and Tony Rudd (BRM) advanced the art beyond Cooper's somewhat crude designs. By 1964 Cooper was no longer a team to be reckoned with, though their designs were still influencing competitors. Carroll Shelby with Dave MacDonald and Parnelli Jones wrote a final American chapter in the Cooper's legacy.

A small bit of irony relative to Shelby's Cobras and the Cooper 500 Formula Three cars: the transverse leaf front and rear suspensions on the John Tojeiro–designed AC/Cobra chassis were pretty much just scaled-up versions of the Fiat Topolino suspension used on the very first Coopers.

Buddies with a Big-Block?

Earl Jones had become my closest friend. We worked side by side at Shelby's as low-level fabricators and wannabe professional race drivers. We lived under the same roof, as did our race cars in adjoining garages. Earl had won the 1964 Pacific Division SCCA C Production championship, allowing him to compete in the end-of-the-year American Road Race of Champions at Riverside in early November.

The C Production class was comprised of Lotus Super 7s and the new Lotus Elans. The only non-Lotus in the race was the Morgan Super Sport of Earl Jones. It didn't look very promising for Earl. Carroll Shelby had come out to watch the Cobras in the A Production race, so I took it upon myself to ask Carroll as the C Production cars were gridded on the track, "Do you see that Morgan, the only non-Lotus in the race?"

"Yes," Carroll answered. "I see it."

I said, "That's Earl Jones. He works for you in the shop and he is going to win this race."

I really didn't believe that myself, but as the race progressed, Earl kept passing Lotuses until there were no more to pass. I was very happy for him, but I don't think Carroll even noticed. To him, good drivers were a dime a dozen and he could have nearly anyone he wanted. He wasn't running a talent contest.

Ed Leslie won the A Production race with Bob Johnson second and poor Dick Guldstrand third as he continued to soldier on in his Corvette Stingray.

Back at the shop, shortly after Earl's Riverside victory, Earl, Allen Grant, and I were given the job of driving to Los Angeles International Airport and picking up four Cobra Coupes. They had arrived from Europe on a Slick Airways DC6. All four of them were painted in the old Viking Blue team color. One of them appeared to be brand new and not quite finished. Another was the stretched one that had been built to accept a big-block engine. The nose was damaged but it had not been run.

The three of us picked out a car and posed with it pretending, "This is the car I'm going to be driving," as Dave Friedman took our picture to prove our claims.

The Coupes were brought into the race shop and each of the four cars was assigned to a chief mechanic and a helper. The Coupe that had been stretched was temporarily stored because they hadn't decided what to do with it. It was not one of the four cars being read-ied for the 1965 Daytona and Sebring efforts.

One night Earl and I were over at the Carter Street building where the 427 Coupe was stored. The car's fate seemed to be in limbo because it just wasn't practical to take on a new project in the shop with all the work to be done before the 1965 season opener at Daytona in February.

That's when Earl and I cooked up the stupidest idea anyone at Shelby American had ever thought of. The two of us would take the 427 Coupe home to our one-car garages, install free of charge a 427 engine that Shelby would provide, and, voilà, a fifth team car at hardly any cost to Shelby American or Ford. Naturally Earl and I would drive the car free of charge. It goes without saying our scheme didn't make it to first base. To this day I'm still astounded by my immaturity back then.

Next Generation

On December 10 I took my wife to her scheduled routine appoint-ment with her obstetrician. The doctor told us it would be at least another two weeks before the baby would arrive. That evening Jan started having pains in her abdomen. She thought it was gas. About midnight the pains had intensified to the point that I was getting very scared. She was adamant that it was not the baby. I got her into the car and drove my practiced emergency route to Santa Monica

Hospital. At the emergency entrance, they put Jan on a stretcher as she protested, "I'm not having the baby." I heard a nurse say, "Not having a baby? Look at those contractions."

They wheeled her inside, and I went to the waiting room. About 5:30 a.m. someone told me I had a daughter and could see her in a little while. I'd never seen a newborn before. It wasn't pretty. Her head was pointed and she was red. They promised all that would change and it did. I was allowed in to see Jan, and she was still pretty dopey but I thought she looked beautiful. I asked if she knew what she had and she said, "Yes, puppies." I laughed and she got embarrassed. "I mean kittens," she responded. She was serious. It is one of my fondest memories of her. We named the baby Leah after a Roy Orbison song. Jan has always denied that is where the name came from, but it did. I sure as hell would not have named her after Rachael's ugly sister in the Bible.

I understand that some race drivers were reluctant to get married and start a family while they were still racing. I've never been sure if it was because they were noble enough not to take the chance of leaving a widow and fatherless children behind or they didn't want a woman pushing them to quit. Or if it was because they were having too much fun to be saddled with the responsibility. In the case of my new family, it just sort of happened.

A few days before Leah was born, *The Turd* with Ken Miles driving made its debut as well as its swan song at Nassau. Nassau was

Allen Grant, myself, and Earl Jones (left to right) picked up four Cobra Coupes after they had cleared customs at LAX. We pretended to pick out our cars for the 1965 season. The car on the right had been stretched to accommodate a 427 engine. It never ran in this configuration. *Dave Friedman*

an end-of-the-year event that was nearly as much a party as it was a race. It took place over several days and counted for nothing much other than bragging rights. I didn't see it in person, but Ken was very fast in his creation. The goal with *The Turd* was to beat the Corvette Grand Sport, the semi-secret Zora Arkus-Duntov backdoor General Motors hot rod that only looked like a Corvette Stingray. Ken led the first race until the aluminum 390 big-block blew. A 427 was installed, but the car failed again, ending its short life as a Shelby team car.

When *The Turd* returned from Nassau, it wasn't alone. It was accompanied by two even more unsuccessful cars, the products of an infinitely more extensive and expensive project than the "in-house" *Turd* effort. They were two Ford GT 40s—so far, the failed collaboration between Ford, Lola, and the John Wyer racing team. Because it was Ford's money, Ford had control of the project. They decided to give Shelby a crack at running them. Carroll Shelby hired Carroll Smith to manage the two-car team. Carroll Smith was eventually given the name Scattershit—Scat, for short. He was smart with good technical skills, but his work habits in the shop left something to be desired. Daytona was in late February, leaving only a couple of months in which to test and improve the cars to the point that they would be competitive with the Ferraris.

This is the last Cobra Coupe chassis as it is being prepared to accept a 427-cubic-inch engine. I'm welding something while Lynn Brewer, Bill Eaton, and another mechanic fit the engine. When it returned from Italy after receiving its body, it sat in limbo and never ran in 427 configuration. *Dave Friedman*

Ken Miles in # 98--the flip-top 427 Cobra hot rod affectionately known as "The Turd"--lines up with Roger Penske's Corvette Grand Sport of at the Nassau Speed Weeks in December 1964. Miles led off the start but the Cobra didn't last long and Penske won. *Dave Friedman*

Ride for a Kiss?

Shelby American planned to run six cars at Daytona: four Cobra Daytona Coupes and the two GT 40s. The preparation of the Daytona Coupes was well underway when the GT 40s arrived. I was assigned to help Mike Donovan on one of the cars. Mike was not as experienced as some of the other crew chiefs, but he worked hard, having moved to the racing team from the production car group. At the September Road America race, Mike took care of our No. 97 that won the race, but this was the first time that he was designated the official crew chief. Allen Grant was assigned as crew chief on the car that he was scheduled to drive at Daytona. His second mechanic was Dennis Gragg, who was more of a body man than a mechanic. Allen was very excited about getting his first chance to drive on the team. He was intent on making his car the best.

I was hoping to get to drive one of the Coupes too. Carroll had a chart on his office wall with all of the team cars listed. Opposite each car was a space for the driver's names to be filled in. Every day I would go upstairs and look at the list. Most of the drivers' names were filled in but not all of them. I lobbied as best I could, but every day there was no John Morton on the wall. Finally there was only one vacant spot left.

In the race shop, Fridays were like any other day. Upstairs, however, things got very casual with the office staff. The day often ended at the Black Whale, a bar/restaurant just a few blocks west on Washington Boulevard. I went up the back stairs that led from the hallway to the offices. Al Dowd had the well-deserved reputation as a womanizer and this day he was living up to his legend when I opened the door into the office suite. As I entered, there was Al locked in an embrace with one of the more attractive ladies of the office. She sprung from his arms upon seeing me as I sheepishly retreated down the stairs and into the race shop where I continued working on the disc grinder.

After a few minutes Al came down and approached me.

"John, you know not to say anything about what you just saw up there, don't you?"

"Oh sure," I smiled. After a pause of a second or two, I added, "Al, I sure do want to drive at Daytona."

Al said, "I'm going to have a meeting with Shelby tonight. I'll try."

As he walked away, I said, "Al?" He turned around. "Try real hard."

I was totally kidding, but to this day, I'm not at all sure that Al knew that. A day or two later, my name was on the wall as a Daytona driver. Then, a few days after that, my name was replaced by Jo Schlesser's. Carroll told me that it was politics, that Ford of France had pulled strings with Ford to get their driver a ride at Daytona. I've always suspected that Al Dowd got Carroll to put my name on the chart because he was afraid I'd blow the whistle on him. Oh well, I was pretty excited for a day or two.

Actually, "Oh well" wasn't how I really felt. I wonder if Carroll thought that because I got married and then had a child at my age it was an indication that I wasn't that serious about racing. It may have indicated a lack of maturity but not a lack of commitment to racing. Hell, it takes some level of immaturity to want to be a race driver in the first place. Carroll didn't seem to have a very good handle on what marriage meant anyway.

904 Lotus

After my race at Monterey, it was clear that my Lotus would have to have a different, more powerful engine if I was going to compete successfully in the under-2-liter class. There were three possible choices as I saw it: the 2-liter Coventry Climax, the BMW, or the Porsche.

My friend Bruce Burness had left Shelby American early in the 1964 season. Bruce was developing a pattern of not sticking around very long at any normal job, or any abnormal one either. He was taking on the odd fabrication job in the garage of his parents' home in Pasadena. When George Follmer, the "He can't be a serious racer if he put a Corvair engine in his Lotus 23" guy, approached Bruce to build a larger gas tank for his car, Bruce said, "I won't waste my time working on a car with a Corvair engine. If you want to remove the Corvair and install a Porsche, we can talk." George took Bruce up on the offer and soon the Follmer/Burness Lotus Porsche was born. I followed the project as something I might want to copy.

Mike Donovan and I continued working on the Coupe, as did the crews on the other three cars. Meanwhile, Earl Jones had decided that his next step toward a career as a professional race driver would be to sell his Morgan and move up to formula car racing. The SCCA was initiating a new class for 1965 called Formula B. The cars were similar to the old Formula Junior cars but with more powerful 1,600cc engines. In 1964 the best source to shop for used race cars was *Competition Press*. Ian Raby Racing in England always had a number of formula cars advertised; Earl decided to give them a call. A call to England from California was very expensive in 1965 but there was a way around this problem. The pay phone in the hallway was still rejecting quarters, or rather ejecting them and making calls free. I learned later that the phone-rigging bandit wasn't Mahlon, as rumor held. It was Ellis Taylor, a former phone company employee. Earl and I made a plan.

Earl came to work equipped with eight quarters. At our morning break he would make the call. The first quarter reached the operator and was returned. She placed the call. Someone at Ian Raby Racing answered. Earl started discussing some of the cars he'd seen advertised. The conversation seemed to go on for a long time considering he was talking to someone in England. I'd never seen anyone talk to England on a phone before; it must be getting expensive. Jack Balch, our shop foreman, told us it was time to go back to work.

I said, "We'll be finished in a minute. Earl's talking to someone in England."

Finally the conversation ended and Earl hung up. On a pay phone back then the operator called back immediately to collect charges. She told Earl, "You talked for twelve minutes. Please deposit fifty-three dollars."

Earl said, "OK." He whispered to me, "Fifty-three dollars."

I did some quick figuring. "Holy shit," I said. "That is two hundred and twelve quarters."

Earl started plugging in quarters eight at a time. I scooped them out of the coin return and handed them back to him.

After quite a while Jack approached again, "Come on, you guys. Back to work."

"Give us just a couple more minutes," I said.

Finally we had circulated 212 quarters through the faulty machine. The operator said, "Thank you," and Earl hung up. We went back to work.

Earl eventually bought an engineless formula car from England called an MRD, which stood for Motor Racing Developments. It was a very early car built by Jack Brabham and his designer, Ron Tauranac. The story goes that a prominent French journalist pointed out to Brabham that saying MRD sounded to a Frenchman very much like *merde*, the French word for *shit*. The name was soon changed to Brabham.

My long search for a more powerful 2-liter engine to replace the 1,600cc Lotus Twin Cam in my Lotus 23 had finally ended. The Coventry Climax engine had been ruled out because parts were scarce and expensive. I'd gone to see Porsche and BMW dealer Vasek Polak about getting a race-tuned BMW engine, but he said he couldn't help me.

Bruce Burness had finished the job of replacing the ill-conceived 2-liter Corvair engine in George Follmer's Lotus 23 with a Porsche 904 engine. It was a very big job, requiring extensive frame modification. On the positive side, the 904 Porsche engine was nearly as powerful as any 2-liter engine, very reliable, and parts were readily available.

I went to see Otto Zipper, a Ferrari and Porsche dealer who had been running a Porsche 904 for driver Scooter Patrick. He said he would sell me a spare engine they had, less carburetors, for $3,100. Shelby had a stock of the 48mm Weber carburetors used on the competition Cobras. I bought a pair for the discounted price of $46 apiece. Earl bought my Lotus engine for his Formula B MRD.

In my single-car garage still in Shelby work clothes, I am installing the 904 Porsche engine in my Lotus 23. The Lotus frame is widened and the motor mounts are welded in. *John Morton Collection*

I purchased a used welding set from shop foreman Jack Balch and, after work at Shelby American, started the daunting project of replicating the Burness/Follmer car in my single-car garage.

Comic Bombs

I never quite understood why there was such an attraction to explosions at Shelby American. It seemed like a disproportionate number of mechanics, fabricators, etc. were bent on setting off large firecrackers and other explosive devices, usually with the goal of terrifying someone. Often it seemed just for the thrill of making an awesome amount of noise. I remember Charlie Agapiou tossing either a cherry bomb or an M-80 (very powerful fire crackers equal to a quarter stick of dynamite) under a Cobra on jack stands while Ted Sutton was working under the car. Ted came out from under the car in a rage. His watch's expansion band had been damaged and he was ready to fight. Ted really wasn't a violent man so his anger at Charlie soon dissipated.

Once Dave MacDonald filled one of the large side exhaust pipes from his Cobra with acetylene gas from a welding torch while it was off of the car sitting on a workbench. When the gas was ignited it gave a very nice report.

From time to time I was asked to make a batch of throttle linkage parts. One of the parts was comprised of a small-diameter steel tube about 6 inches long. A quarter-inch threaded stud had to be silver soldered into each end. I discovered accidentally that when the first stud was in place and the welding torch flame was passed over the still open other end of the tube, a fairly loud pop would occur. The small explosion was caused by residual acetylene in the tube being ignited. Naturally after this discovery, I had to make sure there was another pop from each piece I made, just to keep everybody on his toes.

Mahlon Lamoreaux, the jovial but devilish prankster machinist, gave me some guidance. He said, "If you want to make a really good explosion, get some bubble bath, put it in a bucket with about an inch of water. Then let the unlit torch blow bubbles until they reach the top of the bucket at which time you can ignite the bubbles."

I had no plan to actually do it—that is, until the next morning when I noticed Jan's bubble bath sitting on the bathtub as I got ready for work. I put some in a small bottle and took it to the shop. I found a green rubber bucket and then, per Mahlon's instructions, poured in an inch of water with the bubble bath and submerged the unlit torch in the water until the acetylene bubbles completely filled the bucket. No one in the shop noticed what I was doing.

I couldn't think of a proper fuse so decided to light the torch and, from about 3 feet away, lobbed it into the bucket. I wasn't prepared for the magnitude of the ensuing explosion, nor was anyone else. In shock, I saw a green circle of rubber where a second before, a bucket sat. One of my ears had stopped hearing and the owner of the building across the alley to the west ran from his upstairs office to see what disaster had taken place in his own building. Some of our office personal hurried down to see what had happened. I feared for my job.

The general attitude as I recall was "Boy, that was amazing!" Everyone went back to work as if nothing out of the ordinary had happened. My hearing returned to normal and, after a few days, the ringing stopped. I've always felt lucky that the first bucket I found was made of rubber.

What a Load!
Carroll Smith felt that much progress had been made on the GT 40s. Ken Miles, Bob Bondurant, and Richie Ginther had done a considerable amount of testing at Riverside. The modifications done at Shelby American seemed to be paying off. It was mid-February and time to load the cars for the 1965 Daytona Continental.

Unlike 1964, the race would include prototypes as well as GT cars. The race length would remain the same, 2,000 kilometers—approximately

The Ford GT40 draws a crowd at Riverside, likely during its first test. Shelby American never raced the car with wire wheels. Phil Remington (leaning on car in white shirt) talks to Ken Miles (in car). Behind Remington stands John and Jean Ohlsen. I have my hand on the front fender to the left of Remington. At the rear of the car is engine builder Jack Hoare (far right in photo) with Earl Jones (second from right).

1,220 miles. The coupes would be driven by Jo Schlesser/Harold Keck, Rick Muther/John Timanus, Bob Johnson/Tom Payne, and Allen Grant/Ed Leslie. The GT 40s would be handled by Ken Miles, paired with Indy car driver Lloyd Ruby, in one car; Richie Ginther with Bob Bondurant in the other.

The open car hauler was parked near the Carter Street building just beyond the vacant dirt lot across from the Princeton Drive headquarters. The truck driver, who I recall was Bill Gene, was not present. He was getting some rest before the long trip to Florida. Normally the truck driver is responsible for loading the cars, but in his absence, I was chosen to do the job.

The cars had to be driven up the ramp, which was really no problem for the cars on the bottom. But the cars that had to go on the upper level presented a bit of a challenge because they were geared for the high-speed Daytona tri-oval with a 2.88:1 rear-end ratio. They had to be driven up the steep ramp without slipping the clutch. A damaged clutch would prove disastrous and require a change in Daytona before the race.

I lined the front wheels up with the bottom of the ramp and then accelerated hard without slipping the clutch. It was pretty scary but I

Me (hand on hip), Mike Donovan (hand behind neck), and Earl Jones, all staring in disbelief at the poor job Allen Grant did in loading the Daytona Coupe. He would do a better job driving it at Daytona with Ed Leslie. *Dave Friedman*

successfully loaded two cars on the top level. There was only one car to go, and it would be a tough one because as soon as it crested the top of the ramp, it had to stop immediately to keep from rear-ending the car in front of it.

That car was Allen Grant's. It was running a little late because unlike the other three coupes, it was receiving a color sanding and final polish. When it finally emerged from the Carter Street paint shop, it was beautiful. Dennis Gragg and Allen had succeeded in putting the other three Daytona Coupes to shame.

The car was positioned for loading.

I said, "Allen, I'm not going to load your car."

"Why not?" Allen responded.

"Because if I screw it up, you'll kill me."

I'd known Allen for two years, even roomed with him in 1963. We were good friends, but he could be volatile.

"OK," Allen said. "I'll load it myself."

He removed one work shoe to reach the pedals more easily. He hadn't watched the loading because he had been in the paint shop putting the finishing touches to his car. I told him, "Line the front wheels up with the bottom of the ramp, then really gas it. Don't slip the clutch, but be ready to brake hard at the top or you'll hit the car in front."

Several of us watched as Allen lined the front wheels up with the ramp. But then he inexplicably backed up about 10 feet before charging forward. He hit the ramp hard but his alignment was off. The right side wheels rode up on the outer edge of the right ramp and about halfway up, the left wheels ran off the inside of the left ramp. The car fell between the two ramps and was prevented from falling to the ground by the half-inch rod that crossed between the two ramps to keep them parallel.

Phil Remington yelled to Allen, "Don't get out of the car!" He feared that if the rod holding it up broke as Allen was exiting the car, he would be seriously injured. Allen was in a state of shock. He jumped out of the car and in a frenzy ran in circles in the vacant damp dirt lot, one shoe on, one shoe off, kicking up a rooster tail of mud. Even as I envied his Daytona ride, at that moment, I was glad I was me.

The shop emptied. Everyone helped or at least watched as a forklift was pressed into service to rescue the poor car. Damage was minimal. The nose was quickly repaired and then sprayed in gray primer. The color would have to be applied at the track. When it was ready to travel, I loaded it successfully, a very small consolation prize.

I really wanted to go to Daytona. All was not lost because my parents were visiting my grandmother and other relatives in Savannah and they all wanted to see our new baby. We coordinated a trip with Jan and Leah to Savannah that coincided with the Daytona race. The relatives could play with the baby while I drove to Daytona. My plan was to help the team if needed and see if I might somehow get in the race. I had only seen the track as a college student.

Hoping for an Opening

I carefully studied the entry list looking for a possible vacancy. This time I had my driving gear and license with me. As practice began my attention was drawn to a Ferrari GTO that I had noticed on the entry. Its owner and driver was a Peter Clarke from England. I'd never heard of him but he seemed to be without a co-driver. I introduced myself as a Shelby American driver who was not driving for the team here. He seemed interested but said NASCAR had chosen a driver for him and although he wasn't totally comfortable with the choice, he had to at least give the man a try. The driver's name was Rene Charland from Massachusetts, a champion in NASCAR's Sportsman division, primarily short-track oval racing. I watched closely as he began his practice laps. He drove the GTO with a cigar clenched between his teeth. I assumed it was some sort of trademark or superstition.

Mr. Charland must have been briefed on the importance of downshifting to help slow a road racing car before entering a turn because as he crossed the start-finish line on the tri-oval at 170 miles per hour, he downshifted. The engine screamed in protest as the rear wheels lost traction, sending the red GTO pirouetting down the track toward turn one. Mr. Clarke was not pleased. Mr. Charland missed hitting anything and continued. He spun again but, undaunted, kept going.

I could only see the tri-oval section as the cars entered turn one, but each time the car approached the braking point, the engine revs soared. He finally returned to the pits, cigar still in place. I was pretty sure Rene Charland had failed his driver test. Mr. Clarke was encouraging as I gave him my hotel and room number. I'm sure Rene Charland was a very worthy NASCAR Sportsman driver; this just wasn't his cup of tea.

I was told I would need to get a NASCAR license before I would be allowed to race. I went to the NASCAR office and said to a lady behind a counter, "I'd like to get a NASCAR license. Is this the place?"

She replied, "Yes, this is the place. What kind of license do you want?"

I didn't understand and asked, "What kinds are there?"

"Well," she said, "we have crew licenses and we have driver licenses."

"I want a driver license," I answered.

"What kind of driver?" she asked.

"What do you mean?" I asked, a little confused.

"Are you a Modified Sportsman, a Sportsman, or a Grand National driver?"

"Grand National," I said.

She handed me a form. "Fill this out. That will be fifteen dollars." NASCAR was a little looser back then.

I was now ready for the phone call from Peter Clarke as I sat in my room. It never came. I finally was able to contact him, but he'd arranged a deal with Charlie Hayes. John Timanus was uncomfortable with the high speed on the Daytona banking (over 180 miles per hour). I hoped he would relinquish his ride to me, but he didn't. I was running out of possibilities.

Shelby American had a total of 12 drivers for this race and not a single one was interested in Ken Miles' early morning run. Actually I'm not sure he asked any of them, least of all his co-driver Lloyd Ruby. Ken knew that sort of thing wouldn't appeal to Ruby, so again I found myself at 22 trying to keep up with a 46-year-old man as we ran on Daytona Beach.

The 1042 Princeton Drive race shop shortly before the move to Los Angeles International Airport. It's plain to see that Shelby American had outgrown the building as cars, including a GT 40, are prepared for the 1965 season. *Road & Track* Collection

It rained in one of the practice sessions. Miles was learning how the GT 40 felt in wet conditions. He had a very scary high-speed spin on the banking in plain view of the pits. Apparently it didn't bother Ken much as he continued running. I remember thinking at the time that a driver of his age would normally be slowing down, be more risk averse. But then Miles wasn't really very normal.

John Surtees and Pedro Rodriguez got the pole in their Ferrari, with Bondurant/Ginther second and Miles/Ruby third in GT 40s. Fourth was the white Ferrari of Walt Hansgen/David Piper, followed by the four Daytona Coupes.

At the start, the cars were to run one full lap on the banked stock car track, omitting the road course until the second lap at which time they would enter the road course. The two Ferraris and two GT 40s came by on the first lap in a tight pack, but as they reached the braking zone for the entry into the road course, Bondurant's GT 40 shot into the lead. It only lasted for a second or two as it appeared Bob forgot to brake. It must have been an "Oh shit!" moment for him as he blew through the traffic cones that the course workers quickly installed before the cars finished lap one on the banked track. No harm was done as Bob quickly reentered the course.

Dan Gurney in his 289-Ford-powered Lotus 19B never really showed his hand in practice or qualifying. He soon took the lead.

Gurney and Jerry Grant led until they finally dropped out with engine trouble. The race ended in darkness after more than 12 hours, with Miles and Ruby winning. Rookie crew chief Mike Donovan's Daytona Coupe, driven by Jo Schlesser and Harold Keck, was second and first in GT. Bob Bondurant and Richie Ginther drove their GT 40 to third.

Ironically, at least to me, the first Ferrari to finish was Peter Clarke's GTO in seventh place overall, and first in the obscure under-3-liter GT class. All of the Ferrari Prototypes failed to finish. Shelby American cars occupied positions first through sixth with only the Johnson/Payne Daytona Coupe failing to finish.

LA at Full Throttle

With the production of the GT 350 Mustang and the new 427 Cobra, Shelby American outgrew the Venice facilities. They hired Chuck Cantwell as chief engineer on the GT 350 Mustang. He was the same Chuck Cantwell that I got to know in 1963 when we were both racing in the SCCA, me in my Lotus 7, Chuck in his MGB. I didn't remember that he was an engineer. He worked for General Motors at that time.

The plan was to build the Mustang into a high-performance street car with one version, called the R Model, to be a race car for SCCA competition. Shelby intended to build lots of GT 350s. I still didn't think they looked much like race cars.

The new 1965 427 Cobra looked very similar to the 260/289 cars, except fatter. Some thought it looked more muscular, but to me it just

GT 350s: The GT 350Rs were built in the race car hangar at LAX. They were more extensively modified than the street models, which were built in the production hangar. *Road & Track* Collection

Here mounts for traction bars are welded into place. The SCCA had accepted Shelby's modifications and placed the cars in the B Production class of amateur racing. Road & Track *Collection*

looked fatter. The suspension had been designed in a computer at Ford. It seemed strange that a computer could design a suspension. It must have been a pretty smart computer because it did away with the antique transverse leaf springs and replaced them with modern coil springs. The suspension geometry was also completely revised.

Ken Miles took me for a ride on the street in a big fat red one. When he got on it hard, the rear seemed to squat a lot. The 427 rocketed forward at an unrealistic speed for a street car. These babies could hurt someone; I was sure they were going to.

Right after Daytona, we were moving into two huge hangars at Los Angeles International Airport. The address was 6501 West Imperial Highway. One hangar housed the racing team, as well as the department responsible for building the racing version of the GT 350—the GT 350R. The second hangar contained the assembly line for the street GT 350s. The hangars were about 200 feet apart and separated from the runways by a concrete bunker that created a wide protected area between the hangars and the airport proper. This area would be used to store cars. It also provided a lane on which completed Mustangs and 427 Cobras could be given a brief shakedown run before delivery.

It took quite a few days to complete the move. One that sticks in my mind is the day that all of the completed 289 production Cobras that were stored in the Carter Street building had to be driven to the new facility about 7 miles away, about 15 cars as I recall. I believe these cars were the last 289s ever produced. Five drivers were assigned the task of driving the Cobras. Earl Jones and I were among them. Don Pike would follow in a van, pick the five drivers up at LAX and return us to Venice for another five Cobras. The five of us weren't chosen for our driving skill; it was more like, "We need five guys, how about you, you, you, you, and you." Earl and I were the only ones from the racing department; the other three were from the production side.

They couldn't have found a group of drivers more likely to cause a catastrophe if they'd recruited 16-year-olds on speed. I was by far the most responsible of the bunch and Earl was at least a good driver, but the other three yahoos were serious accidents looking for a place to happen. There was over a mile of open road on Lincoln Boulevard before it merged onto Sepulveda. I was going about 80 while the four Cobras in front of me were pulling away as though I were standing still. I had to laugh out loud at the incredible sight and sound of four Cobras at full throttle and probably 140 miles per hour on a Los Angeles street in the middle of the morning.

Each stoplight, when it went green, signaled a go-for-broke drag race as other drivers and pedestrians watched dumbfounded. There is a long tunnel on Sepulveda where the road passes beneath one of the LAX runways. The sound of Earl passing me inside of it was amazing. The tunnel was dark and Earl told me that when he had let up and started to brake as he reached daylight at the end of the tunnel, he glanced at the speedometer as it was sinking below 115 miles per hour.

All this times three and not even a speeding ticket. They were four lucky speed drunk idiots getting away with murder. Except for Earl; he wasn't an idiot.

Change and Wondering

It didn't take long after the move to the airport to notice that the atmosphere at Shelby American had changed, and it wasn't the smell of jet fuel. It was the smell that occurs when a small company has been absorbed into a much larger company, in this case, the Ford Motor Company.

From time to time, Ford people were ushered through the shop in Venice, usually by tour guide Carroll Shelby. I credit Garry Koike for naming them The Fairlaners, as they sometimes had the appearance of a 1960s singing group with their tidy, dark red blazers. But now there was much more of a corporate intrusiveness as Ford increased its stake in Shelby American, largely the result of Shelby's receiving the GT 40 program and from expansion of Mustang GT 350 production. We were given badges that we had to wear to gain access to the premises. The office suites above the production hangar were soon occupied by people who seemed very far removed from the car people in the race and production departments. Even Carroll Shelby's presence seemed diminished.

The Sebring 12-hour, almost exactly one month after Daytona, would be the first race run out of the new facility. Some of the driver assignments were changed. In the GT 40s, Ken Miles would drive with Bruce McLaren, and Richie Ginther with Phil Hill. In the Daytona Coupes, Allen Grant and Ed Leslie would remain together, as would Bob Johnson and Tom Payne, but now Bob Bondurant would be paired with Jo Schlesser and Lew Spencer with California SCCA racer Jim Adams.

I wondered what criteria Carroll used to make his driver choices. Outside of the regulars—Miles, Bondurant, Leslie, and Johnson—he seemed to have a fairly arbitrary selection process. I used to think he was looking for another Dave MacDonald, but whatever he was looking for, it was becoming clear that he hadn't found it in me.

I was starting to feel anonymous, not sure what my purpose was anymore. I think Earl probably felt that way too, but it didn't seem to bother him as much. Maybe because he had never really been on the team as I had, he wasn't feeling a sense of change as much. On Princeton Drive, I never looked forward to the workday being over, but at the airport, I did. Earl and I would race one another home on the twisty road that ran behind the west end of the LAX runways.

Blizzard in a Coupe!
Donn Allen worked for Jim Hall on his Chaparrals in Texas before coming to Shelby American. He had been involved in constructing the Daytona Coupes almost from the beginning and was now the team manager of that contingent. He installed air jacks in the Coupes for 1965 as well as a fire system comprised of a large extinguisher mounted vertically just to the right of the transmission tunnel. If there was a fire in the cockpit, a driver simply had to hit a button on the top of the extinguisher to activate the system.

The air jacks were to be activated by high-pressure air or nitrogen being applied to the system by a mechanic during a pit stop. The mechanic would attach a hose to a fitting at the rear top of a front fender and the car would rise so tires could be more quickly changed.

The first time the system was tested in the shop, the rear of the car slowly rose, simulating the movement of an old, tired hound dog. The front never quite made it. The system was going to need some work. Eventually it was perfected. The heavier nose of the car would require a different size jack cylinder. At least that's what I remember. It may have just been an increase in pressure.

Before Sebring, Donn decided that the fire system should also be tested. I was picked to be the tester—I guess I can't say I was always overlooked to fill a driver's seat. The car was sitting on the shop floor in the large hangar. I covered my nose and mouth with a bandana made from a red shop rag and got in the car. Before the door closed, I was cautioned that I wouldn't be able to breathe until I exited the car once the system was activated.

Several people had gathered around the car to watch the test. I hit the button. The world went white. I reached for the door mechanism to extricate myself when I realized I couldn't find it in the whiteness. The permanently fixed plastic windows were no longer transparent so the people watching couldn't see that I was in trouble. Worse yet, there were no door handles on the outside of a Cobra Coupe. Just as I was about ready to pass out from holding my breath for so long, I found the door latch and opened the door.

I got out and started to run. I couldn't grasp why it was still white. I knew if it was white, I still couldn't breathe. I was confused and out of air. How could the huge hangar have filled with the white powder? I had to breathe. I tried and I could. Everyone was laughing. I realized that the reason I thought I couldn't breathe after getting out of the car was because my glasses were covered in extinguisher powder.

After the test, I asked Donn, "Why did you have to test a fire extinguisher that you knew would work?"

Donn said, "We wanted to know if the stuff was toxic before we risked an important driver."

I'm pretty sure he was kidding, but I was getting a little sensitive. I laughed anyway.

Sebring 1965 was the first anniversary of my first professional race. This year I didn't even entertain the hope of going, much less driving. Sebring had always been special to me, but this year it was a little depressing. I wondered if I'd ever get to race there again.

The rules were changed for 1965 to allow unlimited engine displacement sports racing cars to compete with the prototypes and the GTs. Jim Hall entered two Chaparrals, John Mecom entered a new

Lola T 70, and Dan Gurney entered his old Lotus 19B powered by Ford; all in the fastest class.

The Chaparrals qualified first and second, the GT 40s third and fourth. There was no way a GT 40 stood a chance of beating the Chaparral, which was an all-out race car, unless the Chaparrals had problems. As it turned out, everyone but the front-running Chaparral of Jim Hall and Hap Sharp had problems because of a torrential rainstorm. They weathered the storm and won with the Miles/McLaren GT 40 second. Bob Bondurant and Jo Schlesser won the GT class in the Daytona Coupe as all of the Shelby American entries finished except for the Phil Hill/Richie Ginther GT 40.

Pipe, Meet Calf

A large number of new 427 Cobras had been delivered and were stored on the apron between the hangars and the bunker. These cars were to be built as race cars to satisfy the FIA's requirement for homologation or certification for international racing in the GT or Grand Touring category. At least a hundred cars had to be built, their construction verified by the FIA inspectors. In April the FIA officials would give

A fresh Daytona Coupe ready for its trip to Europe to contest the 1965 World Manufacturer's Championship waits on the concrete apron outside the race shop at LAX. In the background are unfinished 427 Cobras destined to become race cars. Behind the Cobras, GT 350s to be. *Dave Friedman*

Shelby American a visit to confirm the existence of a hundred cars. The cars didn't have to be finished. The manufacturer just had to show proof that a hundred cars were in process. There had been only about 50 cars delivered from AC Cars in England and most of them had no engines, transmission, or paint yet.

The 427 Cobra project seemed to be low priority until the pending arrival of the FIA. Many of the cars that had been sitting forlorn outside on the apron were moved into the hangar. Every warm body in the shop was pretending to be hard at work preparing the cars so that when the FIA inspectors filed through, they would be impressed. They may have been impressed, but they weren't fooled. The homologation request was denied.

When the GTO was homologated in 1961, Ferrari had duped the FIA. Only 39 cars were ever built, but Ferrari convinced the FIA that there would be a hundred by using large gaps in their serial numbers. They tried to scam the inspectors again with their new mid-engine 250 LM in 1964. That time their ploy failed. Ferrari built 32 250 LMs.

Denied FIA certification, the 427 competition cars were being turned out at a very slow pace. Demand from amateur racers was also weak. When a car was finished, it was given a brief test run up and down the apron between the hangars and the bunker. Bill Eve was given this job. Bill had come to Shelby American from Florida in pursuit of a career as a professional race driver. He was a friend of mine, but a better friend of Earl's, and would help Earl on his race car each night after work.

Bill Eve was the antithesis of Allen Grant. Where Allen's self-confidence rivaled, maybe even exceeded, that of Cassius Clay, Bill was the most self-effacing person I'd ever met. He exuded such a lack of self-confidence that I was never sure it was sincere. A reasonably large ego seemed to be a prerequisite for a race driver.

The competition 427 Cobras had large-diameter exhaust pipes on both sides of the car that ran along the rocker panels just below the doors, ending just before the front of the rear fenders. A driver usually knew how to take a wide step when exiting the car to avoid being burned by the hot exhaust. An inexperienced passenger had to be warned, but surely many were burned. After one of his early test runs when Bill exited the 427, he forgot about the hot pipe. His pant leg had ridden up exposing the calf on his left leg. As he sat there ready to stand up and leave the car, he said, "I smelled something burning before I realized it was my leg. I can thank my lightning fast race car driver reactions." He had a nasty divot burned in his calf.

Sorry

There was a new Cobra Coupe planned for the 427 Cobra chassis. Pete Brock had been in England overseeing the construction of the prototype he had designed. When it arrived, it was without any fanfare and was pushed into a small room in the race team hangar. No one who saw it was very complimentary. It did look a bit large and maybe a little ungainly, but then the first Cobra Coupe was not well received in the beginning either.

But things were different in 1965 from what they had been in 1963. The 427s were only a faint echo of the glory days of the original Shelby American Cobras turned out only two years prior. The 427 Super Coupe was never finished—a sad artifact of the fine work Pete Brock had accomplished for Shelby American. He had started in 1962 with high hopes of being a driver for Carroll Shelby. He became a test driver and the instructor at the Carroll Shelby School of High Performance Driving, where I sealed my commitment to be a race car driver with him as my mentor for the five days of instruction.

Too valuable to Shelby to be just another of many drivers, Pete designed the Cobra emblem and then the Daytona Coupe race car, which would be Shelby American's crowning achievement. Pete left the company not long after it became obvious to him that his latest project was of no interest to the people from Ford. They were calling the shots now.

Shelby American was going to Europe to contest the GT III World Manufacturing Championship. Ferrari wasn't planning a serious

Pete Brock designed a 427 Super Coupe, but Ford had no desire to continue funding the Cobra contingent of Shelby American, instead focusing only on the GT 40s. The Super Coupe was never completed until it was later sold to a collector. *Dave Friedman*

effort to defend their dominance of that class and was leaving it up to private teams running GTOs to deal with the Cobras. Ford's main interest was winning Le Mans with the GT 40s. Shelby Cobras in GT III were of secondary importance.

Ford made a serious effort to buy Ferrari in 1963, which Enzo Ferrari rejected in the 11th hour. This ignited a vendetta from Henry Ford II to defeat Ferrari at Le Mans and deprive them of an overall win. To this end, the GT 40 was born—a collaboration between Lola's Eric Broadly and Ford engineers.

Only Shelby's best people would be traveling to Europe to support the Cobras and GT 40s. I knew I was not one of them. Shop foreman Jack Balch was a good guy and I think he liked me, but one day he came to me and said I was being laid off. I thought there must be some mistake; they wouldn't do that to me. I don't remember who I pleaded my case to but it saved my job. I thought I was just caught up in a mass layoff by accident. There was no explanation given.

Jack was OK with the fact that I'd gone over his head to save my job. It likely wasn't his decision to let me go in the first place. It used to be obvious where decisions came from, but now with the ever-increasing bureaucracy, things were less straightforward.

Not really being a racing mechanic and not being involved with the production of the GT 350s, I was given the job of stripping the paint on one of the Cobra Coupes. I applied paint stripper to a small portion of the car and proceeded to remove paint. When Phil Remington saw what I was doing, he hit the roof.

"Who told you to do that?" he very forcefully asked.

"Jack," I answered.

"Doesn't he know how much filler is in an Italian body?"

It was a rhetorical question. Then he raised hell with Jack.

A week or so after the layoff scare, as the team was about to leave for Europe, Carroll Smith informed me that my services would no longer be needed. This time I had to talk to Shelby in person. There was a small office suite separate from the hangars where Carroll had an office. I went in to see him but a receptionist said, "He's in a meeting."

I felt I had to see him. I said, "I'll wait."

I sat nervously for close to an hour before the office door opened. Carroll and several others filed out. I don't remember who they were or if I recognized any of them.

Carroll glanced down at me as he walked past and said, "Sorry," bringing to an abrupt end my tenure at Shelby American.

CHAPTER SIX

The Shelby Shadow

I felt pretty horrible about losing my job. It wasn't so much about the job itself as it was a feeling of failure, not to mention embarrassment. Jan didn't react with sadness but with anger. She needed a focal point for her anger, someone to blame for a perceived injustice. In this case, it was Carroll Shelby. I couldn't completely blame Shelby. Hell, I don't even know for sure whose decision it was to let me go, but for sure he could have kept me on and he didn't.

Looking back from 47 years later, it is still a little painful to think that, for whatever reason, I blew a golden opportunity. Nobody but myself to blame; I just wasn't ready.

The fact is that none of the people who came to work at Shelby American with dreams of working themselves into the team as drivers succeeded for very long, if at all. Ron Butler for one was too valuable as a mechanic to be wasted as a driver. Allen Grant was good, but my guess is that after three races in Europe on the team, he realized that being the "World's Greatest Driver" was going to take a lot more work with no guarantee of success. He quit Shelby American, went back to school, and became a successful developer like his father. He never raced again. Then there was Joe Freitas, Earl Jones, and Bill Eve.

I felt that I'd lost the foundation of my racing life. Actually I had, even thinking for a few days that they might call and tell me they'd terminated me in error and ask me back. But they didn't. As depressing as the situation was, I never considered for a second giving up on my goal to be a professional race driver. I still owned a race car and had a few thousand dollars left. I'd made friends at Shelby American who were willing to help me.

What's New Is Old
Bruce Burness had finished installing the Porsche 904 engine in George Follmer's Lotus 23. They had decided to compete in the USR-RC series. The first race of the 1965 season was in Pensacola, Florida, only two weeks after Sebring. Jim Hall's Sebring-winning Chaparral would also compete for the USRRC Championship. Two Chaparrals were entered in the 200-mile race, and although the car driven by Jim Hall and Hap Sharp at Sebring had weathered 12 grueling hours in nearly impossible conditions to win, both cars had problems at Pensacola. To everyone's surprise, George Follmer won the race overall in his under-2-liter Lotus Porsche.

George's overall victory was very encouraging because Bruce Burness had allowed me to copy his Porsche engine installation for my car. I knew when mine was finished, it would be nearly a twin of the Follmer car. I worked on the car in my single-car garage every day. Jan didn't complain much and never pressed me to go get a real job. I collected unemployment for a while, but it was degrading so I stopped.

I helped with Leah as best I could, often giving her a bottle. I guess I was a little impatient about how long it took her to finish them. Cutting a much larger hole in the end of the nipple sped up the process tremendously and didn't seem to cause anything worse than a little extra gas. Diaper changing was another duty we shared.

The engine swap in my 23 was taking much longer than anticipated. I'd never done anything this difficult before. The frame of the car had to be extensively modified to accommodate the much wider Porsche engine. The goal was to finish the car in time to run some of the USRRC races before the season ended.

Jeff Schoolfield of Karmann Ghia fame, who left Shelby's before I did, was a big help. He took a machine shop class at Santa Monica City College so he could make a bell-housing to adapt the English Hewland transmission to the German engine. The exhaust system was another difficult project that Jeff took on.

While my project was slowly coming together, out of the next garage, Earl Jones and Bill Eve were campaigning Earl's MRD Formula B car in SCCA races. Their efforts would lead ultimately to Earl's second National SCCA amateur championship at the American Road Race of Champions in late November in Daytona.

Earl and I had been best friends almost since we first met at Shelby's in 1963, but in 1965, although we still lived in adjoining apartments, our relationship started to change. Bill was eager to race himself, but he devoted full time to helping Earl, seeming to put his own ambitions on hold.

It took a while for Jan and me to realize what was creating this distance between us and the Joneses. I started feeling a change right after I sold Earl the engine and transmission out of my car. I sold it to him at a very low price. As I recall it was $1,300. I had always wanted Earl to succeed and was glad to lend any support I could. He needed a lot of support because the driving talent he had was offset by a lack of ambition and perhaps a touch of laziness. Connie possessed the ambition that Earl lacked and had no qualms about using people to further her husband's career. I believe she felt that I had nothing more to contribute; friendship was only important to her if Earl's career would benefit. I would come in contact with other cunning people in racing through the years. She was the first.

The 1965 USRRC season was coming to its end as my car neared completion. I'd spent most of the 1965 season in my garage without running a single race. The only USRRC race left was the September Road America 500 at Elkhart Lake, the race in which I'd had wins in l963 and 1964. The car had to be finished in time for this one.

George Follmer had won all but three of the eight races leading to the final at Road America. In late August, Bruce Burness, who ran the team for Follmer, called and offered me the job of co-driving with Follmer in the 500. I told Bruce I couldn't because I was going to run my own car in the race. I suggested that he give the ride to Earl Jones, which he did.

The headers and a couple of other details had to be finished by morning, and then we would have to leave immediately to get to Wisconsin in time. I'd been working under the front of the car on something when I was awakened by bright early morning sunlight. Jeff was asleep under the back of the car where he'd been trying to finish the header system. We'd been working almost nonstop for days and we just ran out of time.

George Follmer and Earl Jones finished fourth overall and won the under-2-liter class giving George the 1965 USRRC Championship. This wouldn't be the last dumb decision I would make in racing.

By October the Lotus Porsche was finished. We had been to Riverside to test and had made minor changes. I sold what little stock I had remaining, about $700 worth. Jeff, Jan, and I headed for Kent, Washington, for the first of the fall pro races.

Kent was a 1,200-mile drive, but the anticipation of finally getting to race my car again made it easy. Unfortunately the car's debut

The Porsche-powered Lotus finally emerged from the garage nearly six months after the conversion was started. It was a real learning experience. *John Morton Collection*

ended before reaching the first turn of the first practice session when the Porsche engine made a loud rattling sound. On inspection that evening we discovered a large quantity of metal in the crankcase.

Distraught and angry, I phoned Otto Zipper from whom I'd purchased the engine. It had been represented as a new engine that they had carried as a spare for the 904 Porsche, but had never used. I pretty much accused him of screwing me, to which he took great offense. (This is the same Otto Zipper who didn't answer my request to be transferred from the So Cal Division to the Central Division in 1963, depriving me of my B Production Divisional Championship, but was later instrumental in my getting the Cal Club Driver of the Year Award.)

I don't know for sure why the engine failed with so little time on it. It may have been a faulty oil tank, which I modified after our short test at Riverside. But when we tore the engine down in Monterey the following week in hopes of repairing it for the Monterey Grand Prix the week after Kent, we discovered something else: the engine sold as new had considerable time on it and had very early-specification pistons. My teardown verified that I hadn't bought the new engine that I paid for.

I ordered a new crankshaft from Vasek Polak, which arrived just in time for us to make the race. But in our haste to get ready in time for the consolation race, we'd missed practice. The half shafts were installed out of time, causing a huge vibration. Our two weeks of hell were over. It seemed that the good luck I'd had with the Lotus Super 7 in 1963 and early 1964 was truly beginner's luck. Concurrent with being terminated at Shelby American, the real world had closed in.

S.A. Rolls On

Shelby American had a good year in 1965 in spite of the fact that the GT 40s, as well as the new 427 GT 40 MK IIs and the Daytona Coupes, all failed at Le Mans. The Cobras won the World Championship of Manufacturers in the over-2-liter class. It was an important championship but the perennial winner of this class—Ferrari—didn't make much of an effort in 1965, leaving private teams in outdated Ferrari GTOs to battle the Cobras.

The other two classes in the World Manufacturers Championship, the under-2-liter and the under-1.3-liter classes, were won by Porsche and the Abarth Simca respectively. Of course most American fans who followed European racing were not interested in the smaller classes, even though all three manufacturers were in fact World Champions.

With the 1965 season over, there was time to try to find some financial help for the 1966 season. I bought a folder at the drug store for a dime, put a couple of snapshots of my car in it along with a race schedule for the 1966 USRRC series, plus a page explaining all of the wonderful things I would do if someone would only give me $10,000. After showing it around to a few companies, I didn't even get my dime back.

The Shelby American team had started 1966 even stronger than they had been in 1965 by winning the inaugural 24 Hours of Daytona and the 12 Hours of Sebring. Ken Miles and Lloyd Ruby won them both overall in the Ford MK II. The MK IIs were actually highly modified GT 40s with 427 NASCAR-style engines. Dan Gurney and Jerry Grant were second at Daytona in another Shelby American MK II, with Walt Hansgen and his protégé Mark Donohue third in a Holman and Moody–entered MK II.

At Sebring, Gurney and Grant led in a MK II but broke a timing chain on the last lap, allowing the Miles/Ruby MK II roadster to cross the line first. Gurney was disqualified for attempting to push his car to the finish. Hansgen and Donohue were second in the Holman and Moody MK II. Third went to Skip Scott and Peter Revson in a standard GT 40.

Lanced

The first USRRC race was not until late April, so in the meantime I needed to have some sort of income without committing to long-term employment. I met a guy through Jeff named Lance Smith. He had a small shop in Santa Monica where he was making fake roll bars to attach to Corvettes and other open roadsters. They were comprised of a short roll-bar-looking, U-shaped bend with a rearward brace welded on. They were to be attached by drilling three holes in the car's rear deck and would be held in place by rubber grommets.

My job was to weld the braces on. I was to receive a portion of money from each sale. Lance claimed to have an order for several hundred bars from an auto parts wholesaler named Ed Cholakian Enterprises. Jeff and I often witnessed Lance talking to the wholesaler on the phone. We were very encouraged. I probably welded a hundred or so of the bars when Lance informed Jeff and me that the order had been canceled.

A man named Jim Russell, who owned a slot car company called Russkit, had bought one of the now obsolete Cobra Coupes from Shelby. He wanted to drive it on the street, but the gearing was too high because the car had recently run at Bonneville with Daytona gearing—2.88 to 1. I don't remember how he got in touch with me. He hired Lance and me to put a more suitable rear end in the car. I think I made $75, about a month's rent.

One day Lance had a brainstorm.

"I know who'll sponsor your race car. Woody Duke."

"Who's he?" I asked.

Lance said he knew him from drag racing and that he owned Cloverleaf Aviation at the Santa Monica Airport. We drove to Duke's house in Pacific Palisades with my 10-cent folder. Lance showed him the pictures of my car, but made no mention of sponsorship. When we left, I was irritated that Lance hadn't broached the subject of sponsoring me.

I said, "I'm going home right now and calling him."

Lance replied, "No, I'll call him."

We went to my apartment and I listened carefully as Lance set up an appointment with Mr. Duke to discuss helping me financially. I arrived at Duke's office at the appointed time only to be told, "Mr. Duke won't be in today."

Disappointed and angry about being stood up, I went home and called Mr. Duke's home. He answered.

I said, "I thought we had an appointment today to discuss my racing plans."

"What made you think that?" Duke asked.

"Because Lance Smith called you after we left your house and you set up an appointment for eleven o'clock this morning at your office."

He replied, "I never talked to Lance after you left my house."

"But I was sitting right next to him while he was talking," I said.

"I never talked to him after you left my house," he repeated. Then he added, "I have some advice for you. I had Lance do some work for me once on one of my dragsters. There's something wrong with him. Be careful."

It hit me like a shot. I suddenly realized that on all the calls to Ed Cholakian Enterprises as well as Mr. Duke, Lance was carrying on a conversation with the dial tone. I'm sure there is a name for his malady, but crazy is good enough for me.

Just before this incident, Lance begged me to loan him my blue wool Cobra team jacket for just a few days. Reluctantly I did and never saw it again. He worked for several big teams later, including Penske Racing and Newman Racing. At least that's what he claimed.

Poor. Parents.

Jan and I got along pretty well in spite of the fact that we never had any extra money that wasn't earmarked for the race car. She seemed to accept the fact that it was in pursuit of a goal. However Earl Jones and I had gotten interested in slot cars during the slot car craze while we worked at Shelby's. There were slot car tracks springing up everywhere. Earl and I may have gotten a little obsessive about it for a couple of months. Jan chose not to participate though she knew she was welcome to. It became a big deal to her, and she held it over my head forever.

We were pretty good parents considering our youth and inexperience, but of course we made our share of mistakes. When we went anywhere with our baby, we placed her in a plastic carrier. One time our old television was beginning to fail so I removed some of the tubes to test at the drugstore where they had a tube-testing machine. I set baby Leah in her carrier on a wide windowsill near the machine and proceeded to test our tubes. After determining which ones seemed to be bad, we picked out and bought new ones. It was around nine or ten in the evening when we left the store.

As we approached our car, we suddenly remembered we'd left Leah on the windowsill. I ran back to retrieve her but it was closing time and the door was locked. After frantically pounding on the door, Jan and I finally got someone's attention. I said we accidentally left something of ours in the store. He let us in. We picked up our baby and sheepishly left while the man who let us in gave us a very strange look.

We were running very short of money. The start of the 1966 USRRC season wasn't very far off and I still had to upgrade my Porsche engine to have any hope of competing with the under-2-liter Porsche 906. Bruce Burness offered me the job of helping him rebuild a MK I McLaren for a man who had rented it to a movie studio to use in an Elvis Presley movie. The movie was *Spinout*, not one of Elvis's finest hours. Apparently the McLaren was used in a scene at Ascot, a famous half-mile dirt oval in Los Angeles. The deal the car owner made when he rented the car to the studio was that it would be rebuilt when they finished with it. Bruce and I worked on the rebuild, which gave us both a bit of money.

I also used my Lotus in a Wonderbread commercial. The plot was to show how quickly Wonderbread was delivered to market. It was shot at the Pomona racetrack. I remember getting $175 for that and felt like I was stealing.

Jan's parents visited from Illinois to see the granddaughter. Leah was just over a year old. They thought she was pretty special and of course Jan and I did, too, but we were merely parents; they were grandparents. I used to throw Leah up in the air, let go as she flipped over my head, and catch her on the way down. I thought the grandparents would be thrilled to see their granddaughter do a somersault in the air. As they watched intently, I gave Leah the well-practiced toss, except this time I screwed up and released her too soon. She went out instead of up and there was no way of catching her. It was like it was happening in slow motion—a bad dream. She hit the carpeted floor. Everyone was in shock, no one more than I was. Leah cried a little but not much. Thankfully she wasn't hurt, but I felt like a real shithead. I guess we needed more practice before performing in public.

Porsche Faster Still

George Boskoff and Bruce helped me prepare my car for the first race of the season, which was in Las Vegas at Stardust Raceway on April 24. Bruce worked on updating my engine, while George worked with the chassis. George and Jeff Schoolfield would help me at the west coast races.

Bruce had arranged for me to move my car to a friend's large garage nearer Bruce's home in Pasadena so he could more easily rebuild the Porsche engine. One day in early April as George and I were driving to work on the car, we heard on the car radio that Walt Hansgen had been seriously injured during a Ford test at Le Mans. He died a few days later.

Later I learned that Hansgen was trapped in the wreckage of the Holman and Moody MK II after crashing on the wet track in the Dunlop turn, just past the pits. In a panicked effort to free him, a French marshal with a Skil saw was starting to cut through the tub, which contained the fuel cell. Remington forcefully removed the Frenchman and his saw from the scene to stop him from igniting the wreckage with sparks from the steel tub.

Hansgen was 46 years old, a year younger than the oldest man on the Ford team, Ken Miles. I once asked Ken how long he planned to race. He was 46 when I asked. He answered, "Until I stop enjoying it."

It was finally time for me to race again. We had made it to Stardust Raceway for the first USRRC race. But after the opening practice session at Las Vegas, not only was my car's speed disappointing, but the superior speed of the new Porsche 906 with Ken Miles driving was disappointing as well. I'm sure Miles was still enjoying it. Miles was driving for Otto Zipper. Scooter Patrick was in Zipper's 904 Porsche, and George Follmer was in his championship-winning Lotus Porsche.

George Boskoff felt that we had somehow crossed some of the plug wires on the Porsche's dual ignition system. We finally got it running better, but the speed was still a bit below expectations and hopefully short of its true potential.

Bill Eve finally got his chance to race again. He and Earl Jones had bought a used Ford-powered MK 10 Genie from Don Wester. Their plan was to alternate drivers each race. Bill went first. At Stardust he failed to finish.

Miles won with Follmer second, Scooter Patrick third in a 904 Porsche, then me. John Cannon won the overall race in Dan Blocker's MK 10 Genie. I should have easily beaten a 904 if my car was as good as it could be. At least we finished the race first time out. Beating Follmer would be my goal next time.

Next time was just a week later at Riverside. Scooter Patrick took Ken Miles' place in Otto Zipper's Porsche 906 and easily won the under-2-liter class. Follmer was second; I was third. I was close to Follmer's speed but he still had the edge. Overall was won by Buck Fulp in a T 70 Lola.

Fulp was sort of a legendary bad boy from Anderson, South Carolina. I met him when I was in college at Clemson. He often drove Ferraris on Luigi Chinetti's North American Racing Team and had developed into quite a good driver. He also drove a Holman and Moody–prepared 1957 Ford at very high speeds through his South Carolina hometown of Anderson. Legend has it that he drove into the Blue Light, a local joint, and called the police to tell them someone just drove through town at over a hundred. And he said, "You better clear the streets, 'cause he's coming through again!"

Laguna Seca, a week after Riverside, would be my last chance to challenge George Follmer in equal cars. He was not planning to contest the rest of the series with his Lotus Porsche, not only realizing it was futile to run against the 906 Porsches, but because he was offered a ride in John Mecom's Lola T 70. I didn't have any choice but to continue to run my own car against the 906 Porsches.

My pursuit of George lasted less than a second because when I let my clutch out for the standing start, my axle broke and the car sat stationary until I was pushed off the track. Ken Miles won again in the under-2-liter class. Charlie Hayes won overall in his McLaren Chevy.

After the race, Follmer said he was sorry about my axle saying, "Here, John, have a beer." He handed me an empty can and laughed.

Taste of Home

I was determined to stay with the series. There was a bit of a logistics problem because the rest of the races were in the East and Midwest. Jan, Leah, and I gave up our apartment to spend the summer with my parents in Waukegan, which was a much better base from which to travel to the races.

The next race was Bridgehampton out on Long Island, New York. My brother Lyman and Jan went with me, Lyman being my only help. Though he tried and certainly meant well, he had no real experience.

Other than having to buy some new gears to have the correct ratios for the track, everything went fairly smoothly. I finished eighth overall, but only fifth in the under-2-liter class. Again Scooter Patrick won the under-2-liter class, followed by Herb Wetanson and Peter Gregg, all in 906 Porsches. Skip Barber was next in a Brabham BT 8 Climax, then me. There were several under-2-liter cars behind me, but it was a little discouraging trying to keep up with the Porsches. The Brabham BT 8s were faster than my car too. Luckily there weren't many of them. It seemed that every decent driver had a 906 Porsche. Jerry Grant won overall in a Lola T 70.

There was a month before the next race at Watkins Glen. It was a little strange living at home again. Jan and Leah stayed with her parents some of the time. They were less than a block away from my parents' house.

Le Mans took place the week before Watkins Glen. It turned out to be the crowning achievement of the Ford Motor Company and Shelby American. The Ford MK IIs finished first through third, completely dominating the race just as they had at Daytona and Sebring that year. The only problem was that the wrong car won. Ken Miles with Lloyd Ruby drove the winning car at Daytona and Sebring, and Miles was positioned for a dominating win at Le Mans when someone on the Ford Team decided to stage a photo finish of the three-car Ford sweep. Miles and Denny Hulme had a lap on the second-place car when someone in scoring took a lap away from them. Perhaps someone on the team had it out for Miles, who could sometimes be abrasive, or maybe they didn't want the success of one driver to overshadow the achievement of Ford. At any rate, Miles and Hulme got screwed and were awarded second. Bruce McLaren and Chris Amon were declared the winners with Ronnie Bucknum and stock car driver Dick Hutcherson third.

It became painfully obvious that the Lotus-Porsche was not going to be able to beat a reasonably well-driven Porsche 906. Here at Bridgehampton, on Long Island, New York, I was beaten by four of them as well as a BT 8 Brabham driven by Skip Barber. *Dan Miller*

I talked to Ken at Watkins Glen. It had only been a few days after Le Mans and although he didn't point any fingers, it was plain to see he was not happy with what had taken place.

My car ran pretty well in practice and was doing OK in the race. I can't remember what my position was, but early in the race heading into the high-speed esses, flags were waving like crazy. There were yellow flags and then a red flag. A red flag meant stop immediately; I did.

A 906 Porsche was stopped against the guardrail on the right side of the track as the road climbed into a fast left at the top of the hill. Then there was the wreckage of John Cannon's Dan Blocker–owned MK 10 Genie and a burning T 70 Lola. The driver of the Lola was Mark Donohue in only his third race for Roger Penske.

Apparently the Cannon Genie and the 906 Porsche of Joe Buzzetta touched, causing the Genie to spin blocking the track in the very high-speed turn. Donohue came onto the scene and plowed into the Genie and caught fire. Donohue was painfully but not critically burned. The Genie was badly damaged. The Penske Lola was destroyed.

After a long cleanup, the race resumed. A little past the halfway point of the 200-mile race, while going down the back straight at full speed, my engine blew. When a Porsche engine blows, things get very expensive.

Upon examination, it appeared that a connecting rod bolt broke first, sending parts through the crankcase. A piece even got into the cooling fan and destroyed it. Again the overall race was won by Buck Fulp. Bill Eve finished third for the first good result that Eve and Jones had all season.

It was a depressing ride back to Waukegan. I was broke and facing a prohibitively expensive engine rebuild. Fortunately my parents were not charging rent. Lyman had finished school at Clemson and hadn't pissed away all of his money trying to race. He very generously offered to loan me enough money to have my engine rebuilt. I took it to a man in Highland Park who was highly recommended. It was going to take quite a while.

I had lost one of the air horns off of a carburetor at Watkins Glen. Nickey Chevrolet in Chicago had a speed shop at the dealership. I'd never been to Nickey but had seen the race cars they had sponsored since I was in high school. They were always purple and were driven by Jim Jeffords. The Corvette they ran was called the *Purple People Eater*. Later they bought a Scarab from Lance Reventlow and called it *Nickey Nouse*.

A Niche with Nickey

I walked through the service department to get to the Dickey Harrell Speed Shop. To my utter amazement, there were two racing teams busily working on their cars. One was Charlie Hayes, who had won the USRRC at Laguna Seca; the other, Lothar Motschenbacher. Both teams were sponsored by Nickey. There was actually going to be a third Nickey team eventually. This would be the Genie owned by Dan Blocker that John Cannon crashed at Watkins Glen. This car was in California being rebuilt by Joe Huffaker, the builder of the Genies.

I didn't know Charlie Hayes very well and didn't even know if he'd remember me, but he did. He asked what I was doing. I gave a brief account of my woes. He offered me a job; I accepted.

The speed shop didn't have the air horn I was looking for but nevertheless, it had been a very successful trip. This was the first real job I'd had since Shelby American.

Nickey Chevrolet was on the north side of Chicago about 35 miles from Waukegan, about an hour drive each way. The first job I had was repairing the rear bulkhead on Charlie's McLaren. It had

PURE HOSSPOWER...

Al Seelig, the overseer of the three Nickey Chevrolet teams, offered me the opportunity to co-drive in the Road America 500 with regular driver Bob Harris in the Nickey–Blocker Genie if I would agree to be the car's crew chief for $125 per week. *John Morton Collection*

been damaged when a universal joint on a half-shaft failed, a common problem on early McLarens.

Carl Haas was the McLaren distributor and owned Charlie's car. He would come by Nickey and talk to Charlie, which seemed to make Charlie a little nervous. The team was having a run of bad luck after winning the race at Laguna Seca. A highway accident on the way to Bridgehampton was a setback. The team pickup truck was wrecked, so the crew rented another truck and pressed on only to have another accident. This time the truck, trailer, and race car were damaged and one crewmember was seriously injured. I think this misfortune had a profound effect on Charlie, from which he never fully recovered. He was a good driver and I enjoyed working for him, but it ended after only a few weeks.

After the repaired Blocker Genie was delivered to Nickey, Charlie hinted that there might be a driving opportunity for me there. A man named Al Seelig seemed to be the overseer of the three Nickey race teams. He was a rather unpleasant, grumpy fellow, at least that is the way he struck me. He came to me with a proposition: if I would accept the job of crew chief on Blocker's Genie, I could co-drive the car in

the Road America 500 in September. Blocker had terminated his relationship with John Cannon and had given the ride to his friend, Bob
Harris, a Hollywood stuntman who had driven for Blocker several
years earlier.

I took the job knowing that being a crew chief on a major team
was likely over my head, but the lure of a potential driving job was
great. It paid $125 a week.

The next race was in late August at Mid-Ohio. Getting the car
ready for Mid-Ohio was not easy. I was getting about three hours of
sleep a night. The Blocker team consisted only of me and the driver.
Motschenbacher's chief mechanic, Peter Reinhart, would give me a
hand once in a while. Bob Harris was often around but not much help.
He was very funny, very entertaining, but not very mechanical.

One day Charlie Hayes had apparently been on the phone.
When he returned to the work area, he looked disturbed then quietly
announced, "Ken Miles was killed today testing a car at Riverside."

It seemed impossible. Miles was too tough, too old, and too experienced to die in a race car. But it was true. To this day, no one seems
to know exactly why the prototype J car skidded out of control near
the end of the long Riverside straight. Phil Remington, who was there,
is sure that the experimental two-speed transmission locked up. The
car tumbled as it left the track, throwing Ken out before it came to
rest. His 15-year-old son, Peter, was at the track with his dad. It is still
one of the saddest and most haunting events I've ever heard of in all
my years of racing.

Bob Harris, his girlfriend, Ginger, and I drove a pickup towing the
Genie to Mid-Ohio. The car ran pretty well but Bob had some problems shifting. I'd made a new shift linkage for the car and it still
needed a little work. The Genie never got going very fast. Bob was
rusty, but the car wasn't great either. I can't remember what put us
out early.

Mark Donohue led the race from the pole, then with just a few
laps to go, had a flat and Lothar Motschenbacher won in his McLaren
MK II. Lothar used a Traco-built aluminum Olds engine, the same
as Blocker's Genie. Blocker named his race cars *Vinegaroon* after a
scorpion-like insect.

The next race was the Road America 500. I was really looking
forward to the opportunity to drive the Genie. I'd never driven a powerful rear-engine race car so was pretty nervous. It rained on Friday
and sadly a driver in a Lola T 70 was killed when he lost control on

the front straight, hitting the end of the guardrail. His name was Don Skogmo. Jan and I had just arrived at the track from Chicago. It cast a pall over the already gloomy day. I was able to put these things out of my mind pretty well, out of necessity and, unfortunately, experience. I wasn't sure how it affected Jan. I didn't ask her.

On Saturday morning, Bob practiced first before turning the car over to me. I ran a few laps. The car felt really fast, so it was going to take some time to feel completely comfortable. I was amazed to be several seconds faster than Bob and still, there was a lot left in the car. In fairness to Bob, he'd never raced at Road America.

Now we had to get back to the workshop in Sheboygan where our teams were doing final preparation for the 500. The alignment had to be rechecked, the valve clearances checked hot. This meant the engine had to be warmed up and then the complex 180-degree exhaust system removed to access the valve covers. In other words, a hell of a lot of work for one guy.

Bob came by and wanted to help. There wasn't much I trusted him to do, but he offered to install new spark plugs, so I said OK. Bob started changing the plugs as I continued working. After a few minutes he said, "John, one of the plugs doesn't want to tighten. It was real hard at first but now it just turns."

I thought, *Oh shit. He cross-threaded the plug in the aluminum head.*

We were screwed. We had no way of repairing the head that night. Maybe tomorrow at the track someone would have a Heli-coil to repair the stripped threads.

After two hours of sleep, I got to the track early. The Champion spark plug representative had an insert that might work, but the cylinder head had to be removed. It was a huge job given the time we had before the start of the race. A couple of guys from the other two Nickey teams helped.

The race cars were lined up on the track as we finished bolting everything back together. Bob got in and idled out to the grid as the cars left on the pace lap. I had my fingers crossed while watching the first several laps. The car seemed to be running fine.

There would be over an hour before my turn; I was exhausted. Dan Blocker had witnessed our drama. He knew what I'd been through and how little sleep I'd had. He handed me some pills, "Take these, little buddy. You'll feel a lot better."

Taking an unknown drug when I was about to get into the fastest car I'd ever driven didn't seem like a good idea, no matter how tired

I was. "No thanks. I'm going to rest a few minutes in the pickup. Just give me enough warning when he's going to come in."

I put my suit on and tried to get some rest. Someone opened the truck door and said, "He'll be in in two laps." I waited eagerly as they gave Bob the PIT THIS LAP sign, my adrenaline now bringing me up to speed.

A Road America lap is 4 miles but it seemed to be taking longer than usual. Someone said, "He's overdue." Eventually it became obvious that Bob was not going to come in. We were told that the car was off the track in turn one. Bob walked back and told us that the engine "just quit at the end of the straight."

After the race we discovered the problem. Somehow the condenser wire in the distributor contacted the rotor and broke it—one of those bizarre things that can't happen, but did.

Chuck Parsons won in his McLaren. The rest of the Nickey teams did well. Charlie Hayes driving with Earl Jones finished second. Lothar Motschenbacher was fourth.

This was the last USRRC of the 1966 season. It was followed one week later by the first race of a new series called the Can-Am. The Can-Am series of 1966 would be comprised of six fall races in rapid succession, two in Canada and four in the United States. The first was in St Jovite, a beautiful track near a ski area in Quebec, Canada.

Dan Blocker had said, "If Bobby can't cut it anymore, he'll be the first to admit it." I sort of hung my hat on that statement. It wasn't that I wanted Bob to fail, but I'd seen him through two races now and saw that he was having trouble getting up to speed.

It was no different at St. Jovite. Bob ran lap after lap in practice with very little improvement in lap times. He qualified 22nd. Motschenbacher did very well to qualify fourth. Bob ran steadily and finished 15th while Motschenbacher was 8th after having a mechanical problem. John Surtees won the race in a T 70 Lola.

Bridgehampton was a week later. It must have been Thursday evening. Peter Reinhart, Motschenbacher's chief mechanic, and I were having dinner in a restaurant. We had a booth by a window with a view of the highway that led to the racetrack. It was dark. A white pickup caught our attention as it headed toward the track. Behind it on an open trailer was a white race car.

Peter and I looked at one another. "That was a Chaparral, wasn't it?" he asked.

"I think so, but what was that thing on top of it? A tire rack or something?"

The next morning at the track, we got the answer. It was the Chaparral all right, but with a huge wing that looked about 10 feet tall attached to the rear suspension uprights. It was really more like 3 or 4 feet above the car's body, but it was about to dramatically change racing forever.

Bob Harris in the Nickey/Dan Blocker Genie practicing and qualifying for the first ever Can-Am race. It was on September 10, 1966, at St. Jovite near Mount Tremblant, Montreal, Canada. *Tom Stephani Collection*

Bob Harris finished 15th in the Can-Am at St. Jovite. He ran a lot of practice but never got very fast. The car wasn't great, and we were understaffed, to say the least. *Tom Stephani Collection*

It was not a good weekend for the Nickey teams or for me. During practice the small fiberglass door on the driver side of the Genie blew open and slammed shut. It had done it before but I thought it was just a freak thing. This time, when it slammed shut, it hit Bob's arm, causing it to swell to twice its normal size. Al Seelig decided that this was my moment. With some anxiety I hopped in the car. This wasn't the Can-Am debut I'd had in mind, but I was determined to make the best of it. After a couple of laps, I spun. It was an easy spin, but the car left the road and hit a sandbank, bending a front A arm.

We replaced the bent part, but Blocker decided that if Bob couldn't drive, we wouldn't run the car. None of our three cars had any luck at Bridgehampton. Dan Gurney in his Lola T 70 Ford won from the pole. The Chaparral showed great potential in finishing fourth.

Another week later, Mosport was pretty much a disaster. First the Blocker Genie had a dead battery at the start. Then John Surtees came storming through the field from his 10th place starting position and spun as he entered turn one, causing a real mess. Both Hayes and Motschenbacher suffered damage and neither was able to continue. Mark Donohue won his first Can-Am race, driving Roger Penske's T 70 Lola.

So ended the eastern part of the first Can-Am season. There was a three-week intermission before the first western race at Laguna Seca. The decision was made to park the Genie for a while, so I switched to Motschenbacher's team.

The Beverly Hills Motschenbachers

Lothar Motschenbacher and his mechanic Peter Reinhart were Germans and were both accomplished mechanics. Lothar had been in the apprentice program at Mercedes as a young man in Germany. He had his own Mercedes repair business in the Los Angeles area before becoming a full-time racer.

Lothar, whose McLaren had been running the 5-liter aluminum Olds engine, was planning to switch to the more powerful Chevrolet engine like the factory McLarens of Bruce McLaren and Chris Amon. The plan included upgrading the chassis to Team McLaren's

Bob Harris accelerates out of a turn at St. Jovite during the world's first Can-Am race. The car ran a trouble free race here, a feat not repeated until the last race of the season in Las Vegas. *Tom Stephani Collection*

Two forlorn Nickey team cars at the 1966 Bridgehampton Can-Am. The Charlie Hayes McLaren #97 blew in practice, and Bob Harris injured his arm when the car's door blew open on the straight. Neither car started the race. *Tom Stephani Collection*

Dan Blocker (background, blue jacket) and pseudo team manager Al Seelig kibitz while Peter Reinhart and I change gear ratios in Lothar's McLaren at Laguna Seca. Trevor Harris in STP jacket takes a peek. *John Morton Collection*

specification. This required a significant amount of work reinforcing the frame. We also mounted a new lightweight body that Lothar had picked up in Canada.

Lothar, Peter Reinhart, and I worked nearly around the clock. It was a very difficult two weeks followed by a nonstop trip to California in a two-vehicle caravan. The trailer was towed by a Chevy station wagon followed by a rental van. Tied on top of the enclosed trailer was the original McLaren tail section.

Jan and Lothar's wife, Marilyn, had become friends. Marilyn was a beautiful blonde ex–race queen that Lothar met when he was racing Formula Juniors in California. They thought it would be nice if there was communication between the vehicles so Marilyn bought a pair of cheap walkie-talkies.

We left Nickey Chevrolet about 1:00 a.m.: Lothar, Marilyn, and me in the station wagon towing the trailer; Peter and Jan in the van behind. Jan and Marilyn were trying out the walkie-talkies as we got on the westbound expressway. They didn't work very well; a word here, a word there, but nothing very intelligible. Suddenly I heard Jan's voice very clearly. She said, "The body blew off."

"I think she said the body blew off," I told Lothar.

We pulled off the expressway onto the shoulder, debating whether even to go back. It was surely destroyed and if it wasn't, a car would finish it off. We decided to take a look and started walking back along the shoulder. Jan said it flew through the air, spinning like a helicopter, but she didn't see it land.

The tail had come down in the center divider with part of it in the fast lane. It was in perfect condition. We tied it back on—even better than before!—and proceeded to California without further incident.

Laguna Seca didn't go very well either. The Al Bartz–built Chevrolet engine had some teething problems. I remember quite a bit of oil emitting from the engine's breather. This was very upsetting to Lothar, as he was extremely fastidious about cleanliness. I heard him tell Bartz as we installed the engine in Chicago, "This thing better not blow oil!" It did.

Then in the warm-up before the race, the car lost a rear wheel. Peter and I could see the car in the distance on the outside of turn seven. I was beside myself, having put the wheel on just minutes before. Had I forgotten to torque the nuts? I wracked my brain to remember, but couldn't be sure. When the car was brought back to the pits, to my relief, a hub had broken.

The Laguna Seca Can-Am was run in two heats. We replaced the hub, but not in time to make the first heat, which ruined any chance for a good overall finish.

The highlight of the race was the story of Parnelli Jones in the Mecom T 70 Lola. The team made a desperate, last-minute decision to replace the less powerful Ford engine they had started with and install a borrowed Chevrolet. In so doing they missed qualifying and had to run the consolation race, which they won. In the first heat, Parnelli started at the back, but dropped out with a damaged oil pan. The Chevrolet engine was heavier than the Ford, causing the pan to drag the ground.

Between heats the team repaired the oil pan and raised the rear of the car to provide more clearance. In the second heat, Parnelli again started at the back. He drove as if he were possessed. He was. By the end he had passed Jim Hall and then passed Phil Hill—who were running first and second—to win the second heat. It was the most amazing drive

I'd ever seen. Phil Hill was the overall winner, the first for the spectacular winged Chaparral.

Jan and I stayed in the Motschenbacher's Beverly Hills apartment with them while we were between the Western races. Even though they lived in a fancy part of town, they seemed to be in worse financial shape than Jan and I were. At least we didn't owe anyone much money. Lothar was one of those guys who would do anything to race, including getting into serious debt. I guess I was one of those guys too, but didn't ever learn to be comfortably in debt. Marilyn seemed able to handle it pretty well too; she was a very outgoing person who genuinely loved racing.

During practice at Laguna Seca, Lothar watches as Peter Reinhart (kneeling) checks something while I hold up the tail. *John Morton Collection*

There were two weeks between each of the Western races. Riverside was next. Riverside should have been a good race for us because it was our home track. Lothar out-qualified Charlie Hayes as well as Earl Jones, who was driving Charlie's second McLaren. It was

Lothar Motschenbacher entering turn seven at Riverside on his way to a ninth place finish in the 1966 Can-Am race. *John Morton Collection*

small consolation though because we were only 14th overall.

Peter complained that Lothar was braking too early for turn nine, a fast 180-degree turn after the mile-long back straight. He felt Lothar was not driving up to his full potential. Lothar finished a distant ninth. Hayes didn't finish at all; Earl was 11th. Bill Eve was still running the very low-budget Eve and Jones' Genie. He was 16th. There was a great race for the win between John Surtees' Lola T 70 and Jim Hall's Chaparral. In the end, Surtees prevailed.

We got the McLaren ready for Stardust, the final race of the season, early enough to get there for some testing before the race weekend. Lothar gave Jan and me rides around the track in the race car. I thought Jan would be scared to death, but she liked it. She said, "I don't understand how a driver can see to go through those esses that fast. It was just a blur. I wasn't scared though."

It was a little scary to me. It wouldn't have been if I'd been driving, but riding was a different story. The scariest part though was watching the oil pressure gauge. It would go almost to zero on hard acceleration and come back to full pressure on braking. It also lost pressure when turning in one direction but not the other. The wet sump oil pans were unable to keep enough oil at the pickup to maintain pressure in cars that accelerated and cornered as fast as these. I'm surprised all the Chevies and Fords didn't blow up; several did.

The Chaparrals of Jim Hall and Phil Hill attained their rightful positions on the starting grid—first and second—as they had at

During a private test before the Stardust Grand Prix at Las Vegas, the last race of the 1966 Can-Am season, Lothar gave Jan a fast couple laps around the track. She liked it. Nice helmet! *John Morton Collection*

Laguna Seca. The Nickey cars were less impressive. Hayes qualified 16th; Lothar 20th; and Bob Harris, having another crack at the Genie, was 30th.

Surtees got by the Chaparrals at the start and led the entire race. The Chaparrals both suffered wing failures. McLaren finished second with Mark Donohue third. Surtees was the first Can-Am Champion. Donohue was runner up.

Lothar finished fifth in the race. Bob Harris had his best result, coming in 11th. This time the Eve and Jones Genie blew its engine with Bill driving.

With the racing season over, Peter Reinhart was offered a job with Penske, which he accepted. Jan and I had to get back to Illinois, where Leah was with her grandparents. The Chevrolet station wagon we had been using belonged to Nickey; we would return it to Chicago. Lothar gave us his gas company credit card for the trip. I finally learned to spell Motschenbacher out of necessity.

Is There Money in It?

Neither Lothar nor Charlie Hayes ever explained their deal with Nickey or Blocker with me and I never asked, but there was no sign that either one of them was getting rich. It begged the question, "How does one make a living driving race cars?" In the 1957 Road America 500, the first sports car race I ever saw that inspired me to be a race car driver, it occurred to me that Phil Hill who won and Carroll Shelby who finished second probably made damn near nothing for their efforts. Could this even be considered a legitimate profession?

Nearly 30 years later, I asked Phil Hill what sort of money a top road racer made in the late 1950s and early 1960s. He thought for a minute as he converted lira to dollars in his head—lira because he drove for Ferrari. Phil said, "About eighteen hundred dollars a month, before I won the World Championship in sixty-one. I made about a hundred thousand from that, all told."

I asked Dan Gurney the same question. Dan said, "When I drove Formula One and sports cars for Ferrari in nineteen fifty-nine, I got a free roundtrip ticket from California and a percentage of the appearance money."

"A ticket for each race?" I asked.

"No, just one for the season."

"But your food and hotel expenses were paid, weren't they?"

Dan replied with a chuckle, "No, but we got the racers' discount."

After returning the Chevy wagon to Nickey, I retrieved my rebuilt

Porsche engine with $1,700 from my brother, installed the engine in the Lotus, traded my '61 Ford sedan on a '63 Ford wagon, and with Jan and Leah, headed back to California.

My first priority was finding a job and a place to live. I had gotten some encouragement over the phone from Bruce Burness, who with his partner, Trevor Harris, was working on a secret car project for a large automobile company. Bruce said they may have a job for me. Unfortunately when I got to California and went to see him, they were already short of money to complete the project, and hence had nothing left for hiring anyone else. I went by Bill Thomas Race Cars in Anaheim. I had no connections there and so struck out again.

Jeff Schoolfield was helping Pete Brock set up a race shop not far from the LAX Shelby American facility. They were eventually planning to race an obscure little Japanese coupe called a Hino

My Lotus Porsche at the USRRC at Laguna Seca in 1967. I'm standing on the left, listening to Lyman (dark shirt). The tall blonde is Walter Karpinski, a fellow oil pan maker. My boss Tommy Davis, owner of Aviaid Metal Products, is on the right. *John Morton Collection*

After Dan Gurney and A. J. Foyt won the 1967 Le Mans 24-hour, Gurney popped the cork on the winner's champagne and sprayed it over everyone in range, thus starting a tradition that survives to this day. Foyt and smiling second-place Ferrari driver Michael Parks look on. *Dave Friedman*

Contessa, which was completely unknown in the United States. Jeff told me they could use some help. He'd talk to Pete for me. He did, and Pete's answer was another no.

Jan, Leah, and I had been staying in motels while I looked for work. Our money was down to just a few dollars, maybe enough for one more meal, when I went into a pawn shop on Van Nuys Boulevard to see if we could get something for a gold ring Jan had been given by her boyfriend that preceded me. The man offered so little, we didn't take it.

As I returned to the car, the weight of the world suddenly came down on me. It was the most hopeless feeling I'd ever had in my life. I just sat there and cried. When I regained my composure, I contacted my old friend who was no longer at Shelby's, Ole Olsen, to see if he might have some ideas. Ole said Tommy Davis would hire me. Tommy, who I didn't know, owned a company called Aviaid Metal Products that made oil pans for racing cars and boats.

The shop itself could be described as a sweatshop. It was definitely blue collar. But the only white-collar work I'd ever done was when I raced in a white driving suit. Across Van Nuys Boulevard was the GM plant where they built Camaros. We were a cut above those blue-collar boys; at least we were building race car parts.

I was hired for $3.00 an hour, not much but enough to rent a nice little house in Van Nuys with a garage so I could work on my race car. It was $140 a month.

Tommy Davis was a great boss. He really liked racing and after working for him a while, he would pay my entry fees. I had Aviaid

Metal Products painted on the side of my car. At last, a sponsor. But entry fees were only about $50.

In 1963, my first year of racing, I was eager to leave amateur racing for professional racing, which I did in 1964. Now in 1967 I was back to being an amateur except for the spring USRRCs at Las Vegas, Riverside and Laguna Seca. The biggest payoff was at Laguna Seca, where I finished second to the Porsche 906 of Fred Baker, heir to the Tonka Toy fortune. We took home $600.

I still followed the Shelby American team as well as I could through the pages of *Competition Press*. The Ford Mark IIs that were so dominant in 1966 completely struck out at the Daytona 24-hour, most with transmission problems due to a flaw in the manufacturing process. Ferrari finished one, two, three with Lorenzo Bandini and Chris Amon winning.

At Sebring Ford redeemed themselves by finishing first and second. The new American-built Mark IV dominated with Bruce McLaren and Mario Andretti driving. The Ford Mark IV was derived from the J car that Ken Miles died in at Riverside. With Dan Gurney and A. J. Foyt at the wheel, the Mark IV also won Le Mans.

I was a little ambivalent about the Shelby team's successes or their failures, as I still carried some resentment. However, Gurney and Foyt winning Le Mans was pretty cool, especially Gurney.

It wasn't too bad working at Aviaid. I was learning some new skills and working with generally nice people. On the downside, the pay was such that I could never really save any money. And then there was the carburetor cleaner we used to clean the oil pan cores. Carburetor cleaner has a very pervasive smell so every night I would return home smelling like a freshly cleaned carburetor.

A front view of the nicest car I never got to drive. The preparation went slowly but the end came quickly. It even wore my favorite number. *John Morton Collection*

This is the beautiful new Lola T 70 MK 3 and trailer Ole Olsen and I planned to campaign in the 1967 Can-Am series. This photo was taken shortly before the owner pulled the plug and sold the car. *John Morton Collection*

The cockpit of the T 70 Lola I never got to use. I thought I'd never seen a prettier race car. Losing this ride was almost as big a disappointment as losing the job at Shelby's. *John Morton Collection*

L-O-L-A?

One day Ole announced that he had secured a sponsor for the 1967 Can-Am season and I was to be the driver. A stockbroker acquaintance of Ole's had a client he'd convinced to sponsor a Can-Am car. The client was a very nice older lady by the name of Mrs. Duckworth. She would put up $25,000, and then the stockbroker would get two more clients to kick in $25,000 apiece for a season budget of $75,000. She put up the seed money, which enabled Ole to travel to Texas and purchase a brand new T 70 MK 3 Lola. Two 359-cubic-inch Chevrolet engines were ordered from Ryan Falconer, another ex-Shelby employee, who'd started a race-engine building business. Ole paid me to help with the car; I was in heaven. Tommy understood that I had to leave. We bought a very nice custom-built enclosed trailer and ordered a new Ford pickup.

As the car progressed, the stockbroker, whose name was Dick Maxwell, had yet to provide another $25,000 contributor. Mrs. Duckworth was getting nervous. The car was painted a beautiful bright yellow with orange trim. I'd seen a lot of T 70 Lolas but none nearly as nice as this one. It even had my favorite number on it—46.

Unfortunately Maxwell never came up with another sponsor. Mrs. Duckworth had taken up the slack and was now in for $33,000. The car was finished. All that was left to do was bleed the brakes before it could be tested. Mrs. Duckworth came to Ole's garage as she had done many times before. But this time it was to tell us she could hold out no longer and she tearfully told us she had to sell the car.

It was sold for less than half of what she had in it to a man named Chuck Jones. Rick Muther would be his driver. I would go back to making oil pans.

Last for the Lotus

Ford pulled the plug on their endurance racing program after their 1967 Le Mans win, but Shelby was contesting the Trans-Am series with Ford's Mustang. Jerry Titus was now Shelby's number-one driver. It would be yet another championship for Ford and Shelby.

Not wanting to miss out on the biggest road racing series in America, Shelby had his own Can-Am car built. The designer, Len Terry, had designed some spectacularly successful cars, like the Indy winning Lotus 38. The Shelby Can-Am was not one of them. Jerry Titus drove the yellow car at Riverside and Las Vegas with poor results.

With no more racing for me in 1967, I decided to rebuild my car for the 1968 SCCA Nationals in the Southern Pacific Division.

A publicity photo of the beautiful but disappointing Toyota 2000 GT taken at Riverside Raceway. The tower in the background is the old control tower from LAX. Riverside purchased it for $1. *Dave Jordan Collection*

Scooter Patrick (33) and Davey Jordan (3) in the Shelby-prepared Toyota 2000 GTs at Bonneville Raceway near Salt Lake City, Utah. Both drivers were capable of winning, but the cars were not. *Dave Jordan Collection*

At the end of the season, the first three points leaders in each class got to go to the runoffs. There were seven divisions in the country, each producing three contenders in each class. The final showdown is called the American Road Race of Champions. The winner in each class becomes a National Champion. Back then the race alternated between Riverside and Daytona. In 1968 it would be in Riverside.

I read in *Competition Press* that Carroll Shelby would be contesting the same series of races but in a different class. I would be in B Sports

Racing, while the Shelby team would race in the very competitive C Production class. Shelby had made a deal with Toyota to run two of their new 2000 GTs against the class-dominating Porsches and Triumphs. Shelby's Toyota drivers would be Scooter Patrick and Davey Jordan.

George Boskoff worked with me to rebuild my Porsche engine and chassis in my garage at home. He was now working for Pete Brock's racing team in El Segundo, California, just over a mile from the old Shelby airport facility. Pete called his Hino team BRE for Brock Racing Enterprises. George kept me up to date on their trials and tribulations.

Shelby had moved to a smaller facility after Ford ended its international racing program, but still maintained a presence in the original Venice building.

Tommy Davis gave me a raise of 20 cents an hour, which came out to $1.60 more a day. Even though we never let ourselves get into debt very far, we still struggled to make ends meet. I had a Texaco credit card that I got behind on. They canceled the card pretty quickly, but I had no intentions of not paying them. I've avoided Texaco ever since, when I had a choice. One night Jan and I wanted to go to a movie, a drive-in so Leah could sleep in the station wagon. We counted money but were a little short, so

Leah's grandmother took her to the St. Louis Zoo to meet some new four-legged friends. On the weekend Leah and her grandmother watched me race in Olathe, Kansas.

Leah had turned four just before Christmas 1967. It was time to get her interested in racing so she could experience the wonders that I was enjoying. Actually, she did get to Bondurant's driving school in 2012. *John Morton Collection*

we raided Leah's piggy bank. She didn't know how to count money yet anyway.

At Aviaid we made oil pans for lots of race teams. Many of them were special custom pans such as the one we made for Bill Stroppe's Mercury stock cars that Parnelli Jones drove. One day a man named Duane Feuerhelm came in to see if we could make him a pan for a Datsun. I knew who he was; he owned a dealership in nearby Granada Hills called Auto Works. They sold Datsuns and were the West Coast factory Datsun team.

I had no interest in Datsuns. They were ugly to my mind, but still he had a race team so I hinted that if he could use another driver, I was available. I might as well have kept my mouth shut in light of the interest he showed. Oh well, it didn't hurt to ask. I don't think we ever made a pan for him. He had a good driver in Jon Woodner, but I didn't know much about Feuerhelm's driving. Anyway, the Datsuns didn't seem worth a shit.

Our first race was Stardust. I always finished second to Scooter Patrick in Zipper's 906 Porsche until Zipper got an even faster car: a 910 H Porsche. This was an ex-factory car that was built for hillclimbs in Europe. It was the fastest under-2-liter car in the country.

My best race was Willow Springs. Scooter was still in the 906. We swapped the lead a few times. He ended up winning but not by much. Things went much better for Scooter in the Porsches than in the Shelby Toyotas. As good as Scooter and Davey were, they could not beat the 911 Porsches of Alan Johnson and Milt Minter.

We were allowed to get points from two out-of-our-division races to count toward our total. I couldn't afford the travel; the Shelby-Toyota team could and did. They ran out of division until both Scooter and Davey had two wins each. Scooter made the runoffs in third place, barely beating out his teammate who missed the show.

I didn't go to the Tucson National in March for lack of money. There wasn't another race until July.

In April something terrible happened. Jan and I were watching the ten o'clock news. As they went to commercial, the newsman said championship race driver Jim Clark had been killed that day. I couldn't accept what I'd first heard until after the commercial and the details were given. The racing world and I were devastated. The greatest driver on earth—maybe the greatest driver in history—was dead. It felt for a little while that a passion for racing was like a life sentence, punctuated by the death of friends and heroes. I think Jan knew how I felt, but nobody at work had any idea. Life went on.

Driving a 400-horsepower Corvette at Bondurant's driving school, Leah at 47 looks as happy as she did Christmas morning at 4. *Bob Ayres*

At Bondurant's we stayed after school so I could try to show Leah what it was like in the good old days. *Bob Ayres*

We raced at Riverside, then Charger Stadium in San Diego, Riverside again, then Bonneville Raceway—a little Mickey Mouse track outside of Salt Lake City. George gave me $75 so I could make the trip to Salt Lake.

When the smoke cleared, I had won the Southern Pacific B Sports Racing Championship. Scooter should have won. I guess he missed some races, but he should still be impossible to beat at the runoffs.

George volunteered to dyno my Porsche engine at BRE before the big race. He made the required adapters to couple the engine to the Heenan Froude dynamometer then changed the cam timing slightly. After some fiddling, the engine put out 176 horsepower at 7,500 rpm. Porsche claimed 198 horsepower for the 904 engine, which was a gross exaggeration.

A young man named Adrian Gang had a Porsche repair shop next to Aviaid called Edelweiss. He was young for a 22-year-old and a huge race fan. He and his friend rolled a Fiat Abarth in the theater parking lot after watching the movie *Grand Prix*. Adrian would sponsor my car at the runoffs to the tune of $200, plus he paid for the Edelweiss lettering on the door.

Jan and I got a room in Riverside for the race weekend. When Adrian drove out in his van with no place to stay, I said, "You can stay in our room. We have two double beds."

He said, "Great."

I told Jan and she hit the ceiling. "I'm not sharing this room with someone I hardly even know!" She was adamant. I was disgusted with her attitude. I broke the bad news to my sponsor; it was extremely embarrassing. Adrian slept in his van.

The car ran as well as it ever had, thanks to George, but I could only manage fourth after a race-long battle with a Brabham BT 8 Climax. The three cars that beat me were Scooter in the 910 H Porsche and Lew Florence and Don Pike, both in 906 Porsches. This was the last time I would race the Lotus Porsche.

In the C Production race, Scooter had the same result as I had: fourth, behind the two Porsches of Alan Johnson and Milt Minter, and the Triumph of Bob Tullius. This goes to show that the best driver doesn't always end up in the best car. That was the case with the Shelby Toyota. I may have spent as much as $1,000 in 1968 for my fourth-place position. The Shelby team had a budget of a half million dollars I was told. The disparity doesn't really mean a damn thing; it's just an interesting footnote.

A Ride with Teacher

I went back to the Aviaid grind and realities of life. What could I do next with an uncompetitive car and no money to run it, much less to replace it?

George Boskoff visited Jan and me often. Our conversations always included his experiences and observations from work. It was late '68 when he told me that two Datsun roadsters were delivered to BRE for the purpose of being prepared for racing. The driver was to be Frank Monise, a very experienced driver from Pasadena who had raced Lotuses for many years.

George wanted Pete to succeed in this new racing venture, but knew doing so would require a first-rate engine development program. He approached an old friend who he'd worked with years before at McCulloch Corporation during that company's development of Paxton superchargers. His name was Art Oehrli. When George mentioned Oehrli might be available, Pete asked, "Do you think he'd actually take the job?"

"Well, it's worth asking," was George's reply, already knowing the answer. Art was one of the best engine men in the country, whose resume included test engineer for Lycoming aircraft engines and engine builder for Jim Hall's early Chevrolet-powered Chaparrals. He was a close friend of Jim Travers and Frank Coon of Traco Engineering, the foremost builders of Can-Am and Trans-Am engines. I met Art in 1968 when we ran my Porsche engine on the BRE dynamometer. George had Art run the dyno test while Pete was away in Japan.

In addition to Art Oehrli and George Boskoff, Pete had hired Bruce Burness, Mac Tilton, and John Timanus. Work was proceeding on the first of the two cars.

I didn't know at the time but there had been a number of circumstances leading up to the BRE/Datsun relationship. The story started in 1966 when Brock secured a contract with Toyota to build a one-off GT car that he had designed. He contracted with Bruce Burness and his designer friend, Trevor Harris, to build the car. This was the secret project I had hoped in 1966 would provide me with a job after the Can-Am season. In 1968 Toyota took possession of the not-quite-finished car, taking it to Japan and an unknown future, never to be seen again by its builders.

Hino, the company Pete had represented in SCCA amateur racing since 1966, was about to be taken over by Toyota. Toyota wanted to introduce their beautiful new 2000 GT to America with a racing program, and Brock Racing Enterprises was the logical team to carry

Another treat at Bondurant's Driving School was a few demonstration laps in Bob's GT 40. It's a replica of the car Bondurant raced for Shelby, and it was nice of him to let me drive it. Of course, Bob was out of town at the time. *Bob Ayres*

out Toyota's wishes. Pete had a contract to run two 2000 GTs in the 1968 SCCA season.

Joe Cavaglieri, who started with Brock as a teenager in 1966, recalls seeing two Toyota 2000 GTs in the BRE shop entryway in late 1967 or early 1968. He remembers them only being there for a couple of days before they disappeared. The cars were taken to Carroll Shelby's facility, where they were prepared and raced in the 1968 season, culminating in the fourth place finish in the run-offs with Scooter Patrick at the wheel. The disappointing program was terminated.

The perceived defection by Toyota and slide job by Shelby so enraged Pete that he went right to Toyota's competitor, Datsun, making a pitch to run a team of their cars. The powers that be at Datsun in Gardena, California, felt that the Datsun roadster was not a competitive car and that they already employed a team perfectly capable of losing as well as he would, thank you.

Disappointed but not defeated, Pete approached his Japanese contact at Hino for advice. The Hino contact was a friend of the chairman of the board of Nissan Motor Company, Datsun's parent company. This led to Pete being recommended by NMC, and soon the

This was my sixth year of sports car racing, and I was pretty much back where I had started both figuratively and literally. I did win my class in the Southern Pacific Division and made the SCCA Runoffs. Here I compete in the Lotus-Porsche at Riverside in 1968. *John Morton Collection*

two aforementioned roadsters were delivered to the BRE shop at 137 Oregon Street, El Segundo, California.

George had told me that the first roadster had been completed and was racing in the D Production class. Bruce Burness, who'd done much of the work on the car, decided to quit BRE, leaving George as the only highly skilled fabricator. George had helped me from nearly the beginning of my career, as it were, even though he first suggested I purchase a house rather than a race car back in 1962 at Shelby's.

George informed Pete when I won the Southern Pacific B Sports Racing Championship and went on to brag about my welding skills, yet I entertained no thoughts of ever being involved with BRE. I hadn't really stayed in contact with Pete through the years. The only relationship of any consequence we had had was during the five days we spent together at the Carroll Shelby School of High Performance Driving.

One day in early 1969, I think it was February, I was working on an oil pan when I got a call. It was Pete Brock offering me a job. I went to his office the next day to see what he had in mind. Pete told me that Bruce had left and he needed someone to help build the second car; he'd pay me $800 a month. That was about $300 more than I made at

In the BRE shop with a mockup of the first BRE Datsun 2000. Driver Frank Monise is surrounded by crew, left to right: George Boskoff, Steve Delaney, Art Oehrli, Toru Kanbe, John Timanus, Pete Brock, Mac Tilton, and Bruce Burness. Boskoff, Timanus, Brock, and Burness were former Shelby employees. *BRE Collection*

Aviaid. I thought for a minute and then said, "I'll take the job under one condition."

"What's that?" Pete asked.

"That I get a tryout when the second car is finished."

He said, "OK." I remembered something Pete said at Shelby's school in 1962. He said Phil Hill once told him that it takes seven years of driving before a driver really makes it. That meant my time was up. Could it be that in stealing the Toyota deal from Pete Brock in 1967, Carroll Shelby had inadvertently given me a second chance?

Epilogue

This book didn't end with a cliffhanger just so I could write a sequel. And I'm not planning to. It ended where it did because my first experience at Shelby's racing school, which began my relationship with the Shelby organization, was with Pete Brock. My second experience with Pete, the future job offer at BRE, erased any lingering regrets about my tenure at Shelby's and opportunities lost. Pete and I both still had some Shelby wounds to lick.

Bob Tullius in a TR6 pursues my BRE 240Z at Road Atlanta in 1970. I won my first of two National Championships that year. Tullius hired me to drive his GTP Jaguar 17 years later. *Bill Warner*

Pete Halsmer and I drove this BFGoodrich-sponsored Porsche 962 for Jim Busby's team in 1985. Here it is cranking through Laguna Seca's challenging corkscrew. We won at Riverside in this car. *BFGoodrich press-kit*

To put it succinctly, Pete, who now prefers an *r* at the end of his first name, saved my foundering career. Peter put together a team of very talented people whose skill and support helped me win national championships in 1970 and 1971 with Datsun's new 240Z sports car. Also in 1971 and again in 1972, we won consecutive Trans-Am 2.5 championships for Datsun in their 510 sedan.

The only downside was that as my racing career advanced, my marriage began to deteriorate at the same pace. Jan couldn't seem to feel that we were somehow being rewarded for the struggles we'd endured to get to that point. Perhaps because she felt the reward was mine and not hers, she felt she had to compete with it. At any rate, it seemed to be pulling us apart, and in 1973, we separated.

After the 1972 racing season in which the BRE team dominated the 2.5 Trans-Am, the Sports Car Club of America (SCCA) terminated the series. In a way, our team killed the series with our overwhelming success. In 1972, the BRE team had fielded three cars, the third car designated for various "guest" drivers of national repute: Bobby Allison, Sam Posey, Peter Gregg, Hershel McGriff, and Bob Sharp, along with my regular teammate Mike Downs. I fared well against these stars and superstars, enhancing my reputation, but when the series died, the BRE team had to find a different venue. Peter Brock decided on the SCCA's highly competitive Formula A (later renamed Formula 5000) series. But when it was needed, a sponsorship was not forthcoming. Sadly, since there was no longer a professional series in which we could compete for Datsun, the team disbanded.

By that time, I had a companion named Sylvia Wilkinson. We met when she had proposed to the BRE team that they be the subject of a racing book she was contracted to write. We have been together for 40 years, and her support has never wavered. I don't think I could have attained any further significant degree of success without that support.

I was still getting some rides but primarily in small sedans. Although achieving some success in International Motor Sports Association (IMSA) sedan races, it seemed I'd been typecast for a racing part I'd already played. It was past time to move up the ladder.

In 1987, Hurley Haywood and I drove this Group 44 Jaguar XJR-7 to a very satisfying victory in the last Times Grand Prix of Endurance held at Riverside Raceway. Passing Chip Robinson in the Holbert Porsche 962 for the lead with only one lap remaining is a high point in my racing memories. *Jerry Howard, RIAM*

Formula 5000 was my immediate goal. Peter Brock had presented me and the team with a Lotus T 70B Formula 5000 car on my 30th birthday. We ran it as an after-hours, off-budget effort in three races in late 1972. Though we showed promise, finishing third at Road Atlanta behind Brett Lunger and Brian Redman, a freak cloudburst as the race ended caused a three-car pileup after the checkered. I hit the turn-one guardrail, destroying the car.

In 1974, engine builder and former Shelby American employee Ryan Falconer suggested to a new customer who was forming a Formula 5000 team that I would be a good choice for his driver. I got the job. I was also expected to work on the car. My friend, Joe Cavaglieri, became crew chief. The team owner, a lunatic who owned a Ferrari repair shop in Santa Monica about a mile from the race shop, made his money fleecing wealthy Ferrari owners. When he was not at the race shop, he locked Joe and me inside in case we wanted to steal something. I only drove two races for that weirdo.

Later, badly in need of money, Joe and I agreed to put a new roof on a house. We weren't roofers, so the job took ten days. The owner was a ne'er-do-well who reveled in spending his wealthy wife's money. By the end of the job, we had talked him into a new F5000 Lola. Long story short, we ran several races in 1975, including the first Long Beach Grand Prix, after which Sylvia and I scraped together enough money to buy the car. In 1977, we had to convert it to Can-Am configuration, and we ran that series for several years with very limited sponsorship.

Our shoestring effort was the right move because I started getting rides with different teams in various forms of racing, including IMSA, SCCA, and Indy cars. I raced at the 24 Hours of Le Mans nine times: first for Interscope in a Porsche 935, twice in a Ferrari 512 BBLM as a member of Luigi Chinetti's NART team, once in a Mazda-powered Lola T 616 for Jim Busby Racing, once in a Joest Porsche 956, another time in a Nissan 300 ZX Turbo for Cunningham Racing, twice in Vipers, and finally in a GT2 Porsche for Star Air Racing. Two class wins and a third overall in the 956 were highlights.

From 1985 through 1988, I was fortunate to share the winning car in eight IMSA GTP races driving Porsches, Jaguars, and Nissans. An overall and two class wins at Sebring was the fulfillment of a 34-year-old dream. But my favorite race of all was the victory

Johnny O'Connell, Steve Millen, and I drove this Nissan 300ZX Turbo to a class win and fifth overall at Le Mans in 1994. We were slowed a few hours before the finish with a broken camshaft and then a transmission failure, costing us one position overall. *Nissan Motorsports*

at Riverside in 1987 with Hurley Haywood in Bob Tullius' Jaguar: the last LA Times GP before the track was razed for another needless shopping center. This race brought me full circle, as my entry into the sport really began there in 1962 at Carroll Shelby's School of High Performance Driving. My last professional race was in 2002. From that time until now, it has been vintage racing for me.

I was asked recently to test this 1970 Porsche 908/3 for current owner Jerry Seinfeld. Brian Redman and Jo Siffert won the 1970 Targa Florio in this 908/3, chassis 004. It is one of the nicest handling cars I have ever driven. *Joe Cavaglieri*

In 1990, I reconnected with Shelby at a Tribute Roast. I was one of the designated Shelby roasters along with Phil Hill, Dan Gurney, Bob Bondurant, Danny Sullivan, Peter Brock, and Zora Arkus-Duntov. From that point on, Carroll and I maintained a casual friendship.

In 1999, Carroll asked me to drive his Cobra coupe in the historic races in Monterey, California. As I sat in the car pumping the pedal while a mechanic bled the brakes, Carroll stood beside me talking to an Englishman I didn't recognize. After Monterey, we planned to run the Cobra coupe at the Goodwood Revival in England. The Englishman was telling Carroll how some of the cars over there were stretching the rules.

Carroll's response was, "Oh, that's a damn shame. This is not what vintage racing is supposed to be about." Ten minutes later, sitting in the lounge of the transporter, Carroll gleefully explained to me and car builder Mike McCluskey how he was planning to cheat at Goodwood.

Driving Larry Bowman's Daytona Coupe (chassis #2300) at the Goodwood Revival in 2004. The entrant was Carroll Shelby. Carroll passed on the gala Goodwood party and went to a pizza joint with the team's chauffeur. John Lacey

It was comforting to realize Carroll Shelby was still the same Carroll Shelby I'd met so many years ago.

Index

AC Cars, 64
Adams, Jim, 197
Agajanian, J. C., 145
Agapiou, Charlie, 61, 122, 154–155, 166, 187
Alex, Tossie, 13
Alfa Romeo, 94, 132
Allen, Bobby, 25–26
Allen, Donn, 106, 115, 197–198
Allison, Bobby, 241
1910 American Grand Prize race, 1
Amon, Chris, 213, 229
Andretti, Mario, 229
Anfang, Paul, 52, 76–78
Arkus-Duntov, Zora, 183, 244
Aston Martin, 25
Austin-Healey, 7, 60, 116
Austin-Healey Sprite, 25
Auto Works (Datsun dealership), 234

1963 Badger 200, 95
1964 Badger 200, 160, 162, 163
Baker, Buck, 59
Baker, Dan, 19–23, 30–31
Baker, Fred, 229
Balch, Jack, 186, 202
Bandini, Lorenzo, 229
Barber, Skip, 213
Beckett, Scott, 94
Bianchi, Lucien, 32
Blocker, Dan, 216, 218, 220
Bondurant, Bob, 92, 96, 119, 125, 158, 172, 174–175,
     178, 188, 193–194, 197, 199, 244
Bonnier, Joakim, 24, 27, 32
Boskoff, George, 53, 57, 69, 72–76, 106, 118,
     135–138, 141–142, 211–212, 233, 236–237, 239
Bowman, Cecil, 53
Brabham, 173, 186–187, 213
Brabham, Jack, 46–47, 92, 173, 179–180, 186
1964 Bridgehampton Double 500, 158, 166, 168–169
Bridgehampton Raceway, 168
BRM, 180
Broadly, Eric, 180, 202
Brock, Pete, 38–42, 86, 106, 115, 117–119, 122, 201,
     227–228, 233, 237–242, 244
Brock Racing Enterprises (BRE), 233, 237–242
Bucknum, Ronnie, 76, 107–108, 111, 160, 162, 165,
     168, 172, 174–175, 177–178, 213
Burness, Bruce, 53, 57, 70–71, 107, 148, 185, 187,
     204–206, 210–211, 227, 237, 239
Burnett, Stan, 141
Burris, Jim, 173
Butler, Ron, 204
Buzzetta, Joe, 147, 214

1963 Cal Club Dodger Stadium race, 111
Camano, Paul, 45–46
1966 Can-Am race at Bridgehampton, 219–220
1966 Can-Am race at Laguna Seca, 223–224
1966 Can-Am race at Mosport, 220–221
1966 Can-Am race at Riverside, 224
1966 Can-Am race at St. Jovite, 219
1966 Can-Am race at Stardust Raceway, 224–226
Cannon, John, 151, 212, 214
Cantwell, Chuck, 100, 194
Carrera Panamericana, 62
Carroll Shelby School of High Performance Driving,
     35, 37–42, 86
Carter, Duane, 83
Casner, Lucky, 26

Cavaglieri, Joe, 238, 242
Cevert, Francois, 151
Challman, Bob, 51, 58, 64–66, 142
Chaparral Cars, 32, 140–141, 147–148, 153, 198–199
Chapman, Colin, 109, 180
Charland, Rene, 191–192
Bill Thomas Cheetah, 98, 136, 148
Chevrolet Corvette, 82–83, 134
Chevrolet Corvette Grand Sport, 157, 183
Chevrolet Corvette Stingray, 46–47, 62, 79, 157
Chrisman, Jack, 150
Clark, Jim, 83, 92, 126, 130, 145–146, 148, 173–175,
     234
Clarke, Peter, 191–192, 194
Collins, John, 106, 111, 115, 122, 137–138
Collins, Sid, 145
Competition Press, 98, 101, 185, 229, 232
Comstock, 146
Cook, Paul, 146
Coons, Frank, 46
Cooper, Charles, 179
Cooper, John, 179
Cooper Car Company, 26, 33, 35, 46, 48, 101, 106,
     135–136, 141–142, 157, 178–180
Crawford, Eddie, 8
Cro-Sal Specials (modified Cheetahs), 98
Crosser, Jimmy, 149, 151
Crow, Gene, 98
Culleton, Jim, 70, 110, 126
Cunningham, Briggs, 26
Cunningham, Paul, 107–108

Daigh, Chuck, 10, 12, 46, 136
Datsun, 234, 237–239, 241
Davis, Dudley, 99
Davis, Tommy, 228–229, 231, 233
Dayton, Jan. *See* Morton, Jan (Dayton)
1962 Daytona Continental, 31–32
1963 Daytona Continental, 62–63
1964 Daytona Continental, 115, 119–120
1965 Daytona Continental, 184, 188, 191–194
Decker, Sherman, 169
Dibley, Hugh P. K., 174, 176
Doniack, Dan, 77–78
Donohue, Mark, 208, 214, 217, 221, 226
Donovan, Mike, 184–185, 194
Dowd, Al, 63, 125, 154, 160, 167, 184–185
Downs, Mike, 241
Duckworth, Mrs., 231
Duke, Woody, 209

Edgar, John, 69
Elkhart Lake (WI), 7–8, 81
Elva Porsche, 98, 147, 152–153, 173
Erickson, Ernie, 98–99
Ericson, Ryser, 6–7, 27
Eve, Bill, 200, 204–205, 212, 215, 224, 226
Everly, Jon, 48–49

Falconer, Ryan, 242
Fangio, Juan Manuel, 7
Fédération Internationale de l'Automobile (FIA),
     158–159, 167, 199–200
Ferrari, 26–27, 32, 106, 132, 158–159, 167, 194,
     200–202
Ferrari, Enzo, 159, 167, 169, 202
Feuerhelm, Duane, 234
1964 FIA Manufacturers' Championship, 158–159,
     167, 169

1965 FIA Manufacturers' Championship, 207
Fiat, 25, 79, 179–180
Fiat Abarth, 25, 207
Fitch, John, 26
Florence, Lew, 167, 236
Follmer, George, 136, 185, 187, 204–206, 212–213
Ford, Henry, 75
Ford, Henry, II, 202
Ford Motor Company, 83, 126, 135, 147, 183,
     201–202, 213
1970 Formula 5000 Championship, 151
Foyt, A. J., 92, 146, 173, 175, 229
Freitas, Joe, 121, 134–135, 141, 166–169, 204
1961 French Grand Prix, 32
Friedman, Dave, 74, 134, 181
Fulp, Buck, 212, 215

Gamble, Fred, 55–56
Gammino, Mike, 169
Gang, Adrian, 236
Garrad, Ian, 73, 75
Garrad, Norman, 75
Gates, Bud, 98
Gates, Charlie, 69
Gemini Cars, 26
Gendebien, Olivier, 26, 32
Gene, Bill, 189
General Motors, 41, 50
Gerber, Dan, 163
Ginther, Richie, 26, 28, 156, 172, 174, 177, 188,
     193–194, 197, 199
1963 Golden State 400, 135
Goring, Gordon, 44, 59–60, 65, 76, 107–109, 136,
     155, 171
Goring, Rita, 171
Goth, Mike, 147
Gragg, Dennis, 184, 190
Grand Prix, 236
Grant, Allen, 53, 63–64, 67–68, 76, 106, 135–136, 1
     48, 181, 184, 189–191, 197, 200, 204
Grant, Jerry, 194, 208, 213
Greatorex, Tom, 154, 160
Green, Allen, 136
Greenville Pickens Speedway, 59
Greenwood Roadway (IA), 97–98, 153
Gregg, Peter, 213, 241
Gregory, Masten, 23, 26–28
Griebling, Les, 107
Grossman, Bob, 169
1965 GT III World Manufacturing Championship,
     201–202
Guldstrand, Dick, 140, 181
Gurney, Dan
     Carroll Shelby roast, 244
     money in racing and, 226
     1961 racing season, 27–28, 32
     1962 racing season, 48
     1963 racing season, 59–60, 62, 70–71, 83, 92
     1964 racing season, 120, 125, 132, 136, 146–148,
          158, 167, 173–175, 178
     1965 racing season, 193–194, 199
     1966 racing season, 208, 220
     1967 24 Hours of Le Mans, 229

Haas, Carl, 216
Hall, Jim, 26, 32, 140–141, 147, 153, 157, 198–199,
     204, 223–225
Hansgen, Walt, 26, 32, 165, 168–169, 174–175,
     192, 208, 211

Harris, Bob, 216–220, 226
Harris, Trevor, 227, 237
Hart, John, 107
Hawthorn, Mike, 23
Hayes, Charlie, 153, 168, 177, 192, 212, 215–216, 219, 221, 224, 226
Haywood, Hurley, 244
Heimrath, Ludwig, 146
Heuer, Harry, 12–13
Hill, Graham, 26
Hill, Phil, 7–8, 26–28, 32, 70, 72, 120, 125–126, 197, 199, 223–226, 240, 244
Hino, 227–228, 237–238
Hiroshima, Chicky, 45
Hoare, Jack, 111
Holbert, Bob, 96, 106, 119, 125, 132–133, 140–141, 146
Holcombe, Floyd, 21
Holcombe, Lloyd, 21
Holmes, Jackie, 4
Hooper, Doug, 47, 108
Hudson, Skip, 62, 115, 136
Huffaker, Joe, 215
Hulme, Denny, 213
Hurtubise, Jim, 83
Hutcherson, Dick, 213

1955 Indianapolis 500, 4
1962 Indianapolis 500, 34
1963 Indianapolis 500, 50, 62, 83
1964 Indianapolis 500, 135, 141–146
International Motor Sports Association (IMSA), 241
Isetta 300, 9
1961 Italian Grand Prix, 32, 52

Jeffords, Jim, 12, 215
Jobe, Tom, 149–151
Johnson, Alan, 234, 236
Johnson, Bob, 96, 120, 125, 132–133, 139–141, 142, 148, 152–153, 155, 157, 160, 162, 165, 168, 181, 189, 197
Johnson, Junior, 59
Jones, Bill, 76
Jones, Chuck, 231
Jones, Connie, 171, 174, 205
Jones, Earl, 106, 135, 138–139, 142, 155, 171, 174, 180–181, 185–186, 196–197, 200, 204–206, 212, 219, 224
Jones, Parnelli, 83, 153, 172, 173–176, 178, 180, 223
Jordan, Davey, 108

Kaplan, Ron, 141
Keck, Hal, 167, 189, 194
Koike, Garry, 45, 64, 106, 126, 154–155
Kolb, Charlie, 26
Krause, Billy, 41–42, 47, 50, 73, 107
Kwech, Horst, 94–95

Lamoreaux, Mahlon, 53–54, 122, 188
Lance, Frank, 174
Landaker, Joe, 69–70
Lane, Jack, 175
Lang, Craig, 121, 135, 141, 166
Lang, Dick, 87, 98–99
Leslie, Ed, 133, 139–140, 152–153, 155, 157, 160, 162, 165, 168, 173, 181, 189, 197
Likes, Bill, 41
Lincoln, 62
Lions Drag Strip (Long Beach), 149–151
Lola Cars, 147, 180, 183, 202
1975 Long Beach Grand Prix, 242
1960 Los Angeles Times Grand Prix, 41
1962 Los Angeles Times Grand Prix, 46, 48
1963 Los Angeles Times Grand Prix, 101, 106

1964 Los Angeles Times Grand Prix, 172–177
1987 Los Angeles Times Grand Prix, 244
Lotus, 51, 62, 108–109, 142, 180
Lunger, Brett, 242
Lyall, Glen, 88, 91–92
Lynndale Farms, 93, 98–99

MacDonald, Dave
  Chevrolet Corvettes and, 166
  Cooper cars and, 180
  death of, 145
  at 1963 Los Angeles Times Grand Prix, 101, 106
  1962 racing season, 47
  1963 racing season, 60–62, 67, 70–71, 77, 79, 101, 106
  1964 racing season, 119, 125, 132–133, 135, 136, 140–145
  as a racer, 165
  at Shelby American, 51, 121, 187
Maddox, Owen, 179
Maggiacomo, Jocko, 132
Mathewson, Harold, 107
Maxwell, Dick, 231
May, Derry, 85
McAlister, Hubert, 21
McCluskey, Mike, 244
McGriff, Hershel, 241
McLaren, Bruce, 26, 32, 46, 146–148, 173–175, 197, 199, 213, 226, 229
McLaren Racing, 174, 221–222
McLean, Bob, 147
Meadowdale Raceway, 10, 12–13, 81–84
Mecom, John, 198
Mecom Hussein, 175
Melius, Miles "The Mouse", 5
Mexican Road Race, 62
Mid-Ohio Raceway Sports Car Course, 91, 107
Midwestern Council of Sports Car Clubs (MWCSSC), 82
Miles, Ken
  age and racing, 211
  author and, 65–67
  death of, 216–217
  1963 racing season, 60–62, 70, 96
  1964 racing season, 123–126, 133, 136, 139–140, 142–143, 146, 148, 152–155, 157, 160, 162–163, 165–166, 168–169, 172, 175, 182–183
  1965 racing season, 188, 192–193, 197, 199
  1966 racing season, 208, 212–214
  projects at Shelby American, 72–73, 106, 115, 119, 122, 156–157, 188, 195
Miller, Al, 83
Minter, Milt, 234, 236
1964 Monterey Grand Prix, 177–178
Montgomery, George, 98
1964 Monza FIA race, 158–159, 167
Morton, Jan (Dayton), 87–88, 93, 102, 104, 111–114, 153–154, 171–172, 177–178, 181–182, 205, 210, 241
Morton, John
  childhood introduction to racing, 2–5, 7–8
  departure from Shelby American, 202–204
  hiring at Shelby American, 43–44
  1959 Jaguar XK150 coupe and, 35–36, 66–67
  Lotus 23B and, 142
  Lotus Super 7 and, 58–60, 62, 65–66, 82–83, 99, 108
  1952 MG TD and, 11, 13, 33–34
  relationship with Jan, 87–88, 93, 102, 104, 111–114, 153–154, 171–172, 181–182, 205, 210, 241
Morton, Lyman, 11–13, 16–17, 29–34, 82–84, 88, 93, 95–96, 113, 153–154, 213, 215
Mosport International Raceway, 147

Moss, Stirling, 7, 23–28, 32, 93, 174
Motor Racing Developments (MRD), 173, 186–187, 213
1963 Motor Trend 500 NASCAR race, 59
Motschenbacher, Lothar, 215, 217, 219, 221–224, 226
Motschenbacher, Marilyn, 222–224
Mulinax, Connie, 33
Muravez, Bob, 149
Musgrave, Elmer, 5
Muther, Rick, 176, 189, 231

NASCAR, 191–192
1962 Nassau Speed Weeks, 48
1964 Nassau Speed Weeks, 182–183
1964 New York Auto Show, 75–76
Nickey Chevrolet, 136, 215–220, 226
Nickey Nouse, 215
Nissan Motor Company, 238

Oehrli, Art, 237
Ohlsen, John, 106, 115, 119–120
Olsen, Helene, 173, 177
Olsen, Ole, 53, 65–66, 97, 106, 135, 148, 156, 172–173, 177, 228, 231
Olson, Warren, 41, 43
Olson, Simone, 43–44
Opitz, Johnny, 82–84, 91–93, 95–97, 102, 113, 165
Ortega, Leo, 56
OSCA, 52
Ott, Dave, 86, 95, 99

Pabst, Augie, 96, 98, 146–148, 165
1964 Pacific Division SCCA C Production Championship, 180
1963 Pacific Grand Prix at Laguna Seca, 101, 106
Panks, John, 73, 75
Papov-Dodiani, Mark, 115
Parsons, Chuck, 167, 219
Parsons, Leonard, 55
Pat Clancy Special, 3–4
Patrick, Scooter, 187, 212–213, 234, 236
Payne, Tom, 189, 197
Pearman, Fred, 33
Peat, Wally, 51, 77, 121, 136, 141, 145, 154, 166
Penske, Roger, 48, 140, 147, 153, 165, 173–175, 178
Pierce, Red, 143–145, 166
Pike, Don, 45, 46, 49, 236
Pike, Gary, 57
Pike, Leroy, 74
Piper, David, 193
1964 Players 200 at Mosport, 142, 146–148
Polak, Vasek, 186, 207
Pollack, Bill, 107
Porsche, 147, 187, 213
Posey, Sam, 241
Purple People Eater, 215

Redman, Brian, 242
Reinhart, Peter, 216, 219, 221–224, 226
Remington, Phil, 41, 43–46, 48–49, 57, 71, 75, 106, 116, 118, 135, 191, 202, 211
Reventlow, Lance, 10, 41, 45–46, 215
Reventlow Automobile Incorporated (RAI), 10, 41–46
Reventlow Scarab, 10, 41–42, 45–46, 168, 215
Revson, Peter, 208
Richardson, Joe, 33–34
Rickert, Chuck, 10
Ridenour, Dave, 141
Riverside Raceway, 35–36, 39–42, 59, 61–62, 64–65, 106
1963 Road America 500, 95–96
1964 Road America 500, 157, 160, 162–163, 165
1965 Road America 500, 205
1966 Road America 500, 216, 217–219

Road & Track, 7, 39
1972 Road Atlanta, 242
Roberts, Fireball, 70
Rodriguez, Pedro, 26–27, 120, 169, 193
Rodriguez, Ricardo, 12, 26–28, 32, 52
Rootes, Brian, 73
Rootes, Lord, 75
Rootes Group, 73, 75–76
Rose, Red, 53, 62, 135, 143
Ruby, Lloyd, 189, 192–193, 208, 213
Rudd, Tony, 180
Russell, Jim, 208–209

Sachs, Eddie, 83, 145
Salyer, Ralph, 98–99
Sanesi, Consalvo, 132
San Francisco Examiner, 139
Scarfiotti, Lodovico, 72, 168–169
1964 SCCA American Road Race of Champions,
    180–181
1965 SCCA American Road Race of Champions, 205
SCCA Formula 5000 series, 241–242
1968 SCCA Nationals, 231–233
1968 SCCA race at Bonneville Raceway, 236
1963 SCCA race at Del Mar, 76–79
1964 SCCA race at Del Mar, 141–142
1963 SCCA race at Indianapolis Raceway Park (IRP),
    100
1963 SCCA race at Meadowdale, 85–87
1963 SCCA race at Riverside, 61–62, 73
1964 SCCA race at Riverside, 117–119
1968 SCCA race at Stardust Raceway, 234
1964 SCCA race at Tucson, 134–135
1963 SCCA race at Waterford Hills, 94
1968 SCCA race at Willow Springs, 234
1963 SCCA Regional race at Dodger Stadium, 67–68
1964 SCCA Regional race at Laguna Seca, 136
1968 SCCA runoffs at Riverside, 236
1968 SCCA Southern Pacific B Sports Racing
    Championship, 236
Schlesser, Jo, 125, 185, 189, 194, 197, 199
Schmidt, Frank, 46
Schoolfield, Jeff, 106, 122–123, 126, 132, 205, 208,
    211, 227–228
Schwartz, Brooks, 23
Scott, Skip, 147, 152, 157, 160, 162–163, 165, 208
Seavrens, Bud, 98, 101–102
1961 Sebring races, 25–29
1962 Sebring races, 32
1963 Sebring races, 69, 70–72
1964 Sebring races, 120, 122–127, 129–132
1965 Sebring races, 197–199
1966 Sebring races, 208
1967 Sebring races, 229
Seelig, Al, 216, 220
Seneca Speedway, 19–20, 22, 30
Sesslar, Don, 160
Sharp, Bob, 241
Sharp, Hap, 141, 157, 165, 174, 199, 204
Shelby, Carroll
    author and, 68–69, 108–110, 132, 142, 172–173,
        180, 185, 197, 202, 244
    bibbed overalls and, 67
    Cobra prototype and, 38–39, 41–42, 46–47, 49
    Dave MacDonald and, 51, 135
    employee Stingrays and, 166
    Formula Junior racing and, 26
    427 Cobra and, 116–117
    Goodyear racing tire distributorship, 52
    Joan "Shelby" Sherman and, 46, 56
    Parnelli Jones and, 175–176
    racing career, 7–8, 25, 27

roast of, 244
    at 1963 Sebring races, 71
    at 1964 Sebring races, 129
    Sunbeam Alpine and, 69, 74
    Toyota and, 238, 240
Shelby American Inc.
    author's beginning at, 43–44
    Cobra prototype, 38–39, 41–42, 46–47, 49
    Cooper cars and, 101, 106, 110–111, 121,
        156–157, 178–180
    Daytona Coupe project, 106, 110, 114–115, 119,
        121–122
    development of 1965 427 Cobra, 194–195,
        199–200
    explosive pranks, 187–188
    first 427 Cobra and, 115–117, 119, 121
    first production Cobra, 48–49
    Ford Mark IV, 229
    Ford MK II, 208, 213
    Ford Motor Company effect on, 196–197, 201
    Ford Mustang and, 156
    427 engine "Super Snake" project, 157, 182–183
    GT 350 Mustang, 194–195, 197
    Lola Ford GT 40s, 183–184, 188–189
    1964 racing season cars, 110–111
    production Cobras and, 57–58
    Sunbeam Alpine project, 69, 72–75, 108
    Sunbeam Tiger project in 1964, 121, 156, 162–163
    Toyota and, 238, 240
Sherman, Joan "Shelby", 46–47, 56, 67
Sherwood, Bill, 79
Shoup, John, 110, 122–123, 132
Simca, 207
Simmons, Buck, 31
Simpson, Bill, 149
Skinner, Bob, 137, 148–151
Skogmo, Don, 218
Smith, Carroll, 183, 202
Smith, Lance, 208–209
Sorokin, Mike, 149, 151
Spencer, Doane, 74, 108
Spencer, Jim, 100–101
Spencer, Lew, 70, 72, 96, 111, 121, 123, 125,
    134–135, 197
Spinout, 210
Sports Car Club of America, 64–65, 69, 76, 82, 84,
    185, 242
Sports Cars Illustrated, 7
Stardust Raceway (Las Vegas), 211
Stillman, Eddie, 5
Subith, Roger, 74–75
Sullivan, Danny, 244
Sunbeam, 69, 72–75, 108, 133–134, 159–160, 162
Surtees, John, 72, 193, 219–220, 224, 226
Sutton, Ted, 115–117, 121, 126, 134, 187
Sweikert, Bob, 4

Tauranac, Ron, 186
Taylor, Ellis, 186
Terry, Len, 231
Thompson, Dick, 26
Thompson, Mickey, 50, 83, 135, 145
Thompson, Tommy, 23–27, 31–32
Tilton, Mac, 237
Timanus, John, 83, 189, 192, 237
Titus, Jerry, 231
Tojeiro, John, 180
1964 Tourist Trophy at Goodwood, 158
Toyota Motor Corporation, 233, 237–238
1967 Trans-Am series, 231
Travers, Jim, 46
Triumph Motor Company, 69

Tuller, Roy "Goob", 149
Tullius, Bob, 236
TVR, 117
1966 24 Hours of Daytona, 208
1967 24 Hours of Daytona, 229
24 Hours of Le Mans, 25, 99, 242
1964 24 Hours of Le Mans, 158
1965 24 Hours of Le Mans, 202, 207
1966 24 Hours of Le Mans, 213–214

1963 United States Auto Club World Championship, 92
1963 United States Road Racing Championship, 91, 95
Unser, Bobby, 175
1965 USRRC Championship, 206
1964 USRRC Manufacturer's Championship, 158
1964 USRRC race at Augusta, 133
1966 USRRC race at Bridgehampton, 213
1963 USRRC race at Continental Divide, 92
1964 USRRC race at Elkhart Lake, 159
1964 USRRC race at Greenwood Roadway (IA),
    154–155
1964 USRRC race at Kent, Washington, 140–141
1964 USRRC race at Laguna Seca, 136–140
1966 USRRC race at Laguna Seca, 212–213
1967 USRRC race at Laguna Seca, 229
1964 USRRC race at Meadowdale, 156–157
1964 USRRC race at Mid-Ohio, 157
1966 USRRC race at Mid-Ohio, 216–217
1965 USRRC race at Pensacola, 204
1966 USRRC race at Riverside, 212
1967 USRRC race at Riverside, 229
1966 USRRC race at Stardust Raceway, 211–212
1967 USRRC race at Stardust Raceway, 229
1964 USRRC race at Watkins Glen, 151, 151–153
1966 USRRC race at Watkins Glen, 214–215

1911 Vanderbilt Cup, 1
Vanergriff, Chick, 109
Village Sports Car Club, 12
Vinegaroon, 217
Virginia International Raceway, 107
von Dory, Pedro, 40
von Trips, Wolfgang, 26, 28, 32
Vukovich, Bill, 4

Wall, Tim, 46–47
Ward, Rodger, 34, 153
Ware, Peter, 75
Warren, Fritz, 117
Washburn, Harry, 25
Washington, Joe, 55
1964 Watkins Glen 100-mile GT race, 153
1964 Watkins Glen Grand Prix, 153
Watkins Glen race course, 151–152
Watson, Mike, 139
Waukegan Speedway, 5
Weatherly, Joe, 59
Webb, Ralph, 84
Wester, Don, 153
Wetanson, Herb, 213
Wilkinson, Sylvia, 241–242
Williams, Truman, 20–22
Willow Springs Raceway, 107, 152
Wilson, Peter, 75
Wintersteen, George, 147, 157
Wixcel, Don, 76
Woodner, Jon, 234
Wuesthoff, Bill, 96, 147
Wyer, John, 183

Zerex Special, 48, 147
Zipper, Otto, 102, 187, 207, 212

EVERYDAY PRAYER

with the

Reformers

Everyday Prayer series

Everyday Prayer with John Calvin
Everyday Prayer with the Reformers

Forthcoming
Everyday Prayer with the Puritans

Other Devotional Works by Donald K. McKim

Advent: A Calendar of Devotions 2017

Breakfast with Barth: Daily Devotions

Coffee with Calvin: Daily Devotions

Conversations with Calvin: Daily Devotions

Living into Lent

Moments with Martin Luther: 95 Daily Devotions

Mornings with Bonhoeffer:
100 Reflections on the Christian Life

The Sanctuary for Lent 2017:
Devotions with the Protestant Reformers

EVERYDAY PRAYER
with the
REFORMERS

D O N A L D K. M C K I M

P U B L I S H I N G
P.O. BOX 817 • PHILLIPSBURG • NEW JERSEY 08865-0817

Printed in the United States of America

Library of Congress Cataloging-in-Publication Data

Names: McKim, Donald K., author.
Title: Everyday prayer with the reformers / Donald K. McKim.
Description: Phillipsburg, New Jersey : P&R Publishing Companay, 2020. | Summary: "The wisdom of the Reformers shines forth in their teaching on prayer. Drawing from their writings, Donald McKim provides brief, meditative readings with insights to nourish our prayer lives today"-- Provided by publisher.
Identifiers: LCCN 2020011582 | ISBN 9781629957739 (hardcover) | ISBN 9781629957746 (epub) | ISBN 9781629957753 (mobi)
Subjects: LCSH: Reformed Church--Doctrines. | Prayer--Christianity--History of Doctrines. | Prayer--Christianity--Meditations. | Prayers.
Classification: LCC BX9422.3 .M349 2020 | DDC 242/.805--dc23
LC record available at https://lccn.loc.gov/2020011582

To three friends and persons of prayer:

George Barnes
Buzzy Boehme
David L. McClenahan

With appreciation for our friendship, good times together,
and gratitude for your lives and witness to Jesus Christ

Contents

Preface   11

Using This Book   15

Prayer at the Opening of Bible Studies   18

God's Sure and Infallible Promises   19

The Cry of the Heart   20

Longing for God's Promises   21

Pray to Live for the Glory of God   22

A Sure Persuasion   23

First—Ask for God's Pardon   24

A Prayer for All Conditions of Men   25

Soul Speech   26

God Interposes in Due Time   27

Prayer Is Necessary for Our Deliverance   28

Prayer That Pleaseth   29

Ask Great Things of God   30

Leave Success to God   31

A Prayer before Church-Time   32

Fly to God   33

Why Do We Need to Pray?   34

Praying Out Loud   35

Quick Answers to Prayer   36

Throw It in a Pile before God	37
God's Time Is the Best Time	38
A General Confession of Sin	39
Run to God in Prayer	40
All Prayers of the Holy Spirit Are Promises	41
The Time Arranged by God	42
God Is Moved with Our Prayers	43
Put Our Requests in Christ's Hand	44
Persevere and Be Patient	45
A Prayer for Acts of Charity	46
God Is Good	47
Press Hard	48
Faith Is Essential	49
Confidence in the Divine Promise	50
What Is Prayer?	51
When You Seem Forsaken—Pray!	52
A Prayer of Thanksgiving	53
Direct Us by the Word	54
Prayer: Opening of the Heart	55
Reverence for God	56
God Works, Rules, and Governs	57
Praise Arises from God's Mercy	58
God Helps before We Pray	59
A Prayer for Faith	60
A Friendly Talking with the Lord	61
Pray—Everywhere!	62
Assured before We Pray	63
Forgive Others to Be Forgiven	64
We Pray Because God Commands It	65
The Greatest Comfort in the World	66

Contents

A Prayer for Forgiveness of Sin   67

We Ask, Seek, and Live   68

God Appoints the Means to Answer Us   69

Praying for Spiritual and Temporal Things   70

God Hears Our Petitions   71

Pray to the Trinity   72

Abba, Father   73

A Prayer for Humility   74

Transformed in Prayer   75

We Shall Want for Nothing   76

The Hammer of Prayer   77

God Gives What Is Better   78

Pray When Facing Fear and Affliction   79

God Helps in a Better Way   80

A Prayer for Obedience   81

Our Prayers Are Accepted in Christ   82

Pray for the Whole Human Race   83

Pray for Enemies   84

Prayer as a Means of Grace   85

Focuses for Prayer   86

The Holy Spirit Causes Us to Pray   87

A Prayer for God's Help   88

The Holy Spirit: Our Helper and Teacher   89

Hope Works by Prayer   90

God Grants What Is Good for Us   91

God Plentifully Pours Abundance   92

Why Does God Delay in Helping Us?   93

When You Don't Feel Like Praying   94

A Prayer for Strength and Trust   95

Prayer Surpasses All Good Works   96

Contents

Know You Are Empty   97

Building Up God's Children   98

Pray When the Spirit Moves You   99

For What Should We Pray?   100

God's Answers to Our Prayers   101

A Prayer for Living a Christian Life   102

Pray for the Blessing of All   103

Forgive Us Our Debts   104

Thanksgiving in Prayer   105

The Best We Can Do for Those We Love   106

Pray Always   107

Use the Means God Gives   108

A Prayer for Self-Examination   109

Soul-Melting Passion and Affection   110

Our Perpetual Advocate   111

Familiar Communication with God   112

When Our Prayers Are Few and Faint   113

Our Most Powerful Prayers   114

Depending on God's Promises   115

According to God's Will   116

A Prayer for New Life   117

Index of Quotations   119

Writers and Works   127

Selected Resources for Further Reflection   131

PREFACE

THIS book follows *Everyday Prayer with John Calvin* (P&R, 2019) to express the theology and practice of prayer as understood by Protestant Reformers. Calvin's teachings on prayer were deep and robust. His insights were continued and extended by his contemporaries and successors in sixteenth and seventeenth century Protestant movements. This book presents quotations from these Reformers and my comments about their meaning and significance for Christian people who today live lives of faith and who pray.

My approach here is to provide a series of short devotional reflections on quotations from Protestant Reformers that are drawn from a variety of sources. Information on the writers and sources of these quotations is provided at the end of the book. The writers are Protestants who were involved in significant ministries throughout Europe during the sixteenth and seventeenth centuries. In England, a number of these writers served what became the Church of England. Examples of Reformers' prayers are given so that readers can "hear their voices" as they prayed.

My vocational passion for providing books to introduce important theologians through comments on their quotations has grown in the past years. My hope is these books will open the treasures of theologians to those who are not familiar with their writings. The fact that their theological comments can nurture and benefit our Christian lives today shows that their theologies can live in the church and with Christian believers in the present time. Perhaps readers of the devotions will go on to explore more insights from these theologians. I hope so.

Prayer is a prime topic for theological reflection. Christian people pray. They pray in faith and move on toward understandings of prayer, based on Scripture and their experiences. Part of their experiences can be reflection on the nature of prayer as presented by others who have gone ahead in the faith and have provided theological thoughts about prayer.

Prayer begins in faith and is grounded—as Protestant Reformers make clear—in the promises of God. Prayer is commanded by God with the promised assurance that God hears and answers prayer. A key text in the book of Psalms is God's promise: "Call on me in the day of trouble; I will deliver you, and you shall glorify me" (Ps. 50:15). This promise is fulfilled in the experience of Christian believers. Since we "we walk by faith, not by sight" (2 Cor. 5:7) we express our prayers in faith, living according to God's promise—a promise that stands before us for our ultimate salvation (see Heb. 11:13). It also stands before us as a promise of prayer, every day. As one biblical commentator put it: "Each person's action is guided by a promise concerning the future at a time when it is impossible to see the outcome, so that they can only act in faith."[1] As the saying goes, "Faith is seeing light with your heart when all your eyes see is darkness." In faith, we converse with God in prayer, trusting and believing God hears and will act for our good—even when the circumstances of life around us seem dark or perhaps hopeless. Prayer is our "sure persuasion" (see page 23) and brings us, as one of the Reformers put it, "the greatest comfort in the world" (see page 66).

My thanks again go to the fine folks at P&R Publishing for their interest and splendid help with this project. Dave Almack

---

1. Barnabas Lindars, *The Theology of the Letter to the Hebrews*, New Testament Theology (Cambridge: Cambridge University Press, 1991), 111.

has been a great guide. Amanda Martin has been a helpful and very competent supporter, and Emily Hoeksema always provides useful suggestions. I would also like to thank my friend, Bryce Craig, president of P&R Publishing, for his support of these projects.

This book is dedicated to three friends with whom I have enjoyed many conversations in different places.

George Barnes has been my frequent lunch companion and comrade at a number of Memphis Redbirds baseball games. George and I have stimulating conversations about faith, baseball, and much else. He expresses his faith in his words and actions.

Buzzy Boehme has sat beside LindaJo and me at Memphis Grizzlies basketball games for many years. We share interesting conversations about many things, and it is always a delight to be with Buzzy. His Christian commitment is deep.

David McClenahan, a fellow member of the Board of Directors of Pittsburgh Theological Seminary, shares with me a mutual love of Pittsburgh Pirates' baseball. It is always a joy to share board meeting times together; I very much appreciate Dave's Christian convictions and commitment to the Seminary and the church.

My deep joys, as ever, extend to my family. LindaJo and I have shared love and many years of marriage. Her continuing love and support through all life and our experiences is pure grace, for which I am grateful—ever—to her and to God. Our sons and their families are our great blessings and God's wonderful gifts to us: Stephen and Caroline with our grandchildren, Maddie, Annie, and Jack; and Karl and Lauren. They bless us in so many ways, for which we give greatest praise and thanks to God.

My hope is that this book will introduce readers to Protestant Reformers who have important theological and practical things to say about prayer. Their insights can nurture and bless our faith as we are people of prayer who call on God in petition and give thanks to the One from whom all blessings flow. May our faith be strengthened and our devotion deepened, and may we find of God that, through prayer, "in your presence there is fullness of joy" (Ps. 16:11)!

Using This Book

THIS book introduces reflections of Protestant Reformers on Christian prayer. Quotations from the Reformers are drawn from various primary and some secondary sources. This book seeks to present Reformers' understandings of prayer and how these can nourish our Christian faith today. This book can be used for individual devotional reading as well as with groups.

The format of each devotion is the same. A Scripture passage is provided for initial reading. The context and emphases of the passage are mentioned in the text of the devotion. The order of the devotions in the book follows the biblical or canonical order of these Scripture passages. Some prayers of the Reformers are also presented in the book.

The comments of the Reformers on prayer are provided, and reflections on their meaning and importance for contemporary Christians who pray are described.

Each devotion ends with either a prayer point or a reflection question. Prayer points suggest ways that readers can incorporate that devotion's insights into their own prayers. Reflection questions suggest further dimensions to what has been described, for reflection or group discussion.

I recommend the following approach:

1. *Read.* Read the Scripture passage at the top of each devotion. You can meditate on this Scripture before reading the devotion and keep it in mind as you read

the devotion. Each devotion is compact; every sentence is important. Contemplate each sentence as you read it.

2. *Meditate.* After reading the devotion, meditate on its instruction, asking questions such as the following:

- What has the Reformer conveyed here in the comments on prayer?
- In what ways can the church's life of prayer be deepened by the Reformer's insights?
- What do the Reformer's observations mean for my life of prayer?
- What new directions for prayer does this devotional call me to understand?
- What ongoing changes in the practices of my prayer life are pointed to by the Reformer's words?

3. *Pray.* Whether or not a specific prayer point appears at the end of the devotion, spend time in prayer reflecting on the Scripture passage, the Reformer's insights, and the comments in the devotion. Incorporate all your experience in your conversation with God in prayer.

4. *Act.* These insights about prayer may lead you to move into new directions or act in new ways in your life. Be open to the new dimensions of Christian living to which your prayers move you.

The title of each devotion expresses a main point of the devotion. As you read and reread these titles, recall what the devotion says and means to you.

If you keep a journal, incorporate insights about your encounter with prayer daily or at special times in the week. If you keep a prayer list, expand this to include what God's Spirit tells you through your devotional readings. These materials may be reviewed later and appropriated again for your life.

The devotions of the Protestant Reformers and their prayers can be read daily or upon occasion. I entrust this book to God's providence and the work of the Holy Spirit to be read and received in your life—whenever and wherever you read the devotions. When you use the devotions, use them prayerfully and in anticipation that God can—and will!—speak to you through them.

In some instances, I have modified quotations or provided definitions of archaic terms to enhance our understandings today. Citations are provided at the end of the book, indexed by author name and page number. Selected resources for further reflections are also provided to enable additional study of the Protestant Reformers.

ALMIGHTY, eternal and merciful God, whose Word is a lamp unto our feet and a light unto our path, open and illuminate our minds, that we may purely and perfectly understand your Word and that our lives may be conformed to what we have rightly understood, that in nothing we may be displeasing to your majesty, through Jesus Christ our Lord. Amen.

HULDRYCH ZWINGLI

1

GOD'S SURE AND INFALLIBLE PROMISES

Joshua 21:43–45

GOD is "the author of all goodness," said Heinrich Bullinger. He said we can "ask that of him which we know we want; but yet of him certainly to be received." For, said Bullinger, "we believe his sure and infallible promises."

God's goodness is the source of our confidence in praying. God will convey divine blessings upon us. We ask of God what we know we want and what we believe we will certainly receive. God's Word and will can be trusted. God's promises are "sure and infallible." They will be fulfilled. God's Word is certain and will not lead us astray. This is the God to whom we can pray.

The people of Israel found this in very specific ways. In receiving the land God had promised, the people of Israel found that "not one of all the good promises that the LORD had made to the house of Israel had failed; all came to pass" (Josh. 21:45).

God is a God who keeps promises. In prayer, we acknowledge what God has promised and ask God to meet our needs, according to the divine will. Because God is good, we have confidence that our prayers will be heard. God's "sure and infallible promises" provide our confidence in praying. God will act in accordance with who God is—"the author of all goodness."

Have confidence in God's goodness. Pray, believing that God will surely fulfill all God's promises for you!

REFLECTION QUESTION: Reflect on what promises of God are most important for you right now. In what ways do you ask God to fulfill these promises in your life?

that God would give us "our land" back.
That our enemies would not withstand
that goodness would win over evil

Sept 21 - Biden mandating vaccines.
We have lost our land

19

THE CRY OF THE HEART

1 Samuel 1:9–18

W HEN we call upon God, we speak aloud or pray silently. Both are important. Most important is that our prayers proceed from the depths of our hearts. Prayers must be heartfelt to be offered honestly to the Lord.

Archbishop James Ussher pointed to this when he reflected on Hannah, who became the mother of Samuel. She wanted a child desperately and began to pray (see 1 Sam. 1:10). Eli, the priest, saw Hannah's lips moving, "but her voice was not heard" (v. 13). Ussher wrote, "What do you mean by calling upon God? Not the calling of the tongue, but the cry of the heart: as Hannah called upon God, when her voice was not heard (1 Sam. 1:13). . . .What gather you hence? That the heart without the tongue, may pray with fruit and feeling: (1 Sam. 1:10) but the tongue without the heart is nothing but vain babbling"—referring to Jesus's words about those who "heap up empty phrases" in their prayers (Matt. 6:7).

Hannah's prayer was a cry of the heart. She wanted a child urgently and poured out her heart to God. Her anguish was so deep that she did not speak. But her heart was speaking to God, petitioning God to answer her prayer. God did answer her prayer, and Samuel was born.

Jesus warned about prayers that are "just words." Our prayers must be cries from our hearts. Freely and honestly, we express our deepest desires to God who knows our hearts.

PRAYER POINT: Pray to God out loud and then silently. In both forms of expression, look within your heart to express what matters most to you and what you deeply desire.

LONGING FOR GOD'S PROMISES

2 Samuel 7:16–29

G OD established a covenant with King David. This was of God's pure grace. It was a gift given to David and his posterity. God promised David, "Your house and your kingdom shall be made sure forever before me; your throne shall be established forever" (2 Sam. 7:16).

In response, David prayed, "Because of your promise, and according to your own heart, you have wrought all this greatness, so that your servant may know it" (v. 21). David signaled his assent and prayed, "Confirm it forever; do as you have promised" (v. 25). David prayed in acknowledgment of God's promise: "O Lord GOD, you are God, and your words are true, and you have promised this good thing to your servant" (v. 28).

This promise to David shows that God is a God of promises, as we see throughout the Scriptures. These are promises to all of us. They are expressions of God's goodness, help, and ultimately, salvation. When we pray, we look to God's promises. The Reformer William Tyndale said simply, "Prayer is the longing for God's promises."

God is faithful and will keep all God's promises. As we pray, we desire and long for God's promises given to all—and, especially, given to us. Martin Luther is credited with saying that prayer is not overcoming God's reluctance, but laying hold of God's willingness. God gives promises. In prayer, we long to receive God's loving promises . . . to us!

PRAYER POINT: Think of promises of Scripture that are meaningful to you. Go through them and pray that you may receive these promises as God intends.

James -promise of wisdom
We have been given every spiritual blessing
comforts us in our afflictions
God makes all grace abound in the cheerful giver

21

Pray to Live for the Glory of God

Psalm 9:1-14

PSALM 9 celebrates God's power and justice. The focus is on God—who God is (God's "name") and what God has done ("wonderful deeds"): "I will give thanks to the LORD with my whole heart; I will tell of all your wonderful deeds. I will be glad and exult in you; I will sing praise to your name, O Most High" (vv. 1–2).

God was with the psalmist. Even when he suffered, God was the "one who lifts me up from the gates of death" (v. 13). This leads to the psalmist's deep desire to "recount all your praises, and, in the gates of daughter Zion, rejoice in your deliverance" (v. 14).

What else would one want to do to celebrate who God is and what God has done—except praise God, thank God, and express gratitude to God! As the Strasbourg Reformer Martin Bucer noted, the psalmist "prayed that he would celebrate his praises in the gates and gatherings of Zion, in the church of the people of God, and openly testify of his happiness concerning the salvation received from God. So the saints only ask to live for the glory of God."

Today, we celebrate salvation from God—deliverance, mercy, forgiveness. In joy, we "only ask to live for the glory of God." This is our primary prayer. Pray to live for God's glory! Living for God's glory is the pulsating power that means more to us than anything else. We praise God, thank God, and declare salvation by living for God's glory. God's glory is all in all!

REFLECTION QUESTIONS: Ask yourself how often you think of living for the glory of God. In what ways do you see yourself living for God's glory? What are ways you can keep this as a life focus?

A Sure Persuasion

Psalm 17:1–7

W E say prayer is an act of faith. It is faith because it requires us to step out into the unknown, to trust our prayers are being heard—and will be answered—by God. There is no "evidence" in advance of our prayers that our act of faith will be helpful. In faith, we recall God's past help and answers to our prayers. We believe God will continue to hear our prayers in the future. We believe, so we pray.

The psalmist must have felt this way. In praying for deliverance from persecutors, he speaks of his basis for praying and his hope: "I call upon you, for you will answer me, O God; incline your ear to me, hear my words" (Ps. 17:6). Drawing on his experience with the Lord, he calls upon God, confident of receiving an answer. This will include God's showing "steadfast love" since God is the "savior of those who seek refuge" (v. 7).

Many centuries later, Edwin Sandys wrote that "prayer is the pouring out of a contrite heart, with a sure persuasion that God will grant our requests, and give ear to the suits which we make unto him."

We can have "a sure persuasion" that our prayers are heard and answered by God. Our experience and that of others of faith shows us this is true. Our faith is grounded in God's sure faithfulness to hear and answer. Pray with "a sure persuasion"! God hears and answers!

REFLECTION QUESTIONS: Think of times when you have been unsure God would hear and answer you. What did you do? What convinces you today that God hears and answers your prayers?

First—Ask for God's Pardon

Psalm 25

S OME folks have very set forms for the way they pray. They may consciously move through parts of prayer such as adoration, confession, thanksgiving, supplications (sometimes known by the acronym ACTS). Other folks may let prayer take on a "stream of consciousness" form when they pray about whatever comes into their minds, in whatever order the topics suggest themselves.

John Calvin wanted to be sure Christians realized that it is important to order our prayers by asking for God's pardon, as the psalmist did: "Do not remember the sins of my youth or my transgressions; according to your steadfast love remember me, for your goodness' sake, O LORD!" (Ps. 25:7). Calvin wrote, "The right and proper order of prayer therefore is, as I have said, to ask at the very outset, that God would pardon our sins. . . . In order, therefore, that God may be mindful of his mercy towards us, it is necessary that he forget our sins. . . . When God casts our sins into oblivion, this leads him to behold us with fatherly regard."

We may rightly begin our prayers by addressing God with praise. But we should move on to asking for God's pardon of our sins. Then we can know and experience God's mercy, which wipes away our sins—into "oblivion," said Calvin. God's mercies of loving, listening, and providing for us as we pray are blessings we receive along with the great blessing of having our sin forgiven. God in "steadfast love" remembers us, forgiving and blessing us!

> **PRAYER POINT:** Orient your prayers to asking God's pardon toward the beginning of your prayer. When you ask for pardon, confess your sins, and pray for God's forgiving love in Jesus Christ.

O GOD, the Creator and Preserver of all Mankind, we humbly beseech thee for all Sorts and Conditions of Men, that thou wouldst be pleased to make thy Ways known unto them; thy saving Health unto all Nations. More especially we pray for the good Estate of the Catholick [universal] Church; that it may be so guided and governed by thy good Spirit, that all who profess and call themselves Christians may be led into the Way of Truth, and hold the Faith in Unity of Spirit, in the Bond of Peace, and in Righteousness of Life. Finally, we commend to thy Fatherly Goodness all those who are any ways afflicted or distressed, in Mind, Body or Estate, [Especially those for whom our Prayers are desired] that it may please thee to comfort and relieve them according to their several Necessities, giving them Patience under their Sufferings, and a happy Issue out of all their Afflictions. And this we beg for Jesus Christ his sake. Amen.

THE BOOK OF COMMON PRAYER

SOUL SPEECH

Psalm 25

SOMETIMES we slip into praying that does not engage us fully. We may read prayers and just read words on a page. Or we may say certain familiar phrases without thinking of their meaning. We may even engage in a kind of stream of consciousness in which we offer prayer without considering fully and completely what we are saying. Prayers can also become rote.

But the psalmist begins by praying, "To you, O LORD, I lift up my soul" (Ps. 25:1). The psalmist is praying from his soul. This prayer is engaging the totality of the psalmist's self.

George Downame, in discussing prayer, wrote that "in the soul generally it is required, that our prayer be speech of the soul, and not of the mouth only, a lifting up of our hearts (Ps. 25:1) and a powering forth of the soul (Ps. 62:8), a praying in spirit (Eph. 6:18), and in truth (Ps. 145:18)."

Downame has an arresting image. Our prayer should be "soul speech" (see also Pss. 86:4; 143:8). Soul speech engages our whole self—not just words of the mouth, but words of the heart and our innermost being. This is the pouring forth of our heart and soul to God. We are totally focused on God, the One to whom we are praying. In prayer, practice soul speech!

PRAYER POINT: Practice thinking of your prayers as "soul speech." Take that which is deepest within you. Put your deepest feelings into words and offer them as a prayer to God.

GOD INTERPOSES IN DUE TIME

Psalm 27

I N the Psalms, we recognize that dangers are part of life. Not only sickness and grief, but also suffering and pursuit by enemies can emerge during our days. We face some of these difficulties in various ways. So the Psalms are "for all seasons" of life, no matter what we encounter.

But throughout the Psalms, along with the dangers come ringing notes of confidence. When troubles afflict, God is there. God helps. God delivers. This is faith: "The LORD is my light and my salvation; whom shall I fear? The LORD is the stronghold of my life; of whom shall I be afraid?" (Ps. 27:1).

The writer of Psalm 27 prayed for God's gracious help and answer to his prayers (see v. 7). He prayed for deliverance (see v. 12). We may pray for the same. We need deliverances, too. But as the Scottish Reformed pastor David Dickson wrote, "Let us pray 'Deliver,' and let God choose the way of deliverance. When the good cause of the godly and the godly themselves are left to suffer, know that God in that case will interpose himself in due time." This is the psalmist's reason for hope of help.

The Lord will help us in due time. Our faith must lead us to trust God to choose the way or means to deliver us. We trust God to act for us according to God's will. This is our great comfort and confidence in facing life!

REFLECTION QUESTIONS: What are situations in which you prayed for God's help and deliverance? In what ways were your prayers answered?

Prayer Is Necessary for Our Deliverance

Psalm 30

SICKNESS comes. We seek medical help. We turn to those we believe can help us the most. When do we turn to God? Long before medical science had developed, the psalmist prayed to God for help with some sickness or grave illness: "O LORD my God, I cried to you for help, and you have healed me. O LORD, you brought up my soul from Sheol, restored me to life from among those gone down to the Pit" (Ps. 30:2–3). That is a divine physician whose healing power is fantastic!

It is God alone who is the great healer of Israel: "I am the LORD who heals you," said the Lord (Ex. 15:26). The Psalms show how fully God's people understood this as prayers were made for healing (see Ps. 107:17–20). When people were healed, they rejoiced (see v. 21). Our psalmist proclaims, "You have turned my mourning into dancing; you have taken off my sackcloth and clothed me with joy" (30:11).

Through it all, people of faith pray. Philip Melanchthon wrote that "prayer is always necessary for our deliverance." The examples of the Psalms "have been recorded so that we would believe we too will be heard." God heard the prayers of the psalmist for healing, and God hears our prayer for healing as well. God can work through medical science and all that helps human health. But if we keep our faith perspective, when illness comes, we recognize all healing ultimately comes from God and prayer is a necessary part of our healing and deliverance. Rejoice in joy!

> **PRAYER POINT:** Pray for health—for those you know and love; for those you do not know; for yourself. Make prayers for health a regular part of your prayer life.

PRAYER THAT PLEASETH

Psalm 31

A FTER their dismal performance on the baseball field, a manager said to his team, "We've got to go back to basics. This is a 'bat.' This is a 'ball.'" Sometimes things are *that* basic!

In our Christian faith, we also have basics: key things to keep in mind and use. There are basics in our theological beliefs. There are basics in our Christian life. One mark of Christian living is prayer.

What are the "basics" of prayer? What features of prayer are pleasing to God?

One summary of prayer is from William Tyndale: "If thy prayer be thanks in heart, or calling to God for help, with trust in him according to his promise, then thy prayer pleaseth." Put simply, prayer that pleases God thanks God, calls on God, and trusts in God.

Thanks, calls, and trusts. These three aspects of prayer are basics. The psalmist proclaimed, "I trust in you, O LORD; I say, 'You are my God'" (Ps. 31:14). In prayer we affirm God is our God. God is the God to whom we pray with thanks in our hearts—grateful for all God has done.

We call on God—telling God of our needs and desires. We pray with trust in the Lord, who is our God!

PRAYER POINT: Think of these three basics of prayer for your prayers today: give thanks, call on God, and express your trust in your God.

ASK GREAT THINGS OF GOD

Psalm 36

I T is apparent to us: God is God . . . and we are not! This is one of our most basic beliefs. God is our Creator; we are God's creatures.

Thus, the divine goodness to us—when we are aware of it—must be greater than we are and greater than we can imagine. After all, divine goodness comes from God!

The psalmist loved this when he proclaimed, "How precious is your steadfast love, O God! . . . For with you is the fountain of life; in your light we see light" (Ps. 36:7, 9).

Martin Luther picked up the "fountain" image as he vigorously proclaimed God's goodness in prayer: "Because he is God, he also claims from us the honor of giving far more abundantly and liberally than anyone can comprehend—like an eternal, inexhaustible fountain, which, the more it gushes forth and overflows, the more it continues to give. He desires nothing more than that we ask many and great things of him. And, on the contrary, he is angered if we do not ask and demand with confidence."

We need a vigorous life of prayer! We receive steadfast love from God as the "eternal, inexhaustible fountain," who gushes forth and is overflowing. God continues to give to us—and God gives much greater blessings than we can comprehend! God desires us to "ask many and great things." We must confidently pray boldly!

PRAYER POINT: Pray the most bold and confident prayer you can imagine. Imagine God as the great overflowing fountain who wants you to ask for great things!

LEAVE SUCCESS TO GOD

Psalm 37:1–5

W E hear a lot about "success." All around us, people are driving for success—whatever that is for them. It often means financial gain, prestige, accomplishment, or praise.

But "success" itself is not a biblical category. God does not call us to be "successful." God calls us to be faithful, to live out God's will for our lives, whatever that may mean and in which-ever ways our lives are led. In our prayers, we live by faith, entrusting our lives to God's leading and guiding.

The psalmist captured this when he wrote, "Commit your way to the LORD; trust in him, and he will act" (Ps. 37:5). Our prayer should always be that we follow God's will. Then we trust God will act by leading and helping us.

Jeremy Taylor wrote, "We can but do our endeavor, and pray for a blessing, and then leave the success to God." The results of our actions cannot be determined by us. Whether they are "suc-cessful" or not—by human standards—is not ours to establish. True "success" means being faithful to God's will and way. All other standards are not what matter most. We commit our way to God, pray for God's blessing, and leave all else to the Lord.

When we posture ourselves to gain praise, or enact selfish purposes, we are not true to God's call. Our prayers are to be faithful to God's will, and we leave the "results" to God!

REFLECTION QUESTIONS: Reflect on what "success" means to you. What standard do you use to determine "success"? What does this mean for your life of prayer?

O MY God, I humbly beseech thee to prepare my Soul to worship Thee this Day acceptably, with Reverence and godly Fear; fill me with that Fear which works by Love; purify my Heart from all vain, and worldly, or sinful Thoughts; fix my Affections on Things above, all the Day long; and, O Lord, give me Grace to receive thy Word, which I shall hear this Day, into an honest and good Heart, and to bring forth Fruit with Patience.

Hear me, O God, for the sake of Jesus my Savior. Amen, Amen.

THOMAS KEN

FLY TO GOD

Psalm 37:5–7

I N the Bible, trust in God is combined with action. We have faith, believing and trusting God. But also, we listen to God's Word in Scripture, look to Jesus Christ as our guide for living, and rely on the Holy Spirit to lead us into God's ways. We rely on prayer, asking for God's help and thanking God for our blessings.

The psalmist captured this when he urged, "Be still before the LORD, and wait patiently for him" (Ps. 37:7), and "Commit your way to the LORD; trust in him, and he will act" (v. 5). We stand before God, waiting; then we trust in God and commit our way to God, having faith God will act.

Henry Airay commented that we are to "labour and do all that we have to do, as that still we depend upon the Lord his providence and care over us, and in all things fly unto him by prayer and supplication, with giving of thanks. It is he that must bless our labours, and give a good end unto our business. We only can do that we ought to do, and then commend both it and ourselves unto the Lord, in humble and hearty prayer."

We "fly" to God in prayer, trusting God's providence and care and doing what we believe God calls us to do. This is the tempo of our Christian lives for every day. We pray, we trust, we do!

REFLECTION QUESTION: Remember times when you have prayed for direction and help, then trusted that you knew what God wanted and acted. What happened?

WHY DO WE NEED TO PRAY?

Psalm 50:12–15

A DIRECT and most precious promise about prayer comes from Psalm 50: "Call on me in the day of trouble; I will deliver you, and you shall glorify me" (v. 15).

This is a promise for all seasons. We may need to pray to God because we are facing a "day of trouble." When we do, the promise "I will deliver you" is given. Then, our need is to pray to express our deepest thanksgiving for what God has done in delivering and helping us. We shall "glorify" God by giving gratitude to our deliverer!

This is captured by the Heidelberg Catechism. It asks, "Why is prayer necessary for Christians?" The answer is "Because it is the chief part of the thankfulness which God requires of us."

While we need to pray to seek God's help, we also—especially—need to pray to express our most profound thanks for the help we receive. We glorify God with our praise and thanks. We also glorify God by what we do to live out our gratitude in commitment and service to the One who delivers and saves us.

This response of thanks is a primary mark of a Christian, according to the Reformers. We are supremely people of thankfulness. We are those who live in the grip of gratitude to the God who gives us salvation in Jesus Christ, who died for us. We cannot help but pray in praise to our God!

PRAYER POINT: Pray and request help for the "troubles" of your life. Pray also in deep thankfulness and praise for God's help in delivering you.

PRAYING OUT LOUD

Psalm 54

W E are probably most accustomed to praying silently and praying when we are alone. Sometimes we pray aloud. We offer a prayer of thanks before a meal with friends or family. Or, in church, we may pray a congregational prayer or the Lord's Prayer aloud. But when we think of our prayers, we probably think of the prayers we utter to God in the silence of our own hearts.

But there is value to praying out loud, even when we are alone. It appears that the psalmist asked God in Psalm 54 to hear his prayers, which were spoken aloud: "Hear my prayer, O God; give ear to the words of my mouth" (v. 2). The psalmist must have spoken his prayer—because he says "the words of my mouth."

David Dickson commented here that "in fervent prayer, the very voice has use; as with the supplicant to express his earnestness, and his faith in God, and to stir him up and hold him fixed to his supplication; so with God also, for it is an express invocation of him, and a sign of dependence upon him, and of expectation of a good answer from him."

We may not think of the benefits of prayers uttered aloud, but they do focus our minds and hearts on God. They allow us to express earnest faith. We give voice to our dependence on the Lord and our hope for God's answer. Pray aloud!

PRAYER POINT: For a week, pray your prayers out loud. Consciously focus on God and speak freely of your faith in God, your dependence on God, and your hope in God.

QUICK ANSWERS TO PRAYER

Psalm 54

G OD answers our prayers in many ways and in different times. We never know when or how God's answers will emerge. Sometimes the answers do not come forth for a long period of time. We pray and pray . . . and pray some more! We wait and pray that God will "make haste" to answer our prayers (Ps. 69:17).

But sometimes there are quick answers to prayer. Situations can change unexpectedly and rapidly. We may recognize God's answers in events or comments or the ways we look at what we are facing.

We also may experience "quick answers to prayer" when faith bursts into full flame and we know God is with us in real and vital ways. This is what the psalmist found in Psalm 54. He was praying for vindication from those seeking his life, asking God to "hear my prayer" (v. 2). Then he exclaimed: "But surely, God is my helper; the Lord is the upholder of my life" (v. 4). As David Dickson commented: "Fervent prayer often has a swift answer, and sometimes it is wonderfully swift, coming even before one finishes one's speech, as David experiences here. The light of faith is very clear, piercing through all clouds, and when God holds the light of the Spirit beside it, it can demonstrate the presence of God in an instant, ready to help in the greatest trials."

The light of God's presence and help may emerge slowly . . . or quickly! We should always be ready to see ways God answers our prayers, whether we have a long wait or a quick answer!

REFLECTION QUESTIONS: What do you remember as a "quick answer" to prayer? What were the different ways these answers came to you?

THROW IT IN A PILE BEFORE GOD

Psalm 62:1–8

T HERE are few people with whom we feel comfortable expressing our deepest feelings. If we have someone in our life to whom we can express what is in our hearts, we are fortunate.

In Psalm 62, the psalmist expressed his deep conviction of faith that assurance and security are to be found only in God. It is "for God alone my soul waits in silence; from him comes my salvation" (v. 1). The psalmist urged others to "pour out your heart before him; God is a refuge for us" (v. 8). In our vernacular, with God we can "let it all hang out"!

Martin Luther was known for his blunt way of expressing Christian faith. His comments on Psalm 62 are candid—and very good spiritual advice. Luther wrote, "Strength fades, courage fails; God remains firm. . . . If you are lacking something, well, here is good advice: 'Pour out your heart before him.' Voice your complaint freely, and do not conceal anything from him. Regardless of what it is, just throw it in a pile before him, as you open your heart completely to a good friend. He wants to hear it, and he wants to give you his aid and counsel. Do not be bashful before him. . . . Out with everything."

God is always the one with whom we can express our deepest feelings. We can throw out everything before the Lord, said Luther. Don't be bashful. Trust God. Be open with God!

PRAYER POINT: Think of the deepest feelings, desires, regrets, and sorrows of your heart. One by one, bring each of them to God and ask for help.

GOD'S TIME IS THE BEST TIME

Psalm 70

T HE psalmist is in trouble. He prays, "Be pleased, O God, to deliver me. O LORD, make haste to help me!" (Ps. 70:1). This is a prayer of desperation. God must "deliver" and "help" this person. The situation is grim and dangerous. There are those who seek his life, who "desire to hurt me" (v. 2). The psalmist is "poor and needy." Time is running out: "O LORD, do not delay!" (v. 5).

In *The English Annotations*, English Protestant Reformers reminded their readers that along with our earnest prayers to God, "there must also be a resolution of patience and submission. With belief and assurance, we must understand that God's time, be it sooner or later, is our best time, even though present sense and weak flesh suggest the contrary." Our situations may look dire, and we may feel we are at the end of our rope. But we must continue to have patience and submit our wills to God's will, for "God's time"—whether it be "sooner or later"—is "our best time."

This can be hard for us to hear because we are naturally impatient when it comes to God's answers to our prayers. We want God to hurry up and act . . . now! But what matters most is that we have faith and trust God to act when God desires to act—not when we think God should act.

Like the psalmist, we pray for God's deliverance. We even pray God does not "delay." But as we wait, we trust. God's timing is best. Despite our circumstances, we patiently await God's help.

REFLECTION QUESTIONS: When have you felt great need and had to wait for God to answer and help you? What spiritual lessons did you gain from this experience?

38

ALMIGHTY and most merciful Father, We have erred, and strayed from thy ways, like lost sheep. We have followed too much the devices and desires of our own hearts. We have offended against thy holy laws. We have left undone those things which we ought to have done, and we have done those things which we ought not to have done, and there is no health in us: but thou, O Lord, have mercy upon us miserable offenders. Spare thou them, O God, which confess their faults. Restore thou them that be penitent, according to thy promises declared unto mankind, in Christ Jesus our Lord. And grant, O most merciful Father, for his sake, that we may hereafter live a godly, righteous, and sober life, to the glory of thy holy name. Amen.

THE BOOK OF COMMON PRAYER

Run to God in Prayer

Psalm 70:1–5

T HE psalmist was in trouble: "Be pleased, O God, to deliver me. O Lord, make haste to help me! Let those be put to shame and confusion who seek my life" (Ps. 70:1–2). "I am poor and needy; hasten to me, O God!" (v. 5).

In various ways, we have found ourselves in difficulties. We have known we cannot save ourselves. We need help beyond what we can generate. Our only refuge is God.

Nikolaus Selnecker noted that "from this psalm we learn what we are to do when we are doing badly and many foes . . . are against us. We are to run to God in prayer, lament and hope that he is not going to leave us, nor does he desire to do so. . . . We shall not grumble or chide back or take revenge or be impatient, because we are called a people of blessing. The best thing is to call on God and take comfort in this: God can and wants to help us in his time."

From among all the complex ways we deal with life, this prescription is very simple: "Run to God in prayer." We are God's people, "a people of blessing" as Selnecker says. So, we call on God, believing God will and wants to help us in the time God determines. This faith is possible because we further believe with the psalmist, "You are my help and my deliverer" (v. 5). Do it now. "Run to God in prayer"!

Reflection Questions: Think of times when you have been at the end of your abilities to cope with a problem. Did you run to God in prayer? Should you have done so?

ALL PRAYERS OF THE HOLY SPIRIT ARE PROMISES

Psalm 71

OUR prayers are important. They are conversations with God, as Calvin said, that express our faith and trust that God cares, hears, and answers our prayers. We are prompted to pray by the Holy Spirit, our companion in prayer. The Spirit "helps us in our weakness" to pray as we ought (Rom. 8:26). Our prayers in the Holy Spirit are promises that God does, indeed, care, hear, and answer our prayers—all through Jesus Christ our Lord.

The psalmist in Psalm 71 prays for God's lifelong protection and help. He is perhaps a "senior citizen" since he prays, "Do not cast me off in the time of old age" (v. 9). His basic prayer is "Incline your ear to me and save me" (v. 2; see also v. 18). He prays God will pay close attention and help him through his life with all its difficulties. Throughout he expresses his firm faith in God (see vv. 15–16).

The Lutheran theologian Viktorin Strigel noted in relation to this psalm that "all prayers of the Holy Spirit are promises." The psalmist recounts all God has done throughout his life. He believes God will hear and help now; his prayer expresses his faith in the promise of God's help in the future.

Our prayers in the Holy Spirit are signs of God's promise to hear and help us. We cannot receive any deeper assurance of God's protection and help than God's Spirit in us and with us.

PRAYER POINT: Thank God for the Holy Spirit, our companion in prayer. Thank the Spirit for help praying and for assuring us that God cares, hears, and answers our prayers.

THE TIME ARRANGED BY GOD

Psalm 71:12–24

IN his prayer for God's protection and help, the psalmist petitioned, "O God, do not be far from me; O my God, make haste to help me!" (Ps. 71:12). The difficulties and troubles of the psalmist's life were pressing upon him, and he was in need of God's aid—soon!

We know the psalmist's feeling. There are times we pray to God for help, and for us, the sooner that help comes, the better!

But God's aid does not always come as quickly as we hope. We wait . . . and wait.

Yet we do not despair. While waiting, the psalmist recited what God had done that gave him hope and led him to praise (see v. 14). God has done "mighty deeds" (v. 16), "great things" (v. 19), and revived the psalmist in the past (see v. 20). God is faithful (see v. 22)!

Wolfgang Musculus commented that "although he longs for the help of God to come quickly, nevertheless he indicates that he will not despair, even if he is not delivered immediately. Flesh's nature is to demand that deliverance come quickly; however, it is the consideration of the spirit to hope for the time arranged by God."

In ourselves, we want deliverance to come quickly. But we wait for God. When we wait and wait for God, we can rehearse ways God has rescued and helped us in the past, trusting God to do "great things" in our future as well. The time arranged by God is our hope!

> **REFLECTION QUESTIONS:** Reflect on God's timing in your life, the ways your prayers have been answered after a period of time. What hope do you have as you wait? Have you seen that the time arranged by God has been best?

GOD IS MOVED WITH OUR PRAYERS

Psalm 72:12–14

WHEN we speak of prayer and say that God "hears" and "answers" our prayers, we recognize God is a person we can know through the Scriptures and with whom we can communicate through prayer. We know God supremely in the person of God the Son, Jesus Christ. Jesus taught that God loves us, fully and completely.

The psalmist knew God responds to prayers. For God "delivers the needy when they call, the poor and those who have no helper. He has pity on the weak and the needy, and saves the lives of the needy" (Ps. 72:12–13). God helps and saves.

Heinrich Bullinger wrote of God and our prayers: "Prayer is both always necessary unto men, and very effectual. For we plainly see that God is moved with the prayers of his faithful; for he is good and merciful, he loveth us, he took flesh, that he might be touched with feeling of our infirmities, lest we should be dismayed at him: he is true and faithful, performing those things faithfully which he promiseth."

Imagine: God is "moved with" our prayers, said Bullinger! God is good, God is merciful, and God loves us—as we know in Jesus Christ, who feels our weaknesses as those who are needy (see Heb. 4:15). When we pray, God is actively engaged with our words and feelings. God hears and answers. Believe that!

PRAYER POINT: Pray a prayer in which you pray after your expressions of thanksgiving and petition: "O Lord, hear my prayer . . ."

PUT OUR REQUESTS IN CHRIST'S HAND

Psalm 77

THE psalmist in Psalm 77 cries "aloud to God, aloud to God, that he may hear me. In the day of my trouble I seek the Lord" (vv. 1–2). This man's soul "refuses to be comforted" (v. 2). Indeed, "I think of God and I moan; I meditate, and my spirit faints" (v. 3). His situation is grim. He cannot save himself. Only God can help.

As we read, we see that the psalmist recalled God's mighty deeds, and this gave him grounds for new hope. He said, "I will call to mind the deeds of the LORD; I will remember your wonders of old. I will meditate on all your work, and muse on your mighty deeds" (vv. 11–12).

The Anglican theologian Jeremy Taylor commented—picturesquely—on the psalmist's need to realize he could not save himself or extricate himself from his troubles: "Should we not put our requests into Christ's hand to offer them to his father. . . . If we renounce our wretched selves, and imagine not the least intrinsic perfection to be in our prayers, do we sail then by the Cape of Good Hope? Yes, because God is contented to yield upon such addresses."

We realize it is not our prayers, our efforts, or our goodness that can save us. We put our requests "into Christ's hand" to offer them to God. Our prayers are imperfect. Once we realize that only Christ can help, good hope comes to us. Let's give our requests to Christ!

PRAYER POINT: Make it a focus of your prayers to put all your requests in Christ's hands by praying after each request, "I give this request to you, Lord Jesus."

PERSEVERE AND BE PATIENT

Psalm 77:1–3

IN picturesque imagery, the afflicted psalmist conveys his continuing prayer to God: "I cry aloud to God, aloud to God, that he may hear me. In the day of my trouble I seek the Lord; in the night my hand is stretched out without wearying; my soul refuses to be comforted" (Ps. 77:1–2). Day and night the psalmist prays, in the midst of the "trouble" that surrounds him. The Lord is his only hope and help.

He prays throughout the night. Then the psalmist's hand is "stretched out" in prayer—"without wearying." His soul will not be comforted until the Lord answers his prayer.

John Hooper vividly commented, "For the prophet saith, that he 'lifted up his hands all night, and waxed not weary.' Of this continuance in prayer we learn two things: the one, perseverance in prayer; and the other, patient expectation and willing sufferance until God send redress and ease." We should continue in prayer, said Hooper, to teach us that it is God alone who can help us. This continuance also gives us more opportunities to repent of our sins—which may be the source of our troubles.

Persevere and be patient. These two Ps are basic in our lives of prayer. They are not easy for us, but they are crucial. We should not quit out of frustration that God does not answer. We should endure in hope and trust as we wait.

REFLECTION QUESTION: Remember those times when you prayed for help and needed to persevere and be patient. What helped you endure in those times?

2021 mom and dad suffering with dad's sickness ☹
where is God? Lord have mercy!

45

O LORD God, I do from henceforth resolve to love my Neighbour as myself, and to love him not in Word only, but in Deed and in Truth (1 John 3:18).

I do from my Heart forgive all Men their Trespasses; do Thou, Lord, forgive them also.

Lord, bless them that hate me, and do good to them that have any way despitefully used me: O repay them Good for Evil.

O my God, bless all those that I have any way wronged; have Mercy on all those to whose Sins I have been [in] any way accessory, and give them all Grace to forgive me. Amen, Amen.

THOMAS KEN

GOD IS GOOD

Psalm 86

A FAVORITE blessing for a meal begins, "God is great, God is good; and we thank Him for our food." We pray to the God who is "great" and also "good." It is God's goodness that invites us to pray and that is a basis for all our prayers—all through our lives.

The writer of Psalm 86 knew this. In his prayers for help, he acknowledges, "You are great and do wondrous things; you alone are God" (v. 10). God is great and does "wondrous"—and very good—things!

Lutheran theologian Konrad Pellikan put this in perspective for us when he wrote, "God is good by nature, that is, eager to bring kindnesses to the needy, and those who humbly pray to him, as well as ready to forgive sins, because he is propitious and full of goodness. Therefore in every way he will help those who call on him."

This is our great hope . . . and help, isn't it? God's "greatness" means God has the power to answer our prayers and bring about God's purposes for our lives. God's "goodness" means God has the desire to answer our prayers and "bring kindnesses" to those who pray—a great "kindness" being God's readiness to "forgive sins," as Pellikan wrote. God is good "by nature." We can depend on God's goodness since God is faithful, always acting according to the divine nature. So God brings goodness to those who humbly pray to the Lord.

PRAYER POINT: Pray a prayer of thanksgiving for the goodness of God. Recount the wondrous things God has done in the history of salvation and in your own life.

PRESS HARD

Psalm 86:1–7

W E know we should pray daily. Every day we should be in conversation with God, offering praise, thanksgiving, and petitions.

In Psalm 86, the psalmist prays every day, with petitions to God: "Incline your ear, O LORD, and answer me, for I am poor and needy. . . . For to you do I cry all day long" (vv. 1, 3). The needs of the psalmist are great, and he expresses these to the God he trusts and who will be gracious to him (see vv. 2–3). The psalmist prays continually. He prays as he hopes and expects God's answers. "Listen to my cry of supplication," he prays (v. 6). Perhaps we too have felt the need to pray this vigorously—and often!

Wolfgang Musculus commented here: "We are admonished in this passage how we should not fail in praying even if we may not be immediately heard, but rather press hard without interruption until we are helped. Thus Christ teaches his own to pray ceaselessly (*sine intermission*) in Luke 18 with the example of the widow."

God desires us to pray and continue to pray, even when we may not feel that our prayers are immediately heard. Christ instructed us in this same way. We are to "press hard," as Musculus puts it, "without interruption." We continue to express our faith in the God who hears our prayers, even when our faith is tested by our not receiving God's answers to our prayers as soon as we desire. Press hard!

REFLECTION QUESTIONS: Reflect on times when you've pressed God hard for answers to your prayers. Did answers come? How was your faith affected by this continual praying?

FAITH IS ESSENTIAL

Psalm 90:1–2

P SALM 90 is a great psalm proclaiming God's eternity and our human frailty. We must find our security and help in this great God. The psalm begins the prayer majestically: "Lord, you have been our dwelling place in all generations" (v. 1). This sets things in proper perspective: Our refuge, or place of safety, or "home" (NLT) is God. Our complete life is found and secured in God.

To affirm this is a statement of faith. It is a very personal statement of faith. It is not a generalized truth; it is a confession of the reality of who we are as creatures of God. We know our place of security is in God, from God's own Spirit, as our identity is revealed to us.

Martin Luther emphasized that faith is essential to this confession when he wrote, "'You are our dwelling place.' No one can pray this prayer from the heart without faith and without the gift of the Holy Spirit. . . . Faith is essential in true prayer. If faith is present, we triumph. Because of faith in Christ our prayer is acceptable and pleasing to God and is also effective. If you believe that God is your dwelling place, he is truly a dwelling place for you. If you do not believe this, he is not."

Jesus Christ shows us God is our "dwelling place" as we live in Christ (Col. 2:6). Through faith, we are united with Christ and our prayers are his!

REFLECTION QUESTIONS: What comfort does it give you in your prayers to realize God, in Jesus Christ, is our "dwelling place"? In what ways does this affect your life of faith?

CONFIDENCE IN THE DIVINE PROMISE
Psalm 91

T HROUGHOUT the Scriptures, God promises to hear and answer prayers. These divine promises are made to people of faith and their experience showed God was true to this word. One example is God's promise to the psalmist: "When they call to me, I will answer them; I will be with them in trouble, I will rescue them and honor them" (Ps. 91:15). Other great prayer promises are also given (see Ps. 50:15; Isa. 65:24).

Zacharias Ursinus commented that without these promises that we will be heard in what we ask of God, "there is no faith; and without faith, prayer is of no avail. Except we have faith in the divine promises, and have a regard to them in our prayers, they will not avail us any thing, neither can we desire any thing with a good conscience. Confidence in the divine promise produces an assurance of being heard, and of our salvation, which assurance kindles in us a desire of calling upon God, and of making supplication to him."

Faith believes the promises of God. Without faith, why pray? We gain nothing from God and cannot ask anything of God if, in our inner self, we do not believe God hears and answers prayer.

When we pray we show we believe God's promise to hear and answer our prayers. Our confidence is strong! Our assurance is only in God's promise!

REFLECTION QUESTIONS: What are ways you express in your praying your confidence in God's promises to hear and answer prayer? And in your living?

What Is Prayer?

Psalm 102:1–2

WHEN we reflect on our prayer life through the years, we remember specific prayers. We also know we have prayed prayers now forgotten. But prayer has been vital to our lives of faith. We cannot live without prayer!

Most basically, prayer is calling upon God, conversing with God. As the psalmist puts it, "Hear my prayer, O LORD; let my cry come to you" (Ps. 102:1). We cry to God.

We realize our prayers fit into two broad types or categories. Heinrich Bullinger noted that "prayer is an humble and earnest laying forth of a faithful mind, whereby we either ask good things at God's hands, or else give him thanks for those things we have received." Our prayers are to petition or ask "good things" from God. Our prayers also give thanks to God for all the blessings we have received from God.

We may remember the specific petitions we have made to God through the years, those things we have requested from God—covering all manner of needs and situations.

We may also remember the prayers of thanksgiving we have offered to God, thanking God from the bottom of our hearts for ways God has helped us and the answers to prayer God has given.

Prayer is something about which we know. But even more importantly, prayer is that which we have experienced—in times of need and in times of gratitude. Pray!

PRAYER POINT: Pray to God, expressing your needs or petitions and expressing thanksgiving for God's blessings. Orient your future prayers to these two categories.

When You Seem Forsaken—Pray!

Psalm 116

SOMETIMES life can seem to take us to the bottom. There are times when all seems to be giving way and troubles test our faith. No matter where we turn, we cannot find a way out. We cannot free ourselves from things beyond our control— like sickness or job loss or fractured human relationships. We can empathize with the psalmist when he prayed, "The snares of death encompassed me; the pangs of Sheol laid hold on me; I suffered distress and anguish" (Ps. 116:3). He was overtaken and seized. He could find no way out.

The psalmist felt forsaken. All the dangers of life were laying hold of him. In deep agony, he felt forsaken even by God.

So he prays: "Then I called on the name of the Lord: 'O Lord, I pray, save my life!'" (v. 4). God heard and answered his prayer: "For you have delivered my soul from death" (v. 8); "I kept my faith, even when I said, 'I am greatly afflicted'" (v. 10).

Here, as John Calvin noted, "when he seemed to be most forsaken of God, that was truly the proper time, and the right season for him to give himself to prayer."

When life is at its lowest, its toughest, when it seems there is no relief and that even God has forsaken us—pray! This is our only hope and help. We pray when our need is greatest. Then we find that God is gracious; "our God is merciful" (v. 5)!

Reflection Question: Think of times when life has been toughest and you have felt most forsaken. In what ways did God act to save you and bring deliverance?

I GIVE thanks to Thee, Almighty God, for revealing thyself to me, for sending thy Son Jesus Christ, that he might become a sacrifice, that through him I might be forgiven and receive eternal life. I give thanks to Thee, O God, for making me a recipient of thy great favor through the Gospel and the Sacraments, and for preserving thy Word and thy Holy Church. O that I might truly declare thy goodness and blessings! Inflame me, I earnestly beseech Thee, with thy Holy Spirit that thanksgiving may shine forth in my life. . . . Enlighten my heart, I beseech Thee, that I may be more fully aware of thy favor toward me and forever worship Thee with true thanksgiving.

PHILIP MELANCHTHON

Direct Us by the Word

Psalm 119:105–112

T HE psalmist praised God's Word as "a lamp to my feet and a light to my path" (Ps. 119:105). We understand the meaning. God's Word—what God has said and done, known to us now in the Holy Scriptures—is the means by which we know how to live or "walk" in life. God's Word is our illumination, showing us where God wants us to go and what God wants us to do. The Scriptures are vital since they lay before us God's will and desires for the world . . . and for us!

Martin Bucer linked God's Word with prayer when he wrote that "above all we must pray that God would regard us and direct us by his divine Word." God's Word is what we need to know and follow in life. Prayer is our expression to God of what we hear in the divine Word. What we request from God in our prayer petitions gives voice to what we believe God's Word is guiding us toward. We should pray, "Direct us by your Word!"

When we pray, we ask God to direct us by the Holy Word and lead us by the Holy Spirit. Word and Spirit go together. When, through our prayers, we think we know what God's Spirit is saying to us, we should always look at this in relation to how we understand it emerging from God's Word. The Spirit will not lead us in ways contrary to the Word. The Word points us to God's will where the Spirit can direct us. Through prayer, Word and Spirit are joined!

REFLECTION QUESTIONS: In what ways do you see God's Word and God's Spirit relating to each other? What are ways to keep this relationship in mind when you pray?

Prayer: Opening of the Heart

Psalm 119:145–152

THERE are people to whom we can never open our hearts. There are others with whom we feel we can be more open. But there is one to whom we can open our hearts fully and completely.

This trustworthy One is God. The psalmist prayed, "With my whole heart I cry; answer me, O LORD" (Ps. 119:145). We see the intensity here. One opens one's "whole heart" to cry to God, seeking God's answer. Prayer is not a "spectator sport." It involves one fully, wholly, completely—and passionately—crying to God with one's heart wide open.

George Downame expressed this when he defined prayer, indicating the Protestant focuses on prayer, carried out publicly or in private: "Prayer is a simple, unfeigned [sincere], humble and ardent opening of the heart before God wherein we either ask things needful for our selves and others, or give thanks for benefits received: it is either public in the congregation of the faithful; or private, when we pray alone."

The psalmist and Downame indicate prayer should be "ardent." We open our heart to the One who knows our hearts (see Luke 16:15). We can trust God with our deepest petitions and deepest thanks. In prayer, we tell God what we want God to take control of in our lives. When we do not pray, we are trying to keep things under our own control. It is best to open our heart to God!

PRAYER POINT: Pray a prayer that is as fully open to God as possible. Intensely present your petitions; ardently thank God for the benefits you have received.

REVERENCE FOR GOD

Psalm 124

W E believe prayer is conversation with God—which it is. But as with our human conversations, we can approach God nonchalantly or offhandedly. We may not focus on the God who hears our prayers. We may instead focus on trying to express our current concerns. God hears us. But we may not turn our attention directly on the God to whom we are praying. Who is this God?

To put things in perspective, the psalmist speaks of God in the greatest way imaginable: "Our help is in the name of the LORD, who made heaven and earth" (Ps. 124:8). The One to whom we are directing our prayers—our words—is the "maker of heaven and earth," as the Apostles' Creed puts it. Imagine that!

John Knox asked, "What is to be observed in prayer" and how do we respond? He answered, "The consideration in whose presence we stand, to whom we speak, and what we desire, should excite us to the greatest reverence in doing this; standing in the presence of the omnipotent Creator of heaven and earth, and of all that is thereof."

In prayer, we approach the creator of all things, and we dare address this great God. This is the highest privilege possible! We come with greatest reverence before God. No one else can call forth this kind of reverence from us: awe, worship, and devotion. Keep in mind who God is, and revere this God!

REFLECTION QUESTIONS: What images of God do you have when you pray? What images do you have of yourself? In what ways do you try to express reverence for God?

GOD WORKS, RULES, AND GOVERNS

Psalm 145

PSALM 145 proclaims the greatness and goodness of God: "Great is the LORD, and greatly to be praised; his greatness is unsearchable" (v. 3). God's greatness is accompanied by God's goodness: "The LORD is good to all, and his compassion is over all that he has made" (v. 9).

The faith of Israel and the faith of Christians today rests in this God who is great and good. Part of both God's greatness and God's goodness is that God works, rules, and governs the universe and all within it. The psalmist wrote, "They shall speak of the glory of your kingdom, and tell of your power" (v. 11). This reminds us of the doxology, or "praise," at the end of the Lord's Prayer: "for thine is the kingdom, and the power, and the glory, for ever. Amen" (Matt. 6:13 KJV). John Bradford noted that in this praise, "I should so consider . . . especially in prayer, that I should not doubt but that thou workest, rulest, and governest all things everywhere, in all persons and creatures, most wisely, justly, and mercifully."

God is truly great and truly good. God is at work in the world, in all wisdom. God rules the world with justice and mercy, according to God's nature. God governs all things, everywhere. What greater God, what more wonderfully good God, can there be! We pray in praise to God: "Every day I will bless you, and praise your name forever and ever" (Ps. 145:2).

PRAYER POINT: As you pray, acknowledge and praise God for working in wisdom in the universe, ruling in justice and mercy, and governing all things.

Praise Arises from God's Mercy

Isaiah 63:7–9

THE Protestant Reformers recognized two types of prayer: prayers of petition and prayers of praise and thanksgiving. These form the rhythms of our prayer lives today.

Archbishop Ussher noted that "as Petition arises from the feeling of our misery: so praise from the feeling of God's mercy: Petition begs what we want, and praise acknowledges what and whence we have it (Rev. 15:3; 1 Chron. 29:12)."

Do we spend as much time in praise of God as we do in petitioning God?

David praised God: "And now, our God, we give thanks to you and praise your glorious name" (1 Chron. 29:13; see also vv. 10–13). Isaiah praised God, acknowledging God's mercy to Israel: "I will recount the gracious deeds of the LORD, the praiseworthy acts of the LORD, because of all that the LORD has done for us, and the great favor to the house of Israel that he has shown them according to his mercy, according to the abundance of his steadfast love" (Isa. 63:7).

Praise acknowledges God's greatness and goodness, expressed to us in mercy. Our praise arises from God's mercy. In praise we thank God for all we have been given, ways in which we have been blessed. Our prayers should always include this praise, acknowledging who God is and what God has done.

What God has done most is give us mercy and salvation in Jesus Christ. For the gift of Christ, we give God greatest praise!

REFLECTION QUESTIONS: In your prayer life, what is the balance of praise and petition? What are specific things for which you regularly praise God?

God Helps before We Pray

Isaiah 65:17–25

J ESUS Christ makes God known to us (see John 1:18). Jesus Christ is God incarnate, "the image of the invisible God" (Col. 1:15). In Jesus, we see the human face of God.

Jesus raised the son of the widow of Nain (see Luke 7:11–17). The boy had died. When Jesus saw his mother, he "had compassion" for her and raised her son: "Young man, I say to you, rise!" (vv. 13, 14). Without the boy's mother saying a word, Jesus's compassion overflowed, and he immediately raised her son.

Johannes Brenz commented, "And so it is made clear in Christ that the Father is so full of pity and compassion that he will help the lowly, the afflicted and the oppressed even before they pray. For so he speaks through the mouth of the prophet, saying, 'And it shall come to pass that before they cry I will hear them.'"

This remarkable promise—"Before they call I will answer, while they are yet speaking I will hear" (Isa. 65:24)—means we never pray in vain. God works to help and aid us while we are unaware. Before the widow could ask for help, Jesus showed the compassionate heart of God and raised her son!

God listens to our prayers. But God also helps us by the Spirit to sustain and preserve us . . . even before we pray!

REFLECTION QUESTIONS: Have you become aware of ways God is at work on your behalf before you come to pray about a certain need or situation? When has this happened?

O LORD God, suffer us not to lean to our own wisdom, nor to believe as blind flesh fancies, nor to seek salvation where superstition dreams; but let our faith only be grounded on thy word, and give us grace truly to believe in thee, with all our heart to put our trust in thee, to look for all good things of thee, to call upon thy blessed name in adversity, and with joyful voices and more merry hearts to praise and magnify it in prosperity. Suffer us not to doubt neither of God thy heavenly Father, nor of thee God his Son, nor of God the Holy Ghost, but earnestly to believe that you, being three distinct Persons in the Deity, are notwithstanding one very God, besides whom there is no God, neither in heaven nor in earth. Grant also, that we may assuredly believe whatsoever is contained in the holy scriptures, and by no means suffer ourselves to be plucked from the verity thereof, but mainly and steadfastly abide in the same even unto death, rage world, roar devil. And this faith, O sweet Jesu, increase thou daily in us more and more, that at the last, through thy goodness, we may be made perfect and strong men in thy holy religion, and shew ourselves both before thee and the world truly faithful, by bringing forth plenty of good works, unto the glory and honour of thy name, which with God the Father and God the Holy Ghost lives and reigns true God, worlds without end. Amen.

THOMAS BECON

A FRIENDLY TALKING WITH THE LORD

Jeremiah 29:10–14

WE pray in all seasons of our lives. We pray when times are good. We pray when times are bad. Prayer is the heartbeat of our faith. Our prayers are our lifeline with God. No wonder prayer is so central and important to us!

We are invited by God to pray, and we receive assurance that God hears and answers our prayers. This promise was made clear to Jeremiah: "Then when you call upon me and come and pray to me, I will hear you" (Jer. 29:12). No promise could be more important and more inviting!

What is prayer? Archbishop Sandys wrote, "Prayer is a lifting up of the mind unto God, or a friendly talking with the Lord, from a high and a kindled affection of the heart. In the word God speaketh unto us, in prayer we speak unto him."

We can talk with God as we would a friend. God invites us. Our hearts propel us to express what is in our minds and hearts to our Lord. Sandys simply noted that in the Word (Scripture), God speaks to us. In prayer, we speak to God.

What greater blessing can we have than to pray? Our friendly talking with the Lord is our most important conversation. We hear God's Word (breathing in), and then we speak to God (breathing out). Prayer is our breath of life!

PRAYER POINT: Think of Scripture passages that are especially meaningful to you. As you think of each one, pray about how you can live its truth.

Pray—Everywhere!

Jonah 2:1–9

W E'RE familiar with the story of Jonah. Jonah was swallowed by a big fish. Then he prayed from the belly of the fish and was thrust out on to dry land—most memorable! As someone said, this is "a whale of a tale"!

Of all people, Jonah needed to depend on the power of prayer. In the direst of circumstances, Jonah prayed to God (see Jonah 2:1–9). In the depths of danger Jonah called on God and even expressed his thanksgiving: "I with the voice of thanksgiving will sacrifice to you; what I have vowed I will pay. Deliverance belongs to the LORD!" (v. 9).

Jonah was not the only biblical character who prayed in the midst of great dangers. Bishop John Hooper listed some of these and drew an important conclusion: "Our prophet says, The Lord has no respect to the place, but unto the heart and faith of him that prays: and that appears; for penitent Jonah prayed out of the whale's belly, and miserable Job upon the dung-heap, Daniel in the cave of the lions, Jeremiah in the clay-pit, the thief upon the cross, Saint Stephen under the stones. Wherefore the grace of God is to be prayed for in every place and every where, as our necessity shall have need and wanted solace."

We can pray to God in every place and in every situation. Our need is met by God's grace and help. Pray—everywhere!

REFLECTION QUESTION: If you have had times of danger and prayed for God's help, reflect on them and thank God. When has God's grace and help made a difference for you in difficult situations?

Assured before We Pray

Matthew 6:1–8

WE realize we are not "worthy" to pray. We are flawed people—sinful people—who can never on our own earn or deserve a loving relationship with God. Yet God has reached out to save us and give us this relationship of trust and love. Through the death and resurrection of Jesus Christ, we are reconciled to God and have our sin forgiven. This is the good news of the gospel!

Now, when we come to pray, we can believe Jesus's promise that "your Father knows what you need before you ask him" (Matt. 6:8). God knows our needs before we ask. Now we can be assured God will meet our needs, even before we pray! Theodore Beza wrote that "before we pray . . . let us be assured that for as much as we be reconciled to God by his son, which is our only sufficient intercessor and advocate, we can not fail but to obtain those things which we desire by him, so that it be expedient for us."

This is a "blessed assurance"! We are assured of the blessings of the triune God, with whom we are reconciled through God the Son, who died for us. We can pray in joyful freedom, trusting God will provide for our needs and what is "expedient for us" through Jesus Christ. Our prayers are answered, not because of our "worthiness," but through what Jesus Christ has done for us. This is the confidence for prayer we need now . . . and always!

PRAYER POINT: When you begin your prayers, envision God having heard and answered them. Pray, believing—and praising Jesus Christ.

Forgive Others to Be Forgiven

Matthew 6:7–15

Forgiveness is a need for us. We need to be forgiven by God; to be forgiven by others for our sins against them; and to forgive those who have wronged us. Lots of forgiveness!

In the Lord's Prayer, Jesus gave us the petition "Forgive us our debts, as we also have forgiven our debtors" (Matt. 6:12). Then, "if you forgive others their trespasses, your heavenly Father will also forgive you; but if you do not forgive others, neither will your Father forgive your trespasses" (vv. 14–15). There is a relationship here: we must forgive others to be forgiven.

Thomas Becon showed us this when he wrote, "Forgive thy neighbor thy hurt that he hath done thee; and so shall thy sins be forgiven thee also, when thou prayest. A man that beareth hatred against another, how dare he desire forgiveness of God? He that showeth no mercy to a man, which is like himself, how dare he ask forgiveness of his sins?" Then, "except we forgive them that have offended us, although we pray never so much, yet shall not our prayers be heard of God."

When we pray "forgive us our debts, as we also have forgiven our debtors," the word *as* means "in proportion to." We can only hope for forgiveness for ourselves to the degree that we are willing to forgive others. Forgive others to be forgiven!

Prayer Point: Take time to think of forgiveness in your life—who you need to forgive and who needs to forgive you. Pray about forgiveness. Then request and act on forgiving!

WE PRAY BECAUSE GOD COMMANDS IT

Matthew 6:8–13

S OMETIMES people feel unworthy to pray. We recognize our sinfulness and guilt before God. We know that we certainly are not worthy in ourselves to pray to God.

So, why pray?

We pray because God wants us to pray. God desires to be in a relationship of trust and love with us. Prayer expresses this relationship. Conversation with God comes from the command in Scripture to pray, even when we feel unworthy.

Thomas Becon wrote: "For God neither for our worthiness nor for our unworthiness heareth us; but for his commandment and promise sake. He hath commanded us to pray; therefore ought we to pray. For if we should never pray till we were worthy of ourselves before God to pray, so should we never pray: but we therefore pray, because God hath commanded us so to do. Our worthiness is the humble confession of our unworthiness; and our obedience unto the commandment of God to pray maketh us most worthy."

Regardless of who we are or what we have done, God commands us to pray. Jesus said to his disciples, "Pray then in this way" (Matt. 6:9). Then follows the Lord's Prayer. When we confess we are "unworthy" to pray, we become "worthy" in the sense that we are recognizing prayer comes at God's command and invitation. Prayer is a gracious gift to us. We obey God's command and desire that we pray!

REFLECTION QUESTION: What difference does it make to recognize that our prayers are offered because of God's command, rather than because of any "worthiness" in ourselves?

THE GREATEST COMFORT IN THE WORLD

Matthew 6:9–13

OUR prayers to God bring us comfort. Our conversations with God sustain us because God hears and answers our prayers. In prayer, we commit ourselves to doing God's will. Being in God's presence through this means of grace is one of the deepest joys of our Christian lives.

The Lord's Prayer brings us comfort. Here we pray for those things about which Jesus cared most. This prayer is a model for our own prayers, and it opens us into the heart of God.

The Protestant martyr Hugh Latimer spoke of our comfort in prayer when he wrote, "Truly it is the greatest comfort in the world to talk with God, and to call upon him, in this prayer that Christ himself has taught us; for it taketh away the bitterness of all afflictions. Through prayer we receive the Holy Ghost, which strengthens and comforts us at all times, in all trouble and peril."

In the Lord's Prayer, the bitterness of all our afflictions are removed. They are cast on God and entrusted to God's care. The Holy Spirit joins us. The Spirit's presence strengthens us for all the needs we face. The Spirit comforts us in all times of our lives. We can trust that when we are in trouble or danger, the Spirit is with us. We never face life alone. God's Spirit is in us. This assurance is truly "the greatest comfort in the world"!

PRAYER POINT: Pray the Lord's Prayer. As you do, thank God for the ways each petition comforts you and leads you into ways of serving Jesus Christ.

O MY Lord and only Saviour Jesu Christ, which came into this world to take away the heavy burdens of them that were loaden, to seek that was lost, to call sinners unto repentance, to give everlasting life to the faithful, and to be a Mediator between God the Father and us; I, poor and wretched sinner, from the very heart lament and inwardly bewail my sinful and wretched life, desiring thee, for thy promise sake, according to thy merciful wont, to be my Mediator and Advocate unto God the Father that he may forgive me all mine old sins, and so wholly possess my heart by his blessed Spirit, that he may defend me against all perils to come, which the devil, the world, or the flesh, imagineth against me, and so change me into a new man, that, my old sins being wiped away in thy precious blood, I may walk from virtue to virtue, unto the glory and praise of his blessed name. Amen.

THOMAS BECON

WE ASK, SEEK, AND LIVE

Matthew 6:25–33

P RAYER is not simply an exercise we go through or a litany of wants that we offer to God. Nor is it segregated from what we do in the rest of our days.

We see these approaches countered by Jesus's comprehensive command: "Strive first for the kingdom of God and his righteousness, and all these things will be given to you as well" (Matt. 6:33). Our most strenuous efforts are devoted to living for the kingdom of God and to conveying God's righteousness. When we do this, all that we have been concerned about—food, clothing, all else!—will be given to us. This is the great compass for our lives, our "marching orders," our deepest desire: strive for God's kingdom and righteousness!

This means, according to George Downame, that "what we are to ask in prayer, we are to seek and to labour for in our practice, and to endeavour in our lives, lest we may seem to tempt God."

We do not simply ask for things in prayer and then sit back and wait for God's answer to appear. Instead, we seek these things in life and endeavor—work!—for them. If we do not, we are tempting God. When we know what God wants, we seek the kingdom before us. So we ask, seek, and live for God's great reign!

REFLECTION QUESTION: Think of ways you try to follow through with your prayers, ways in which you act on the things for which you pray. Do you consciously try to put "feet" to your prayers, living out God's answers to your prayers?

GOD APPOINTS THE MEANS TO ANSWER US

Matthew 7:7–11

S OMETIMES we may wonder, What's the use of praying? God knows all things. God's will is being done. Why do we need to pray if God is at work, knowing what we want, and determining what to do in the world and in our lives? Why pray?

On prayer, Jesus instructed, "Ask, and it will be given you; search, and you will find; knock, and the door will be opened for you" (Matt. 7:7). Jesus tells us to pray, asking God for what we need and believing God hears and answers our prayers. Ask and knock.

Archbishop James Ussher said in relation to this verse that "for as God hath fore-appointed all necessaries to be given us; so hath he also appointed the means whereby they should be brought to pass, whereof Prayer is a chief."

God appoints the means by which our prayers are answered. As we ask and knock, we are participating in what God is doing to answer our prayers. When we pray, we do not know in what ways God will answer our prayers. So we "ask and knock." Our prayers are a major means God uses to bring forth the answers to our prayers. As we pray, we are doing what God desires. Through our prayers—and our actions—our prayers can be answered.

This makes prayer exciting for us! We ask and knock, not knowing *how* God will answer, but believing God *will* answer our prayers!

REFLECTION QUESTION: Think of when you have continued to "ask" and "knock" with your prayers. When have you seen how God used your prayers as a means of answering your prayers?

PRAYING FOR SPIRITUAL AND TEMPORAL THINGS

Matthew 8:1–4

J ESUS healed many people. One was a leper who petitioned Jesus, saying, "Lord, if you choose, you can make me clean." Then, Jesus "stretched out his hand and touched him, saying, 'I do choose. Be made clean!' Immediately his leprosy was cleansed" (Matt. 8:2–3). This man prayed for what was most important to him—his health. When he asked Jesus for his cleansing, he said, "Lord, if you choose . . ."

Zacharias Ursinus, in describing "acceptable prayer," wrote, "For faith submits itself to every word and desire of God. But the will and pleasure of God consist in this, that we desire and pray for spiritual things simply, and for temporal things conditionally, and that we be fully persuaded that we shall receive the former particularly; and the latter in as far as they contribute to the glory of God and our salvation. Praying in this way, we do not doubt in regard to our being heard."

Ursinus meant we should pray for what is necessary for salvation, fully believing God will give these spiritual things. We may pray for "temporal things," which are not necessary for salvation, with the same condition as that of the leper: "Lord, if you choose . . ." Things like the forgiveness of sins and eternal life are spiritually necessary for our salvation. Temporal things we ask for should be submitted to God's Word and will, if they will be profitable for us and contribute to God's glory. God will hear our prayers and answer!

PRAYER POINT: Pray in a straightforward way for those things necessary for salvation. Pray for your needs and desires with the provision "Lord, if you choose . . ."

GOD HEARS OUR PETITIONS

Matthew 21:18–22

FAITH is key to prayer. We believe our prayers are heard and answered by God. Our Christian faith is centered in Jesus Christ. Through Jesus Christ we can approach God. Through Christ our prayers are presented to God, and Christ is our great intercessor (see Rom. 8:34; Heb. 7:25). We pray in the name of Jesus Christ our Lord (see 1 Cor. 1:9).

Jesus himself invites us to pray—to pray in faith. In the incident of the fig tree, Jesus said, "Whatever you ask for in prayer with faith, you will receive" (Matt. 21:22). This is an open promise to us as believers who trust Jesus's invitation: "I will do whatever you ask in my name, so that the Father may be glorified in the Son" (John 14:13). Our prayers are made in the name of Jesus, and we want what we ask for to be in line with Jesus himself and Jesus's will for us.

John Bradford reminded us that God hears our petition when he wrote, "In prayer I should in no wise doubt of being heard, but be assured that thou which hast commanded me to pray, and hast promised to hear me, dost most graciously for thy mercy's sake and truth's sake hear my petitions according to thy good will, through Jesus Christ thy dear Son, our Lord and only Saviour."

Our prayers are heard by God, who hears us through Jesus Christ our Savior.

PRAYER POINT: Think of the life of Jesus, what he taught and what he did. Pray to God to help you to live in light of Jesus. Make all your petitions to God in Jesus's name.

PRAY TO THE TRINITY

Matthew 28:16–20

W HEN we pray, sometimes we address God the Father, or Jesus Christ the Son, or the Holy Spirit. We may have images in our mind of the One to whom we direct our prayer.

Regardless of where our direct focus may be, as Christians we are always praying to the Trinity: Father, Son, and Holy Spirit.

God is one God. God is three persons. The term *Trinity* expresses our confession that God is one God in three persons. This has been the church's view since the early centuries. All three members are equal in power, in glory. They all share the same divine "substance"—each one is fully God. The three members of the Trinity work in their various ways. But their divine intercommunion unites them as one God.

Archbishop James Ussher posed the following question and answer: "Whether must we direct our prayers, to the Father, or the Son, or to the Holy-Ghost? We must pray to the Trinity of Persons in the Unity of the Godhead; that is to say, to one God in Trinity."

When we pray, we have the deepest assurance that our one God in three persons hears our prayers. The holy Trinity assures us that Jesus Christ truly shows us who God is. The Trinity assures that the Spirit will never lead us in ways that contradict what we know of God in Jesus Christ. The Trinity assures that God the Father hears our prayers and answers us. Pray to the triune God!

PRAYER POINT: Pray a portion of your prayer to each member of the Trinity. Close by praising and glorifying God as "God in three persons, blessed Trinity"!

ABBA, FATHER

Mark 14:32–42

S EVERAL times in the New Testament, we find the words *Abba, Father* (see Mark 14:36; Rom. 8:15; Gal. 4:6). In Aramaic, the language Jesus spoke, *Abba* is the word for "Father." It is a term that expresses the closest and deepest intimacy of the relationship of parent and child.

No wonder Jesus prayed "Abba, Father" on the eve of his crucifixion as he struggled in the deep agony of prayer in Gethsemane (Mark 14:36). Jesus was addressing God the Father with the term that expressed his deepest recognition of who God is and the relationship of love between God the Father and God the Son.

Philip Melanchthon said, "'Abba, Father.' By this he taught us that these two things are required in prayer, namely, the ardent affection of the mind and the faithful trust of children toward God: these two words testify that both of these aspects were present in Christ."

Our minds and hearts are joined in prayer. We know we pray to God, and we express our deepest trust in our loving Father in heaven. Without a firm knowledge of God—our creator and Lord—our prayers are vacuous, hollow. Without the deep trust of a child for a parent, our prayers have no meaning.

Mind and heart are joined as we pray in the deepest way we know—"Abba, Father."

REFLECTION QUESTION: Reflect on what it means that the great creator has also called us into a loving relationship of parent and child.

WHAT have we, O heavenly Father, that we have not received? Every good gift, and every perfect gift, is from above, and cometh down from thee, which art the Father of lights. Seeing then all that we have is thine, whether it pertain to the body or to the soul, how can we be proud and boast ourselves of that which is none of our own; seeing also that, as to give, so to take away again thou art able, and wilt, whensoever thy gifts be abused, and thou not acknowledged to be the giver of them? Take therefore away from me all pride and haughtiness of mind, and graff in me true humility, that I may knowledge thee the giver of all good things, be thankful unto thee for them, and use them unto thy glory and the profit of my neighbor. Grant also, that all my glory and rejoicing may be in no earthly creatures, but in thee alone, which dost mercy, equity, and righteousness upon earth. To thee alone be all glory. Amen.

THOMAS BECON

TRANSFORMED IN PRAYER

Luke 9:28–36

UNEXPECTED things happen when we pray! Take the example of Jesus. We read that Jesus took Peter, John, and James with him and "went up on the mountain to pray" (Luke 9:28). What happened next? Nothing less than the transfiguration! The appearance of Jesus's face changed, "and his clothes became dazzling white" (v. 29). Moses and Elijah appeared and a voice came from heaven saying of Jesus: "This is my Son, my Chosen; listen to him!" (v. 35).

Philip Melanchthon took this experience of Jesus's transformation to encourage us to pray. He wrote of Jesus, "Because he was transformed while he was at prayer, it shows how we are transformed into God when we are praying, which should cause us to be that much more earnest to pray." Melanchthon cited examples of transformations that occurred when people were praying: Daniel in Daniel 9, Paul in Acts 9, Peter and Cornelius in Acts 10.

We never know what might happen when we pray . . . we might be "transformed"! Melanchthon spoke of these biblical figures being "so often rapt and carried into heaven during prayer." Our transformations can be less dramatic, but very powerful. God's Spirit can give us new understandings, new visions, or new things to do—for God and for others. In prayer, we realize that we are transformed into new life!

REFLECTION QUESTIONS: Think of your experience of prayer through the years. Have there been times when you were aware of being "transformed" by your prayers? What resulted?

We Shall Want for Nothing

Luke 11:1–4

I n Luke's version of the Lord's Prayer, we have the basic request that God will "give us each day our daily bread" (Luke 11:3). This is a petition we may overlook. Many of us are not used to asking God directly to provide our "daily bread"—whatever form that takes.

Philip Melanchthon said our "bread" is not ours by "right and as if it were owed to us like a debt, but rather that it is necessary for us and appointed to us by that providence of our life by which the Lord feeds all things out of his goodness. He gives it to us freely, because he does not want us to be in need." Our bread is God's gift, given so we will not be in need.

Melanchthon went on to say that "in many places in Scripture we are commanded to cast all our cares on God, and he promises most liberally on his part that we shall want for nothing."

God's great promise is to provide for our needs. In the Lord's Prayer, we express our dependence on God. We request our basic needs. We are casting a "burden" of our lives (Ps. 55:22) on our Lord who "promises most liberally" to provide so we shall "want for nothing"!

Prayer Point: Spend time in prayer remembering all the necessities you have and bringing them one by one before the Lord. Ask God to meet these needs.

THE HAMMER OF PRAYER

Luke 11:5–8

To teach perseverance in prayer, Jesus told of the friend who knocks at midnight (see Luke 11:5–8). When he arrives, he leaves the host in need of bread. The host approaches another friend at midnight to ask for three loaves of bread, but the friend refuses, replying, "Do not bother me; the door has already been locked, and my children are with me in bed; I cannot get up and give you anything" (v. 7). But, said Jesus, when the friend persists, the man in bed will give the bread.

The Lutheran pastor Johann Spangenberg wrote, "This sleeping friend is God our Lord, for when we call on him in times of trouble or danger and he does not answer us so quickly, he seems to us to be asleep. And so we continue to knock on the door of his fatherly heart with the hammer of prayer. For the prayer that flows from a faithful heart is such a hammer that it will be heard loud and clear in the highest heaven."

If the sleepy friend will eventually grant the request for bread, how much more will our good God answer our prayers! Spangenberg calls prayer a "hammer" that God will hear! His point is that while God appears to be "asleep," our prayers will still be heard. God's "fatherly heart" will lead God to answer the heartfelt prayers of those who pray . . . and persist in praying. Use "the hammer of prayer"!

REFLECTION QUESTION: Reflect on times in your life when you have prayed and had to be persistent in prayer. What did the persistence teach you about prayer . . . and God?

GOD GIVES WHAT IS BETTER

Luke 18:1–8

A BASIC belief when we pray is that God knows what is best for us. This is, in part, why we pray. We want to ask for what is best for us, believing that God knows what is best and will give what is best for us. Prayer is a primary means to know and understand God's will for us.

As we wait for God to answer our prayer, we may get discouraged if we think God is not hearing us or concerned with us. Waiting can wear on us, especially on our faith.

But Jesus spoke about our "need to pray always and not to lose heart" (Luke 18:1). His parable indicated God will, indeed, answer our prayers. While our faith may be tested, it should not be overthrown. We ought always to pray and believe God will answer. Faith must persevere!

Archbishop James Ussher commented about God's delays in answering prayers: "If we faint not in praying, we shall in due season be sure of a blessing (Lk. 18:7, 8) and that when our God denies us, or delays us in that which seems good unto us, even then he gives us that which he knows is better for us (2 Cor. 12:8, 9)."

When God says no, God gives us something better! This is the persevering faith we need in prayer. Don't lose heart! God knows best what we need, and God will give us what is best!

REFLECTION QUESTION: Reflect on when your faith has flickered as you waited for God to answer your prayers. Have you found God's answer to be better than that for which you prayed?

Pray When Facing Fear and Affliction

Luke 22:41–44

Jesus's anguished prayer in the garden of Gethsemane is most poignant. On the eve of his crucifixion, with the weight of the sins of the world upon him, Jesus withdrew from his disciples on the Mount of Olives to pray. He prayed, "Father, if you are willing, remove this cup from me; yet, not my will but yours be done" (Luke 22:42). His agonizing prayer meant "his sweat became like great drops of blood" (v. 44).

From this example of Jesus, the Lutheran preacher Veit Dietrich said we see "how we should behave when fear, trials and affliction are at hand." Jesus was "grieved and worried." The cross was before him. But "he did not simply dwell on his problems. Instead he went out, fell on his face and prayed." His prayer was intense. But Jesus entrusted himself fully to the will of God.

Dietrich wrote that Jesus's example teaches us "not [to] let affliction bother you so much that you forget to pray. For when we are facing fear and affliction, it is very pleasing to God if we do not give up hope but rather turn our hearts toward him and seek for help from him."

In the times we need God most, we pray as Jesus did. We pray when we face fear and affliction.

Reflection Questions: Think of the times you have been most afraid or most afflicted. What was your attitude? Did you pray? Did you find help from God?

GOD HELPS IN A BETTER WAY

Luke 24:13–35

THE story of the travelers on the road to Emmaus is one of the loveliest short stories in the world. On Easter evening, the risen Christ was revealed to two travelers "in the breaking of the bread" (Luke 24:35).

The two travelers were setting out for Emmaus when "Jesus himself came near and went with them, but their eyes were kept from recognizing him" (vv. 15–16). When they came near their destination, it appeared Jesus was going further. But the travelers "urged him strongly," saying, "Stay with us" (v. 29).

Martin Luther interpreted this "strong urging" as a kind of prayer, writing, "God inspired [these pious people] to invite Christ, but they did not yet know that this would be salvation. The prayer is good, but God rejects the means that we suggest to him. Likewise it also happens with us; God comes to help us sometimes through another way or a better way."

The travelers invited or strongly urged or "prayed to" Jesus to stay, practicing hospitality. But God had a more important function in mind when the travelers came to realize who Jesus was—as they broke bread together. Luther said God rejected the "means" the travelers suggested and that God helped the travelers—and us!—through "another" and "better way."

We never know how God will take our prayers beyond our imaginings or how they "should" be answered. God helps in a better way!

PRAYER POINT: As you pray, be open and alert to unexpected ways God may help you—ways that can be better than your own prayers themselves!

G RANT, Almighty God, that as thou hast hitherto shewn to us so many favours, since the time thou hast been pleased to adopt us as thy people, —O grant, that we may not forget so great a kindness, nor be led away by the allurements of Satan, nor seek for ourselves inventions, which may at length turn to our ruin; but that we may continue fixed in our obedience to thee, and daily call on thee, and drink of the fullness of thy bounty, and at the same time strive to serve thee from the heart, and to glorify thy name, and thus to prove that we are wholly devoted to thee, according to the great obligations under which thou hast laid us, when it had pleased thee to adopt us in thine only-begotten Son.—Amen.

JOHN CALVIN

OUR PRAYERS ARE ACCEPTED IN CHRIST

John 16:16–24

CHRISTIAN prayer is marked by calling upon God through God the Son, Jesus Christ. Our prayers are made in the name of Jesus Christ. We believe it is through the work of Jesus Christ—who was God in human flesh (God incarnate) and who died on the cross for the forgiveness of human sin—that we may now come to God in prayer. Jesus Christ is the "mediator" between God and humanity (1 Tim. 2:5). He was the mediator through his cross, and he now is the one through whom we can come before God as he intercedes for us (see Rom. 8:34) and continues to do so (see Heb. 7:25). We approach God in Jesus Christ, through faith.

George Downame explained that a requirement for prayer is "faith: for as we are in our prayers to call upon God in the name of Christ; so are we to believe, that for Christ his sake the Lord will hear us, and so far forth grant our requests as shall be most for his glory, and our good. . . .We and our prayers shall be accepted of him in his son. This faith is to be grounded also on the gracious promises of God made unto us in Christ."

We now can claim the gracious promise Jesus made to his disciples: "I tell you, if you ask anything of the Father in my name, he will give it to you" (John 16:23). Our prayers are accepted in Christ, and our prayers are answered through Christ!

REFLECTION QUESTION: In what ways do you think of Jesus Christ as the one through whom we can come to God and the one through whom God accepts our prayers?

Pray for the Whole Human Race

John 17:6–19

P RIOR to his crucifixion, Jesus prayed for his disciples. He prayed for those who "have believed that you sent me" (John 17:8). He said, "I am asking on their behalf; I am not asking on behalf of the world, but on behalf of those whom you gave me, because they are yours" (v. 9).

Our prayers should also be for the church, Christ's disciples throughout the world. We are joined by faith in Jesus Christ with believers all across the earth.

At the same time, we should be praying for all people. John Calvin wrote that "we ought to pray that this and that and every man may be saved and so embrace the whole human race, because we cannot yet distinguish the elect from the reprobate." That is, we should pray for all persons—that they come to faith in Jesus Christ and that they know the love of God. This would include the meeting of their needs since we desire others to know it is God who provides for them and gives them salvation through the death and resurrection of Jesus Christ.

We pray for all who are "created in God's image," and "we leave to God's judgment those whom He knows," Calvin went on to say. It is not our job to determine who has or will have faith and who will not. So we pray for all, leaving God's will and work up to God. We are to pray "for the whole human race"! Let us pray . . .

PRAYER POINT: Pray vigorously for all the earth's people. Pray they may know Jesus Christ as their Lord and Savior. Pray for God's Spirit to bring them faith and meet their needs.

Pray for Enemies

Acts 7:54–60

In the whole Bible, one of the hardest commands to obey is the command of Jesus to forgive our enemies (see Luke 6:27). Our urge is to hate our enemies, not love them.

Relatedly, it is a hard command to pray for your enemies. As Jesus puts it, "Bless those who curse you, pray for those who abuse you" (Luke 6:28). On our own, we realize we do not have the strength—or the will—to pray for enemies. We need the power of God's Spirit to enable us to utter those prayers.

Thomas Becon put it simply: "Yea, though he be your extreme enemy and seeketh your life, yet wish well unto him, pray for him, and desire God to forgive him, as Christ and Stephen did."

Becon refers to the stoning of Stephen, when Stephen, "filled with the Holy Spirit" (Acts 7:55), was enabled by the Spirit to pray for his enemies: "Lord, do not hold this sin against them" (v. 60). The Spirit enabled enemy-forgiving prayer. Stephen is a great example of forgiving enemies—even as they were putting him to death!

So also is Jesus. We remember his words from the cross: "Father, forgive them; for they do not know what they are doing" (Luke 23:34). Jesus prayed for those who crucified him.

We must pray for the Spirit to give us this enemy-forgiving love. We pray for those who do us harm and then forgive them for even the deepest wounds.

Prayer Point: Think of all those who have done you harm, in whatever ways. Pray for them. Ask God's Spirit to help you offer forgiveness to them.

Prayer as a Means of Grace

Acts 9:10–19

THE story of Saul's dramatic conversion on the road to Damascus, told in Acts 9:1–9, is followed by his blindness. Saul (later known as Paul) was healed and his sight returned when Ananias, as directed by God, came to Saul and laid his hands on him (see v. 12).

Ananias had a vision in which God told him to find Saul. Meanwhile, Saul was praying—"At this moment he is praying" (v. 11)—and saw in a vision that Ananias would come to restore his sight (see v. 12). He prayed and was prepared for Ananias to come and heal him. Saul was expecting Ananias because of his prayer.

John Wesley wrote that "when we say, 'Prayer is a means of grace,' we understand, a channel through which the grace of God is conveyed." We see in this story that prayer prepared Saul for the reception of God's grace. Prayer was a means or channel of God's grace when God used Ananias to restore Saul's sight.

When we pray, we put ourselves in the position to receive God's grace through our prayers. We never know what God will do when—and while—we pray. He may bring new blessings, new visions, or new life. We should pray expectantly, casting all things in humble trust before God. God can use our prayer as a channel of blessing to do for us and in us what God desires. God's grace comes to us!

> **PRAYER POINT:** Pray in complete dependence on God. Pray expectantly, believing that God's grace will come to you and bless you in unexpected ways!

FOCUSES FOR PRAYER

Romans 5:1–5

O UR lives of prayer can take us in many directions. There is much to pray about, and much to pray for, each day. We have many specifics for which to pray—whether we are thanking God for them or requesting them. These are good focuses for us, what some have called ESP—"Experiments in Specific Prayer"!

But sometimes we need to stand back a bit. We need to let the focus of some of our prayers be on "the big picture" or the "umbrella" under which all our other prayers are set. John Wesley provided us with several good focuses for prayer when he wrote his requests for prayers for himself. His words apply to our own prayers as well: "Pray, that the love of God and of all mankind, may be more largely poured into my heart; that I may be more fervent and active in doing the will of my Father which is in heaven; more zealous of good works, and more careful to abstain from all appearance of evil."

Romans 5:5 gives us this image: "God's love has been poured into our hearts through the Holy Spirit that has been given to us." And Wesley gives us this advice: pray to love God and all humankind more fully, to fervently do God's will, to be passionate about doing good works, and to avoid all appearance of evil.

These are focuses for prayer that can help to keep our whole Christian life in focus!

PRAYER POINT: Use the elements Wesley highlighted as a basis for your prayers on a regular basis. Pray them . . . and live them!

THE HOLY SPIRIT CAUSES US TO PRAY

Romans 8:26–27

O UR prayers take place in many places, at many times. We may have set times for prayer while at other times our prayers are more spontaneous.

But one thing is true of all our prayers: All are initiated by the Holy Spirit. No matter when or where or why we pray, the impulse to prayer comes from God's Spirit within us.

Paul focuses on this: "The Spirit helps us in our weakness; for we do not know how to pray as we ought, but that very Spirit intercedes with sighs too deep for words" (Rom. 8:26). Since we "do not know how to pray as we ought," it is the Spirit who sets our manner of praying and originates prayers in our hearts. We need the Spirit's help with our prayers, including initiating our prayers.

This was emphasized by Heinrich Bullinger when he wrote, "Though there be many causes concurring which move men to prayer, yet the chief [origin] of prayer is the Holy Ghost; to whose motion and government, in the entrance of all prayers, whosoever pray with any fruit do beg with an holy preface." In short, the Spirit is the origin of our prayers, and all who pray should beg for the Spirit to stir us up to begin to pray.

Ask for God's Spirit to help you to pray—anytime and anywhere!

REFLECTION QUESTION: Think about your prayers and what led you to pray the prayers you prayed. Do you associate your impulse to pray with God's Spirit?

O MERCIFUL Father, we cry unto thee in all trouble, and call upon thee through the crucified Jesus. Suffer us not to sink in great afflictions, give us not over unto our own strength; but the more the enemy presseth upon us, the more be thou our assistance: for in all anguish and trouble thou art the right helper and most faithful friend. If temptation then come upon us by thy fatherly will, grant us grace, O Lord, patiently to bear it, and to lay the burden upon thy mercy; that in all trouble we, being else destitute of all consolation, may put our whole trust only in thee. Amen.

MILES COVERDALE

The Holy Spirit:
Our Helper and Teacher

Romans 8:26–27

O UR times of prayer are special because they focus us
directly on God, and we recognize they are prompted for
us by the Holy Spirit. In these times we are aware of a "spirit of
prayer" that enables us to concentrate on what we are saying to
God and what God is saying to us. This time provides opportunities to thank God and petition God as we trust the One who
hears and answers our prayer.

To the question "What is the spirit of prayer?" James Ussher
answered, "An especial grace and operation of the holy Ghost
(Jude 20), called therefore the Spirit of grace and Supplication
(Zech. 12:10), enabling us to pour out our souls unto the Lord
(Ps. 62:8), with sighs that cannot be expressed (Rom. 8:26). For
the holy Ghost must be our helper in prayer, to teach us both
what to pray, and how to pray (Rom. 8:26)."

The Holy Spirit, who calls us to prayer, helps us in prayer by
teaching us what we should pray and how to present our prayers
to God. The Spirit surrounds us in prayer and is our helper and
teacher in prayer.

This is exactly what we need for our prayers. Paul's words
are deeply meaningful to us. He wrote, "The Spirit helps us in
our weakness; for we do not know how to pray as we ought, but
that very Spirit intercedes with sighs too deep for words" (Rom.
8:26).

Prayer Point: As you pray, think of the Holy Spirit as
your helper and teacher. Ask the Spirit for help in your
prayers—to teach you what to pray for and how to pray
for it.

HOPE WORKS BY PRAYER

Romans 12:9–13

I N the closing part of Paul's letter to Christians at Rome, he speaks about the marks of a true Christian (see Rom. 12:9–21). He instructs his readers, "Rejoice in hope, be patient in suffering, persevere in prayer" (v. 12). Here, hope is linked with prayer.

Lancelot Andrewes explored this connection when he wrote that "the fruit of faith is hope, and the fruit of hope is prayer . . . hope works by prayer. And so the property of hope is to stir us up to prayer, and the property of prayer is to . . . express the desires of our hope."

We sense this in our own lives, don't we? Our faith—in God's loving salvation in Jesus Christ—produces our hope in God's future, in eternal life, in knowing God. Hope leads us to pray because "hope works by prayer." Because we hope, we pray to God in thanksgiving and in petitions. In our prayers, we express the "desires of our hope"—what we hope God will be and do for us and for the world.

Without hope, there would be no prayer. Without prayer, we would not hope. In hope we pray for God's great works in Jesus Christ, and God's ongoing presence and work in our own lives.

Realizing the connection of hope and prayer energizes us. In prayer, we have a way to express our hope honestly and fully before God. Our hope draws forth our prayers, bringing us into God's presence—which brings deepest joy and blessings!

REFLECTION QUESTIONS: Think about the hope we have in Jesus Christ and also that for which you hope. In what ways does this hope urge you to pray? Do you pray for those things for which you hope?

GOD GRANTS WHAT IS GOOD FOR US

Romans 16:25–27

MOST of the time we think we know what is good for us. We make our choices and seek to achieve our desires. We may pursue this path in our prayers. We let God know what we want and what we think is good for us.

But God does not always answer our prayers the ways we want or give us what we desire. That's a good thing!

Our prayers usually focus on what will make things go well with us. But Heinrich Bullinger pointed out that "God, since he is only wise, knows what can profit and what can hurt us, and does not give us what we ask; yet by not giving he in very deed grants that which is good for us. Therefore the lawful prayer of the faithful is always effectual, and evermore obtains his purpose; the Lord granting to his that which he knows to be good."

God gives us what is good for us—even when God says no to our prayer requests. God knows what is good for us better than we do ourselves. For God is "the only wise God," as Paul proclaims (Rom. 16:27).

We need to trust that even when our prayers are not answered as we think we want them to be, God is still granting what is good for us. God knows best. Trust "the only wise God"!

REFLECTION QUESTION: When have you found that God has given you not what you asked for in prayer, but what was ultimately good for you?

God Plentifully Pours Abundance

1 Corinthians 2:6–13

OUR confidence in prayer is based on God's greatness and goodness, seen in God's love shown to us in Jesus Christ. We believe in God's providence—that God leads and guides, working in our lives to carry out good purposes and help us do God's will. In prayer, we receive the grace of conversation with God and blessings God gives. We hold to this faith even as we await God's answers to our prayers.

While awaiting death in the Tower of London, the Protestant martyr John Bradford wrote a letter to his mother on February 24, 1554. He wrote about a reason God may put off answering our prayers: God "doth put off our prayers, that he might recompense it with abundance, that is, that he might more plentifully pour upon us the effect of our petitions."

We can imagine that no one would seek an answer to his prayers more ardently than Bradford while awaiting death. Yet he believed that even with no apparent answers to prayers, God plentifully pours abundance on those who pray!

At the end of his letter Bradford mentions God's promise—which believers receive and anticipate, even in the midst of their sufferings and afflictions. Paul recorded the promise: "What no eye has seen, nor ear heard, nor the human heart conceived, what God has prepared for those who love him" (1 Cor. 2:9) Plentiful abundance! Now and forever!

REFLECTION QUESTION: When have you found that God has plentifully poured out abundance to you, even as you waited for an answer to your prayers?

Why Does God Delay in Helping Us?

2 Corinthians 12:1–10

AFTER we pray and pray, we wonder, Why doesn't God hurry to answer my prayers? Our faith seems tested while we wait for God to answer—in whatever ways God chooses. Waiting is hard for us. While we wait, our faith can flicker when we feel that God does not hear us or care about us or remember us.

Archbishop James Ussher responded to this question of why God—who sees and hears us pray—may delay in helping us. Ussher wrote that reasons may be "because we are sometimes too haughty, and he will humble us; sometimes too hasty, and he will curb us (2 Cor. 12:7–9). Sometimes we fail in the matter, asking we know not what; sometimes in the manner asking, we know not how; and sometimes in the end, asking we know not [why]."

What Ussher is pointing toward is illustrated by Paul seeking relief from his "thorn in the flesh," which he asked God three times to take from him (see 2 Cor. 12:7–9). Through his prayers, Paul could see this was given "to keep me from being too elated" (v. 7). Other reasons for God's delay can be that we are not asking for what is best for us or we are not realizing that God is giving what is best for us.

When an answer is delayed, we should hear God's answer to Paul: "My grace is sufficient for you, for power is made perfect in weakness" (v. 9).

REFLECTION QUESTION: Reflect on the times when you have fervently prayed for God to hurry to help you. When you look back at the experience, what do you learn about the ways of God?

When You Don't Feel Like Praying

Galatians 4:1–7

T HERE are times when we simply don't feel like praying. We have a power failure of the spirit—our spirit! Theologically, we know it is God's Holy Spirit who prompts us to pray. In John Calvin's Catechism, he wrote that "the Spirit of God helps us with groanings that cannot be uttered, and forms in our hearts the affection and zeal that God requires as Paul says (Rom. 8:26; Gal. 4:6)."

Then Calvin went on to ask, "Does this mean that we have not to incite and urge ourselves to pray?" The answer is "By no means. On the contrary, when we do not feel such a disposition within us we should beseech the Lord to put it into us, so as to make us capable and fit to pray as we ought."

When we don't feel like praying, we should ask God's Spirit to stir in us and enable us to pray. We cannot create our own urge to pray. But we can ask for God's Spirit to establish the desire to pray within us. We pray in faith, believing God's promises. With the promise that God's Spirit is sealed in our lives (see Eph. 1:13; 4:30), we can appeal to that Spirit to help us pray!

Reflection Question: Think of the times when you did not feel like praying. What changed things? Try asking God's Spirit to move you to pray, and see what happens!

BEHOLD, Lord, an empty vessel that needs to be filled. My Lord, fill it. I am weak in the faith; strengthen thou me. I am cold in love; warm me and make me fervent that my love may go out to my neighbor. I do not have a strong and firm faith; at times I doubt and am unable to trust thee altogether. O Lord, help me. Strengthen my faith and trust in thee. In thee I have sealed the treasures of all I have. I am poor; thou art rich and didst come to be merciful to the poor. I am a sinner; thou art upright. With me there is an abundance of sin; in thee is the fullness of righteousness. Therefore, I will remain with thee of whom I can receive but to whom I may not give. Amen.

MARTIN LUTHER

Prayer Surpasses All Good Works

Galatians 6:7–10

Sometimes we can have a view of prayer that is too narrow. When we pray, we petition God for our needs; we thank God for our blessings. We also pray for others. But very often, our prayer is focused mostly on ourselves.

We need to realize that prayer is also an action that touches others—in fact, our prayers can touch the whole world!

Hugh Latimer was preaching about good works—especially giving alms or charitable contributions to others. He noted that by giving alms, he could help only one or two people. But "with my faithful prayer I help all." He went on to say, "What an excellent thing prayer is, when it proceedeth from a faithful heart; it doth far pass all the good works that men can do." Latimer said he desired God to "comfort" all living people and that "we ought to pray with all our hearts for the other, which believe not, that God will turn their hearts and renew them with his Spirit."

So our prayers can reach the whole world! Paul urged the Galatians to "work for the good of all" (Gal. 6:10). Through our prayers for others, we can reach out for God's blessings to them—which "far surpasses all the good works" we can otherwise do.

This ought to be a great motivation to pray for others. We work for their good and express deep care for them!

Prayer Point: Pray a prayer that expresses concern for someone in all facets of their life. When you pray, think of specific things you can do to help them.

Betty + Lindsey   Aug 2021

96

Know You Are Empty

Ephesians 2:1–10

W E pride ourselves on being self-sufficient. We like to think we have a "can-do" attitude to get things done in all the various parts of our lives.

This attitude can carry over into views about our relationship with God. We may think we "deserve" blessings from God and that these blessings should come to us by virtue of what we do.

Our Protestant tradition, however, is clear that we are all sinners before God (see Rom. 3:23) and unable to deserve or merit a relationship with God on our own. A basic conviction of our faith is that "by grace you have been saved through faith, and this is not your own doing; it is the gift of God—not the result of works, so that no one may boast" (Eph. 2:8–9). It is only when we recognize and admit our sinful unworthiness that God's grace can save us.

Likewise, we need to confess our inadequacy before praying. James Pilkington wrote, "Let us therefore in all our supplications and prayers unto the Lord first confess our beggarly poverty and unableness to help ourselves, the want of his heavenly grace and fatherly assistance; and then our gracious God will plenteously pour his blessings into our empty souls, and fill them with his grace."

When we pray, we must know we are empty. We have "empty souls." Our sins separate us from God so that we have no relationship with God on our own. Only when we recognize our emptiness and confess it in prayer will God's grace fill us!

PRAYER POINT: As Christians, we recognize our need of God's grace. Empty yourself before God, confessing your sin and need of gracious love to fill your life.

Building Up God's Children

Ephesians 4:1–16

E PHESIANS 4:1–16 presents a great vision of unity in the body of Christ. The church is united in the one body by the one Spirit who brings unity and peace in "one Lord, one faith, one baptism" (v. 5). We move toward the "unity of the faith and of the knowledge of the Son of God," Jesus Christ, the great "head" of the church (vv. 13, 15). From Christ, the "whole body" of the church is "joined and knit together" as the body grows "in building itself up in love" (v. 16).

God desires this vision of the church, and every Christian should pray for this every day. James says, "pray for one another" (James 5:16), a command as wide as the world and the whole church of Jesus Christ. We pray for the church, for sisters and brothers in faith. These prayers should be fervent . . . and constant.

John Wesley wrote that "God, in answer to their prayers, builds up his children by each other in every good gift: nourishing and strengthening the whole 'body, by that which every joint supplieth.'" God answers our prayers for nourishing and strengthening the body of Christ with its members joined together by faith in Christ as the ligaments of our physical bodies are "joined and knit together," to allow the body to live and grow. This is how important our prayers can be for the building up of God's children!

PRAYER POINT: Make prayers for the church a constant part of your daily prayer life. Pray fervently for the building up of God's children and the unity of the church in Jesus Christ.

PRAY WHEN THE SPIRIT MOVES YOU

Ephesians 6:18–19

WHEN we think of our prayers, we may think we pray when we choose to—and we do. However, as we noted in an earlier devotion, it is God's Holy Spirit who moves us to pray. Our prayers are the action of God's Spirit in our lives, leading us to pray at set times and other times. As Paul wrote, "Pray in the Spirit at all times" (Eph. 6:18).

There are times we feel like praying—and we do—but it is always with the help of the Spirit!

The Spirit may move us in different ways at different times. Praying when the Spirit moves us gives us great freedom to pray. In some moments we may ask the Spirit to lead us to pray.

Heinrich Bullinger wrote, "Pray therefore as oft as the Spirit moveth thee, and as often as necessity itself or matter provoketh thee to pray. Yet let nothing here be of constraint; let all things proceed from a willing and free spirit."

The lyrics to a spiritual declare, "Every time I feel the Spirit moving in my heart I will pray." We do "feel the Spirit moving" at times. Then we can pray! We may face necessities or needs in our lives. We know we need help, and we respond to the Spirit who leads us. In all times and places, we can be aware of the Spirit—who moves us to pray!

PRAYER POINT: As you pray, realize the Holy Spirit is at work in initiating your prayers, leading you in prayer, and enabling God to speak to you in your prayers.

For What Should We Pray?

Philippians 1:3–11

P AUL's affection for sisters and brothers in Christ at Philippi was deep and joyful! A measure of that affection is found in Paul's opening words where he mentions "I thank my God every time I remember you, constantly praying with joy in every one of my prayers for all of you" (Phil. 1:3–4).

We may wonder what Paul prayed for when he prayed for the Philippians. Surely there are some basics for prayer that all our prayers—for others and for ourselves—may include.

Jeremy Taylor suggested a few of these basics of prayer when he wrote, "And thus we must always pray for the pardon of our sins, for the assistance of God's grace, for charity, for life eternal, never giving over till we die: and thus also we pray for supply of great temporal needs in their several proportions; in all cases being curious, we do not give over out of weariness, or impatience, for God oftentimes defers to grant our suit."

These prescriptions for prayer mark prayers that encompass spiritual and physical needs. Most essential is prayer asking God to pardon our sins—a pardon we always need. We need also God's grace to assist us in resisting temptation. We pray for love toward others, for eternal life, and for our earthly needs to be met. These prayers are constants for us.

Through all circumstances we persevere in prayer—not becoming weary or impatient, even as we await God's help!

PRAYER POINT: Pray for the pardon of your sins, God's grace to help, love toward others, and life eternal. Then pray for your temporal needs for living.

GOD'S ANSWERS TO OUR PRAYERS

Philippians 4:2–7

WHEN we pray, we usually know what we want to ask from God. Our prayers emerge from our needs, and we think we know what we need! But do we?

We expect God to hear and answer our prayers. We anticipate that these answers will correspond with our needs and will clearly show God has heard us and acted on our behalf. This is often our "normal procedure" in prayer. As Paul said, "In everything by prayer and supplication with thanksgiving let your requests be made known to God" (Phil. 4:6).

But Luther helps us realize that as we look for God's answers to our prayers, we should recognize "God's way of hearing our prayers surpasses our understanding—it is not like we have imagined it, or thought of it, or, so it seems, prudently chosen."

In other words, God's hearing and answering our prayers may occur in ways that exceed our understandings. We may not recognize God's answers, or those answers may go over and beyond what we were anticipating! When we pray, it's not as if we know the best way for God to respond. We cannot imagine how God may choose to answer us. We may not even be choosing the best things to request. We may not know the best way for our prayers to be answered. But God knows, and God's ways bless us!

REFLECTION QUESTIONS: Think about those times you were sure about what you wanted when you prayed to God. Did you receive the answer you anticipated? In the way you anticipated it?

Dear God and Father, we thank thee for thine infinite goodness and love to us. You do continually keep us in the Word, in faith, and in prayer that we may know how to walk before thee in humility and in fear, and that we may not pride ourselves on our own wisdom and righteousness, skill and strength, but glory alone in thy power who is strong when we are weak and does through us weaklings daily prevail and gain the victory. We pray thee so to nurture us that we may please thee willingly . . . that many people may enjoy our fruits and be attracted by us to all godliness. Write into our hearts by thy Holy Spirit what is so abundantly found in Scripture and let us constantly keep it in mind and permit it to become far more precious to us than our own life and whatever else we cherish on earth. Help us to live and act accordingly. To thee be praise and thanks in eternity. Amen.

MARTIN LUTHER

PRAY FOR THE BLESSING OF ALL

Colossians 1:3–8

ROBERT Rollock wrote that "self-love draws us so near our selves, that it maketh us forget others." We don't like to admit this, but it is true.

In contrast, Paul wrote to the Colossians, "In our prayers for you we always thank God, the Father of our Lord Jesus Christ" (Col. 1:3). Commenting on this verse, Rollock wrote, "Thou art not bound only to pray for thy self, but if thou be a member of Christ, thou art bound to pray for the body in general, and particular: and all the benefits of God bestowed on any person on the earth temporal or spiritual, should be to thee a matter of praising God. Brethren, if we had that zeal to the glory of God, and that love to our neighbours which we ought to have, there would not be a blessing of God that fell to our neighbour, but we would glorify God for it, as if it had fallen to our selves."

This speaks to us, doesn't it? As "member[s] of Christ," we are to pray for the church and for all the blessings of God "bestowed on any person on the earth"! We pray for all other people in the world and for their blessing. Then, if we have zeal for God's glory, we will glorify God for our neighbors' blessing—as much as if the blessing had come to us! Are we loving neighbors and living this way?

> **PRAYER POINT:** Make it a practice in your prayers to pray for others to be blessed. Thank and glorify God for their blessings, as much as you do for your own blessings.

Forgive Us Our Debts

Colossians 1:13–14

We are all familiar with monetary debts. These are monies owed to all manner of institutions and people for purchases. These are debts that must be paid, or the borrowers face the consequences.

In the midst of the Lord's Prayer, Jesus instructs his disciples to pray, "Forgive us our debts, as we also have forgiven our debtors" (Matt. 6:12). We owe debts—and especially "debts" to God. These debts, too, need to be paid in some way. In our prayers we must acknowledge this need and ask for forgiveness of the debts we owe when we sin against God.

Thomas Becon wrote, "We [are] all debtors unto God; so that in this petition we desire him to forgive us these debts, yea, the pain and punishment also, which is due to us for not paying our debts, and not to lay unto our charge those our sins which we daily commit in thought, word, and deed; but rather most graciously both to forgive and to forget them."

The forgiveness of our debts takes place in Jesus Christ. In his death, our debt for sin in thought, word, and deed is forgiven. As Paul wrote, God has "rescued us from the power of darkness and transferred us into the kingdom of his beloved Son, in whom we have redemption, the forgiveness of sins" (Col. 1:13–14).

Pray today, "Forgive us our debts"!

Prayer Point: Spend time in prayer considering your "debts" or sin against God. Ask God's forgiveness for each sin, through Jesus Christ.

Thanksgiving in Prayer

Colossians 4:2–6

W E all need to hear one instruction from the apostle Paul that he wrote to the Colossian Christians: "Devote your-selves to prayer, keeping alert in it with thanksgiving" (Col. 4:2). Do we "devote ourselves to prayer"?

Prayer is key to our Christian lives. Our prayers include our petitions to God. They also include what Paul notes to the Colossians: thanksgiving. Do we make thanksgiving to God a vital part of our prayers?

John Calvin noted here that Paul "adds *thanksgiving*, because we must ask God for our present necessity in such a way that we do not forget benefits already received. And also we ought not to be so importunate as to murmur and be resentful if God does not immediately meet our wishes, but we must accept con-tentedly whatever He gives. Thus a twofold giving of thanks is necessary."

Our prayers ask God for our necessities. But as we do, we remember all the great benefits God has given us. These show us how active and generous God has been, and we are thank-ful. Sometimes we have to wait for God's answers. As we do, we should not be resentful. We need to accept whatever God gives. For whatever God gives . . . we are thankful also! So there is a "double thanksgiving" in our prayers—for blessings in the past and blessings in the present, as we wait for blessings from God in the future. No wonder our prayers are filled with thanksgiving!

PRAYER POINT: Pray with portions of your prayer being "petition" and "thanksgiving." Thank God for all the ben-efits God has given and continues to give in the present as you wait for an answer to your petitions.

The Best We Can Do
for Those We Love

Colossians 4:10–18

T UCKED away in the final greetings Paul gives to the Colossians is mention of Epaphras in Colossians 4:12. He showed up earlier when he is said to be "our beloved fellow servant," a "faithful minster of Christ" (1:7). Now, at the end of the letter, Paul said Epaphras is "always wrestling in his prayers on your behalf, so that you may stand mature and fully assured in everything that God wills" (4:12).

Epaphras was a person of prayer. It is telling for our friends to recognize we are persons of prayer. Paul certainly knew and appreciated the ministry of prayer that Epaphras carried out for the sake of the Christians at Colossae.

Reflecting on this verse, Jean Daillé, a French Huguenot pastor, wrote: "Paul says first that Epaphras always strives in prayer for them 'that you might abide perfect and complete in all the will of God.' Prayer is the best office that we can perform to those we love."

Have we thought of prayer like this before? "Prayer is the best office that we can perform to those we love." There are many ways we can serve others. This takes shape at different times and in different places. But one way we can serve—at all times and in all places—is by praying for them. This is our ministry. What if this really *is* the best thing we can do for those we love!

PRAYER POINT: Take seriously Daillé's comment and pray for those you love, commending them to God and praying they may do God's will in their lives.

PRAY ALWAYS

1 Thessalonians 5:12–22

IN his final exhortations, greetings, and benediction to the Thessalonians, Paul wrote, "Pray without ceasing, give thanks in all circumstances; for this is the will of God in Christ Jesus for you" (1 Thess. 5:17–18).

We may think this instruction is impossible to carry out. We cannot literally "pray without ceasing"—as if the only thing we should do in life is pray!

So we know Paul means here that we should be people who make prayer a consistent, ongoing part of our lives. Jesus spoke of our "need to pray always and not to lose heart" (Luke 18:1). Paul also urged the Romans to "persevere in prayer" (Rom. 12:12).

Heinrich Bullinger gave a perspective on this when he wrote, "The Lord commandeth to pray always; that is to say, as often as we conveniently may, at all times and in all places . . . and give him thanks for benefits received; which should also continually ask favour of him."

Our prayers should be "at all times and in all places"— pointing toward a continuity of prayers throughout our entire lives. Someone said prayer should be as natural for us as breathing, which we do rather continually!

And Bullinger reminds us that our prayers consist of giving thanks for God's benefits and "continually" asking favor of God. So let us "pray always"!

> **REFLECTION QUESTION:** Think of the times you pray. In what ways do you believe you are fulfilling the command to "pray always"?

USE THE MEANS GOD GIVES

2 Thessalonians 3:6–13

I N a Christmas Eve blizzard, a man was trapped by rising snow. He prayed to God for safety. Then a sleigh came along with a driver who offered him a ride. But the man refused, saying he had faith God would help him. Later, the same thing happened. The man refused a ride. When the snow was up to the man's chin, a sleigh came again. He still refused, saying God would help him. But the man died. When the man met God, he said, "Why didn't you help me? I had faith." But God replied, "Sir, I sent the sleigh three times!"

We are to use the means God gives for answering our prayers. We have to use the sleigh!

James Pilkington wrote that "it is not sufficient to pray, and then to neglect such means as God hath appointed us to use for our defense and comfort, no more than it is to say, when he hath prayed, I will live without meat and drink, and God himself shall feed me." Prayer and God's providence go together.

We pray for our daily bread (see Matt. 6:11). Yet "anyone unwilling to work should not eat" (2 Thess. 3:10). Working is a means God gives us through which our prayer for "daily bread" is answered. It is our "sleigh." We receive God's gifts, even when we work for them—as a means of God's grace.

Watch for that sleigh and use it!

REFLECTION QUESTIONS: Reflect on times when you recognized God's answers to your prayers. Were they unexpected? Did you realize what was happening was God's answer?

G RANT, almighty God, since our minds have so many hidden corners that nothing is more difficult than thoroughly to cleanse them of all inventions and falsehood, grant, I say, that we may rightly examine ourselves; and shed the light of your Spirit upon us that we may truly recognize our hidden vices and drive them far from us, so that you alone may be our God and true piety may win the victory in us and we may offer you sound and unblemished service; and also that we may live with a sound conscience in the world; each of us so engaged in our own lot as to care for the good of others rather than ourselves, so that at the last we may become partakers of the true glory which you have prepared for us in heaven through Christ our Lord. Amen.

JOHN CALVIN

SOUL-MELTING PASSION AND AFFECTION

Hebrews 4:14–16

J ESUS Christ is our Great High Priest who sympathizes with us in our weaknesses and provides mercy and "grace to help in times of need" (Heb. 4:16). This is our immense comfort, assuring us of God's ongoing grace and help for us through our Savior, Jesus Christ.

For this grace, given in Jesus Christ, we approach God in our prayers with thanksgiving. For what greater gift could we be thankful than Jesus's provision of grace to help us? Our prayers of thanksgiving lead us to say, as Paul said, "I thank my God" (Phil. 1:3–4).

Henry Airay wrote of how intense and deeply felt our thanksgiving to God should be: "The apostle to the Hebrews exhorteth, saying (4:16), 'Let us go boldly unto the throne of grace,' be it in prayer or in thanksgiving; 'Let us go boldly unto the throne of grace, praying and giving thanks unto God through Jesus Christ our Lord.' . . . Our thanksgiving unto God should be offered up with such soul-melting passion and affection, that . . . we should say, 'I thank my God' (Phil. 1:3)."

Are the prayers of thanksgiving we offer to God prayed with "soul-melting passion and affection"? Are they ardent prayers, thanking God for grace given and blessings received? Do we pray with the psalmist: "Bless the LORD, O my soul, and all that is within me, bless his holy name" (Ps. 103:1)? Does the depth of our affection for God emerge with "soul-melting passion"? Thank God passionately!

PRAYER POINT: Pour out your deepest feelings, thanking God for Jesus Christ and the blessings you have received.

OUR PERPETUAL ADVOCATE

Hebrews 7:23–25

W E know the stories of Jesus from the gospels. These tell us about Jesus's earthly life, what he said and did. When it comes to prayer, we know Jesus taught his disciples they should always pray (see Matt. 6:5, 7), and that when they pray in faith, they will receive (see 21:22). We also know that Jesus prayed for his disciples (see Luke 22:32).

Now that Jesus has ascended to heaven and sits at "the right hand of the power of God" (Luke 22:69; Acts 5:31), what is Jesus doing in relation to prayer?

Jesus is doing far more than we can know or imagine! What we know is that Jesus Christ makes continual intercession with God the Father on behalf of those who pray. Hebrews says of Jesus, "He is able for all time to save those who approach God through him, since he always lives to make intercession for them" (Heb. 7:25). Through Jesus Christ, our prayers are brought to God and are heard and answered.

Theodore Beza highlighted this when he wrote that "Jesus Christ [is] our only perpetual Advocate . . . [also Intercessor . . .]. And who shall be sooner heard of God the Father than his own dearly beloved Son, in whom he most delights, and without whom nothing is acceptable."

What wonderful confidence this gives us for our prayers! Jesus Christ, God's "dearly beloved Son," advocates and intercedes for us. What greater assurance that God hears and answers our prayers than that they are presented by Jesus—our "perpetual Advocate"!

REFLECTION QUESTIONS: Do you think of your prayers as being presented to God by Jesus Christ? What new dimensions to prayer may emerge for you when you think of your prayers this way?

Familiar Communication with God

James 4:1–9

SOMETIMES we take prayer for granted. We may pray half-heartedly or distractedly, or without thinking or feeling. Think of what we are missing!

James says, "Submit yourselves therefore to God. Resist the devil, and he will flee from you. Draw near to God, and he will draw near to you" (James 4:7–8). Imagine that when we come to God in prayer, God comes to us! We draw near to God, and God draws near to us.

Who is this God to whom we can draw near? Thomas Becon wrote, "What a treasure then is it to talk with the King of kings and Lord of lords." Imagine—we can draw near to this God!

Then, said Becon, "This thing cometh to pass by true and Christian prayer. For what other thing is prayer than a familiar communication with God, wherein we may freely pour out the troubles of our hearts, and declare all our matters boldly to him, as the child doth unto his father, and obtain at his hand all good things?" For, "we are our own enemies, if we neglect and despise this great commodity and singular pleasure."

In prayer, we may freely pour out our hearts as a child does to a parent. We can have "familiar communication with God." No privilege or blessing could be greater for us. The great God is also the God who loves us!

REFLECTION QUESTION: In what ways does realizing prayer is "familiar communication with God" energize your prayer life?

WHEN OUR PRAYERS ARE FEW AND FAINT

James 5:13–18

AT times our lives of prayer are difficult. We face a power failure of the spirit, a season when our prayers are few . . . and faint.

When these periods occur, what can we do?

Archbishop James Ussher addressed this question and suggested some special helps: "None better than to pray for the Spirit of Prayer, which helpeth and healeth our infirmities, and teacheth us both for manner, measure, and matter, to lay open all our necessities (Rom. 8:26; Luke 11:13). And secondly call others who are best acquainted with the practice and power of prayer, to pray with us, being present (James 5:14) and for us, being absent from us (Rom. 1:9)."

Helpfully, when we pray, we can ask God to give us "the spirit of prayer," to spark and renew within us the work of the Holy Spirit, who leads us to pray and leads us in prayer. Pray for the Spirit's work.

Also, we can "call others who are best acquainted with the practice and power of prayer, to pray with us." James says leaders of the church should be called to pray over someone who is sick (see James 5:14). We often think we need to get out of our spiritual difficulties by ourselves. But others can pray for us (see Rom. 1:9). Surrounding ourselves with those who know the practice and power of prayer to pray over us can be used by the Holy Spirit to strengthen our faith and energize our prayers!

> **PRAYER POINT:** Pray always for the Spirit of God to lead your prayers and lead you into prayer. Be strengthened in your prayers when you pray with others.

Our Most Powerful Prayers

1 Peter 4:7–11

W E may think our most powerful prayers are those where we ask God for something and then receive it. It seems we have come, we have prayed, and we have "conquered"—receiving what we desired for ourselves.

But what if our most powerful prayers are those we pray on behalf of others?

Peter urges people of prayer to "maintain constant love for one another" (1 Peter 4:8). We are also to "serve one another" (v. 10). Love and service are crucial; they are expressed in our prayers.

Lancelot Andrewes wrote that "our prayers are most powerful with God, when we express in them a fellow-feeling of the Necessities of our Neighbors, and Sympathize with them in their misery. This is Charity [love]. Let every one of us therefore be as willing and careful to pray for others, as well, and as heartily as for himself; considering, that in so doing, he prayeth for him, whom Charity hath made as himself. Christ bare us, and all our sins in his body. Let us do the like to one another in word and deed."

Pray for others as vigorously as you pray for yourself. We love our neighbor as ourselves (see Mark 12:31). As Christ loved us and carried our needs, so our most powerful prayers are love for others.

Prayer Point: Devote a whole prayer to the needs of others. Think of what their needs are and how you can help meet their needs, as expressions of Christ's love.

DEPENDING ON GOD'S PROMISES

2 Peter 1:3–11

P RAYER and God's promises go together. We pray because we believe God hears and promises to answer our prayers. In prayer, we depend fully and completely on God. We depend on God's care for each of us; God's providence in leading and guiding our lives; and God's faithfulness in providing for our salvation by faith in Jesus Christ.

God's saving message in Christ is God's "precious and very great promises," as the second letter of Peter says: "Thus he has given us, through these things, his precious and very great promises, so that through them you may escape from the corruption that is in the world because of lust, and may become participants of the divine nature" (2 Peter 1:4). Through Jesus Christ, we can participate in the life of God!

In prayer, we depend on God's promises, not any "righteousness" or merit of our own. John Knox offered a wish for Christians who pray: "This consolation I would wish all Christians in their prayers: the testimony of a good conscience to assure them of God's promises. But to obtain what they ask must only depend upon him, all opinion and thought of our own [righteousness] being laid aside."

In prayer, we depend completely on God's promises, in Christ. We have no "righteousness" before God on our own—only in Christ. We depend on God solely through Christ in whom all the promises of God are "Yes" (2 Cor. 1:20).

> **REFLECTION QUESTIONS:** Think of promises God makes in Scripture. Which ones are most precious to you? In what ways do you depend on God's promises?

According to God's Will

1 John 5:13-17

OUR prayers to God can be spontaneous and free. They can reflect what is in our hearts and mind as we unburden our souls to our loving God. God wants us to pray in humility and trust, expressing our needs and desires.

But as we pray, we must always keep in mind that our prayers should be offered as prayers submitted to God's will. Our prayers to God should reflect the attitude of Jesus in Gethsemane—"not my will but yours be done" (Luke 22:42). We want our wills to correspond to God's will. Our greatest prayer should always be for this to be so. This is what we pray in the Lord's Prayer—"Your will be done" (Matt. 6:10).

This direction is also given in 1 John: "This is the boldness we have in him, that if we ask anything according to his will, he hears us" (1 John 5:14). When we ask in accord with God's will, God hears and answers our prayers. John Calvin indicated this when he wrote, "Christ dictated that form of prayer, 'Thy will be done,' setting limits round us, that we should not preposterously prefer our desires to those of God, nor ask without deliberation what first comes into our mouth."

What we desire most from God should be what God desires most for us. As we pray, we express our desires to God, always seeking that our requests be according to God's will. Doing God's will is our greatest desire and joy!

REFLECTION QUESTION: Think about how you see your prayer requests in relation to God's will. Do you always express that your desires be God's desires?

To thee, O Son of God, Restorer of the defaced and deformed image of God in man, who died for our sins and was raised up for our righteousness, to thee we pray with all our heart. Create in us a new life through thy Holy Spirit. Inflame us with true knowledge, prayer, and love. Be our protection, O Christ, lest the burning wrath of God fall upon us; lest we, unclean and impure, stand judged before God. Clothe us with thy righteousness, and cleanse us from our sin that we may be acceptable to th[ee] eternal Father. Strengthen now our faith, that in the next life, made whole again, we may give thanks to thee and with all the righteous angels as well as men forever praise thee and the Father and thy Holy Spirit. Amen.

PHILIP MELANCHTHON

INDEX OF QUOTATIONS

U NLESS otherwise indicated, all works were written by the author whose name appears in bold above them.

Airay, Henry

33   *Lectures upon the Whole Epistle of St. Paul to the Philippians* (London, 1844), 352.

110   *Lectures*, 18.

Andrewes, Lancelot

90   *The Pattern of Catechetical Doctrine at Large, or A Learned and Pious Exposition of the Ten Commandments* (London, 1675), 142.

114   *Holy Devotions, with directions to pray also a brief exposition upon [brace] the Lords prayer, the creed, the Ten commandments, the 7 penitential psalms, the 7 psalms of thanksgiving: together with a letanie* (London, 1663), 89.

Becon, Thomas

60   *Prayers and Other Pieces*, ed. John Ayre (Cambridge: Cambridge University Press, 1844), 46.

64   *The Catechism of Prayer*, in *The Catechism of Thomas Becon with Other Pieces*, ed. John Ayre (Cambridge: Cambridge University Press, 1844), 141.

65   *Catechism of Prayer*, 130.

67   *Prayers and Other Pieces*, 75.

74   *Prayers and Other Pieces*, 82.

84   "The Pleasant New Nosegay," in *The Early Works of Thomas Becon . . . being the treatises published by him during the reign of Henry VIII* , ed. John Ayre (Cambridge, 1843), 228.

104 "The Catechism," in *Catechism of Thomas Becon*, 178.

112 Preface to *The Pathway unto Prayer, full of muche godly fruite and Christen knowledge*, in *Early Works*, 128.

Beza, Theodore

63 *A Briefe and Pithie Summe of Christian Faith*, trans. Robert Fills (London, 1589), 58.

111 *Summe*, 57.

The Book of Common Prayer

25 *The Book of Common Prayer and Administration of the Sacraments, and Other Rites and Ceremonies of the Church, According to the Use of the Church of England* (Cambridge, 1666), after C2.

39 "The Book of Common Prayer and Administration of the Sacraments, and other Rites and Ceremonies in the Church of England, 1559," in *Liturgies and Occasional Forms of Prayer Set Forth in the Reign of Queen Elizabeth*, ed. William Keatinge Clay (Cambridge: Cambridge University Press, 1847), 55.

Bradford, John

57 *Meditation on the Lord's Prayer*, in *The Writings of John Bradford*, ed. Aubrey Townshend (Cambridge: Cambridge University Press, 1848), 1:138.

71 *Meditation*, 1:138.

92 "Letter to His Mother," in *The Writings of John Bradford*, ed. Aubrey Townshend (Cambridge: Cambridge University Press, 1853), 2:73.

Brenz, Johannes

59 Commentary on Luke 7:13–15, in *Luke*, ed. Beth Kreitzer, Reformation Commentary on Scripture (Downers Grove, IL: IVP Academic, 2015), 154.

Bucer, Martin

22 Commentary on Psalm 9:7–14, in *Psalms 1–72*, ed. Herman J. Selderhuis, Reformation Commentary on Scripture (Downers Grove, IL: IVP Academic, 2015), 86.

54 Commentary on Psalm 13:1–6, in *Psalms 1–72*, 106.

Bullinger, Heinrich

19 *The Decades of Henry Bullinger*, ed. Thomas Harding (Cambridge: Cambridge University Press, 1852), 5:168.

43 *Decades*, 5:170.

51 *Decades*, 5:163.

87 *Decades*, 5:174.

91 *Decades*, 5:171.

99 *Decades*, 5:183.

107 *Decades*, 5:182.

Calvin, John

24 Commentary on Psalm 27:5, *Commentary on the Book of Psalms*, trans. James Anderson (Edinburgh, 1845), 1:319–20.

52 Commentary on Psalm 116:4, *Commentary on Psalms*, trans. James Anderson (Edinburgh, 1847), 4:361.

81 *Commentaries on the Book of the Prophet Jeremiah and the Lamentations*, trans. and ed. John Owen (Edinburgh, 1850), 1:106.

83 *The Gospel According to St. John 11–21 and The First Epistle of John*, trans. T. H. L. Parker, ed. David W. Torrance and Thomas F. Torrance (Grand Rapids: Wm. B. Eerdmans, 1994), 140–41.

94 *The Catechism of the Church of Geneva* (1541), questions and answers 244–45, in *The School of Faith: The Catechisms of the Reformed Church*, ed. and trans. Thomas F. Torrance (New York: Harper & Brothers Publishers, 1959), 42.

105 *The Epistles of Paul the Apostle to the Galatians, Ephesians, Philippians and Colossians*, trans. T. H. L. Parker (Grand Rapids: William B. Eerdmans, 1996), 356.

109 *Daniel I (Chapters 1–6)*, trans. T. H. L. Parker, Calvin's Old Testament Commentaries (Grand Rapids: William B. Eerdmans Publishing Co., 1993), 20:116.

116 Commentary on Psalm 145:18, *Commentary on Psalms*, trans. James Anderson (Edinburgh, 1849), 5:283.

Coverdale, Miles

88 *Writings and Translations of Bishop Coverdale*, ed. George Pearson, (Cambridge: Cambridge University Press, 1844), 305–6.

Daillé, Jean

106 Commentary on Colossians 4:10–18, in *Philippians, Colossians,* ed. Graham Tomlin, Reformation Commentary on Scripture (Downers Grove, IL: IVP Academic, 2013), 249.

Dickson, David

27 Commentary on Psalm 27, in *Psalms 1–72,* ed. Herman J. Selderhuis, Reformation Commentary on Scripture (Downers Grove, IL: IVP Academic, 2015), 220.

35 *A Brief Explication of the Psalms* (Glasgow, 1834), 1:323.

36 Commentary on Psalm 54:4, in *Psalms 1–72,* 399.

Dietrich, Veit

79 Commentary on Luke 22:41–44, in *Luke,* ed. Beth Kreitzer, Reformation Commentary on Scripture (Downers Grove, IL: IVP Academic, 2015), 436.

Downame, George

26 *An Abstract of the Duties Commanded, and Sinnes Forbidden in the Law of God* (London, 1620), unnumbered.

55 "The Doctrine of Libertie," section 4, in *The Christians Freedom wherein is fully expressed the doctrine of Christian libertie* (Oxford, 1635), 14.

68 *The Christian Arte of Thriving* (London, 1620), 5.

82 *The Christians Sanctuarie* (London, 1604), 39–40.

The English Annotations

38 Commentary on Psalm 70:1, in *The English Annotations,* ed. John Downame (1657), in *Psalms 1–72,* ed. Herman J. Selderhuis, Reformation Commentary on Scripture (Downers Grove, IL: IVP Academic, 2015), 478.

Heidelberg Catechism

34 Question and answer 116.

Hooper, John

45 *Later Writings of Bishop Hooper*, ed. Charles Nevinson (Cambridge: Cambridge University Press, 1852), 317.

62 *Early Writings of Bishop Hooper*, ed. Samuel Carr (Cambridge: Cambridge University Press, 1843), 491.

Ken, Thomas

32 *A Manual of Prayers for the Use of the Scholars of Winchester College, and All Other Devout Christians*, 28th ed. (London, 1755), 45–46.

46 *Manual*, 75–76.

Knox, John

56 "A Treatise on Prayer," in *Writings of the Rev. John Knox* (Philadelphia: Presbyterian Board of Publication, 1842), 73.

115 "Treatise," 77.

Latimer, Hugh

66 *The Works of Hugh Latimer: Sermons*, ed. George Elwes Corrie (Cambridge: Cambridge University Press, 1844), 1:444.

96 *Works*, 1:338–39.

Luther, Martin

30 "The Lord's Prayer: The Second Petition," in "The Large Catechism," *The Book of Concord*, ed. Robert Kolb and Timothy J. Wengert (Minneapolis: Fortress Press, 2000), 447.

37 Commentary on Psalm 62:5–8, in *Psalms 1–72*, ed. Herman J. Selderhuis, Reformation Commentary on Scripture (Downers Grove, IL: IVP Academic, 2015), 437.

49 Commentary on Psalm 90:1–2, in *Psalms 73–150*, ed. Herman J. Selderhuis, Reformation Commentary on Scripture (Downers Grove, IL: IVP Academic, 2018), 112.

80 Commentary on Luke 24:28–32, in *Luke,* ed. Beth Kreitzer, Reformation Commentary on Scripture (Downers Grove, IL: IVP Academic, 2015), 489.

95   Quoted in Charles E. Kistler, *Luther's Prayers, Bethüchlein* (Reading, PA: Pilger, 1917), quoted in *Prayers of the Reformers*, comp. Clyde Manschreck (Philadelphia: Muhlenberg Press, 1958), 79.

101 Commentary on Philippians 4:2–9, in *Philippians, Colossians*, ed. Graham Tomlin, Reformation Commentary on Scripture (Downers Grove, IL: IVP Academic, 2013), 111.

102 Quoted in Kistler, *Luther's Prayers*, quoted in *Reformers*, 79.

Melanchthon, Philip

28   Commentary on Psalm 30:11–12, in *Psalms 1–72*, ed. Herman J. Selderhuis, Reformation Commentary on Scripture (Downers Grove, IL: IVP Academic, 2015), 234.

53   Quoted in Clyde Leonard Manschreck, *Melanchthon: The Quiet Reformer* (Nashville: Abingdon Press, 1958), 312.

73   Commentary on Luke 22:41–44, in *Luke*, ed. Beth Kreitzer, Reformation Commentary on Scripture (Downers Grove, IL: IVP Academic, 2015), 437.

75   Commentary on Luke 9:28–36, in *Luke*, 203.

76   Commentary on Luke 11:1–4, in *Luke*, 233.

117 Quoted in *Prayers of the Reformers*, comp. Clyde Manschreck (Philadelphia: Muhlenberg Press, 1958), 75.

Musculus, Wolfgang

42   Commentary on Psalm 71:12–24, in *Psalms 1–72*, ed. Herman J. Selderhuis, Reformation Commentary on Scripture Series (Downers Grove, IL: IVP Academic, 2015), 483.

48   Commentary on Psalm 86:1–5, in *Psalms 73–150*, ed. Herman J. Selderhuis, Reformation Commentary on Scripture (Downers Grove, IL: IVP Academic, 2018), 90.

Pellikan, Konrad

47   Commentary on Psalm 86:1–5, in *Psalms 73–150*, ed. Herman J. Selderhuis, Reformation Commentary on Scripture (Downers Grove, IL: IVP Academic, 2018), 90.

Pilkington, James

97   *The Works of James Pilkington*, ed. James Scholefield (Cambridge: Cambridge University Press, 1842), 411–12.

108   *Works*, 412.

Rollock, Robert

103   *Lectures upon the Epistle of Paul to the Colossians*, ed. H. Holland (London, 1603), 5.

Sandys, Edwin

23   *The Sermons of Edwin Sandys*, ed. John Ayre (Cambridge, 1842), 76.

61   *Sermons*, 76.

Selnecker, Nikolaus

40   Commentary on Psalm 70:1–5, in *Psalms 1–72*, ed. Herman J. Selderhuis, Reformation Commentary on Scripture (Downers Grove, IL: IVP Academic, 2015), 479.

Spangenberg, Johann

77   Commentary on Luke 11:5–8, in *Luke,* ed. Beth Kreitzer, Reformation Commentary on Scripture (Downers Grove, IL: IVP Academic, 2015), 235.

Strigel, Viktorin

41   Commentary on Psalm 71:1–24, in *Psalms 1–72,* ed. Herman J. Selderhuis, Reformation Commentary on Scripture (Downers Grove, IL: IVP Academic, 2015), 482.

Taylor, Jeremy

31   *The Rule and Exercises of Holy Living*, 25th ed. (London, 1739), 235.

44   Commentary on Psalm 77:1–9, in *Psalms 73–150,* ed. Herman J. Selderhuis, Reformation Commentary on Scripture (Downers Grove, IL: IVP Academic, 2018), 32.

100   *Holy Living*, 234.

Tyndale, William

21   *The Obedience of the Christian Man*, ed. Henry Walter (Cambridge: Cambridge University Press, 1848), 300.

29 *Expositions and Notes on Sundry Portions of the Holy Scriptures*, ed. Henry Walter (Cambridge: Cambridge University Press, 1849), 96.

Ursinus, Zacharias

50 *Commentary on the Heidelberg Catechism*, trans. G. W. Williard, 3rd American ed. (Cincinnati, 1851), 624.
70 *Commentary*, 624.

Ussher, James

20 *A Bodie of Divinitie, or The Summe and Substance of Christian Religion* (London, 1653), 346.
58 *Divinitie*, 350.
69 *Divinitie*, 347.
72 *Divinitie*, 343–4.
78 *Divinitie*, 347.
89 *Divinitie*, 343.
93 *Divinitie*, 347.
113 *Divinitie*, 348.

Wesley, John

85 "The Means of Grace," in *The Works of the Rev. John Wesley in Ten Volumes* (New York, 1826), 5:159.
86 "Catholic Spirit," in *Works*, 5:417.
98 "Fourth Discourse on the Mount," in *Works*, 5:262.

Zwingli, Huldrych

18 Quoted in Gottfried W. Locher, *Zwingli's Thought: New Perspectives* (Leiden, Netherlands: E. J. Brill, 1981), 28.

WRITERS AND WORKS

Henry Airay (ca. 1550–1616) was an Anglican priest and theologian.

Lancelot Andrewes (1555–1626) was an Anglican bishop who was also a scholar, pastor, and prominent preacher.

Thomas Becon (1511/1512–1567) was an Anglican ecclesiastical leader who was a renowned popular preacher.

Theodore Beza (1519–1605) was a French pastor and professor who became the successor of John Calvin in Geneva. He was a New Testament scholar, church Reformer, and theologian.

The Book of Common Prayer (1549; 1552) was the liturgical manual produced for the English Protestant church to convey the theology and worship practices that distinguished the Church of England from Roman Catholicism.

John Bradford (1510–1555) was an English Reformer, Prebendary of St. Paul's Cathedral, and Protestant martyr.

Johannes Brenz (1499–1570) was a German Lutheran theologian and pastor.

Martin Bucer (1491–1551) was an influential German Reformed theologian and a leader of the Strasbourg Reformation.

Heinrich Bullinger (1505–1575) was a Swiss Reformed pastor and important Reformed theologian who succeeded Zwingli as leader of the Reformation in Zurich.

John Calvin (1509–1564) was a French Reformer who was the leader of the reform movement in Geneva and developed what became known as Reformed theology through his theological writings and biblical commentaries.

Miles Coverdale (1488–1569) was an Anglican bishop and Bible translator.

Jean Daillé (1594–1670) was a French Reformed pastor.

David Dickson (1583?–1663) was a Scots Reformed pastor, preacher, professor, and theologian.

Veit Dietrich (1506–1549) was a German Lutheran preacher and theologian who worked with Melanchthon to reform churches in Germany.

George Downame (1560–1634) was an English professor and bishop who had a long preaching ministry.

The English Annotations (1645; 1651; 1657) was an English language collection of significant biblical resources from Continental biblical scholars.

Heidelberg Catechism (1563) was a Reformed theological catechism authored by Zacharias Ursinus and Caspar Olevianus and became one of the most widely used Reformed catechisms.

John Hooper (ca. 1495–1555) was an Anglican bishop, Reformer, and martyr.

Thomas Ken (1637–1711) was an Anglican bishop who was one of the most prominent of English hymn writers.

John Knox (1514–1572) was a Scots Reformed pastor, preacher, and a leader of the Reformation in Scotland.

Hugh Latimer (ca. 1485–1555) was an Anglican bishop and preacher. He was tried for heresy and burned at the stake.

Martin Luther (1483–1546) was a leading Protestant Reformer whose work is considered to have originated the Protestant Reformation.

Philip Melanchthon (1497–1560) was a German Lutheran theologian, educator, and Reformer who was a close collaborator of Martin Luther and highly influential for Protestantism.

Wolfgang Musculus (1497–1563) was a German Reformed pastor and theologian.

Konrad Pellikan (1478–1556) was a German Reformed Hebrew scholar and theologian.

James Pilkington (1520–1576) was an English Protestant bishop and professor at the University of Cambridge.

Robert Rollock (ca. 1555–1599) was a Scots Reformed pastor, theologian, educator, and prolific writer of sermons, biblical commentaries, and theological treatises.

Edwin Sandys (1519–1588) was an Anglican bishop and Bible translator, many of whose sermons were published.

Nikolaus Selnecker (1530–1592) was a German Lutheran pastor, hymnist, and theologian.

Johann Spangenberg (1484–1550) was a German Lutheran pastor and theologian also known as a catechist.

Viktorin Strigel (1524–1569) was a German Lutheran theologian.

Jeremy Taylor (1613–1667) was an Anglican theologian, author, and preacher.

William Tyndale (1494–1535) was an English Reformer, theologian, and Bible translator.

Zacharias Ursinus (1534–1583) was a Reformed theologian who taught at the University of Heidelberg and was coauthor with Caspar Olevianus (1536–1587) of the Heidelberg Catechism.

James Ussher (1581–1656) was an Archbishop in the Church of Ireland and Primate of all Ireland who wrote extensive theological works.

John Wesley (1703–1791) was an English Protestant clergyman and theologian who led a revival movement in the Church of England and is known as the founder of Methodism.

Huldrych Zwingli (1484–1531) was a Swiss Reformed pastor and theologian who led the Protestant Reformation in Zurich.

Selected Resources for Further Reflection

Battles, Ford Lewis, trans. and ed. *The Piety of John Calvin: A Collection of His Spiritual Prose, Poems, and Hymns*. 1978. Reprint, Phillipsburg, NJ: P&R Publishing, 2009.

Beeke, Joel R. "Calvin on Piety." In *The Cambridge Companion to John Calvin*, edited by Donald K. McKim, 125–52. New York: Cambridge University Press, 2004.

Bloesch, Donald G. *The Struggle of Prayer*. New York: Harper & Row, 1980.

Calvin, John. *On Prayer: Conversation with God*. Louisville: Westminster John Knox Press, 2006.

Kao, Chaoluan. *Reformation of Prayerbooks: The Humanist Transformation of Early Modern Piety in Germany and England*. Refo500 Academic Studies, edited by Herman Selderhuis. Göttingen, Germany: Vandenhoeck & Ruprecht, 2018.

Kolb, Robert, Irene Dingel, and L'Ubomír Batka, eds. *The Oxford Handbook of Martin Luther's Theology*. Oxford: Oxford University Press, 2014.

Nelson, Derek R., and Paul R. Hinlicky, eds. *The Oxford Encyclopedia of Martin Luther*. 3 vols. Oxford: Oxford University Press, 2017.

Spear, Wayne R. *The Theology of Prayer: A Systematic Study of the Biblical Teaching on Prayer*. Grand Rapids: Baker Book House, 1979.

Wengert, Timothy J., et. al. *Dictionary of Luther and the Lutheran Traditions*. Grand Rapids: Baker Academic, 2017.

ALSO BY DONALD K. MCKIM

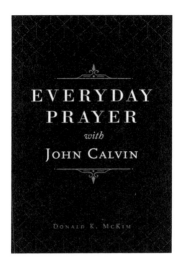

Drawing from the *Institutes* and Calvin's Old and New Testament commentaries, Donald K. McKim comments on Calvin's biblical insights on prayer and intersperses his short readings with Calvin's own prayers. Reflection questions and prayer points help you to meditate on Scripture, understand Calvin's teaching, and strengthen your own prayer life.

"Donald McKim draws on Calvin's prayers to help us with our own. . . . This guide breathes spiritual passion, energy, and wisdom. If, like mine, your prayer life could use a little help, this book will be of immense value to you."
—**Michael S. Horton**, Professor of Systematic Theology and Apologetics, Westminster Seminary California

ALSO FROM **P&R** PUBLISHING

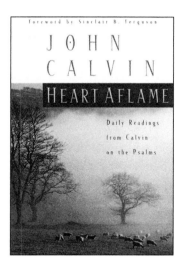

"In these pages you will find the Spirit-inspired biblical anatomy of the Psalms and the hands of an outstanding physician and surgeon of the spirit. Reading them on a daily basis can hardly fail to bring you spiritual health and strength. . . . Calvin seems to come to us from within the Bible, from inside the reality described in the text. He had learned the meaning of the command to love God 'with all your mind.' You will find him to be a sure-footed and wise guide, and I suspect you will come to love him—as well as the Psalms—better before the year is ended."
—**Sinclair Ferguson**, Chancellor's Professor, Reformed Theological Seminary; Teaching Fellow, Ligonier Ministries

Did you enjoy this book?
Consider writing a review online.
The author appreciates your feedback!

Or write to P&R at editorial@prpbooks.com
with your comments. We'd love to hear from you.